PHILIP GARDINER

Secret Societies:

GARDINER'S
FORBIDDEN
KNOWLEDGE

Revelations About the Freemasons,
Templars, Illuminati, Nazis, and
the Serpent Cults

NEW PAGE BOOKS
A division of The Career Press, Inc.
Franklin Lakes, NJ

SECRET SOCIETIES: GARDINER'S FORBIDDEN KNOWLEDGE
EDITED BY KATHRYN HENCHES
TYPESET BY EILEEN DOW MUNSON
Cover design by Dutton & Sherman
Printed in the U.S.A. by Book-mart Press

To order this title, please call toll-free 1-800-CAREER-1 (NJ and Canada: 201-848-0310) to order using VISA or MasterCard, or for further information on books from Career Press.

The Career Press, Inc., 3 Tice Road, PO Box 687,
Franklin Lakes, NJ 07417
www.careerpress.com
www.newpagebooks.com

Library of Congress Cataloging-in-Publication Data

Gardiner, Philip.
   Secret Societies : Gardiner's forbidden knowledge : revelations about the
Freemasons, Templars, Illuminati, Nazis, and the serpent cults / by Philip Gardiner.
      p. cm.
   ISBN-13: 978-156414-923-7
   ISBN-10: 156414-923-4
   1. Secret societies. 2. Secret societies—History. I. Title.

HS125.G37 2007
366--dc22

                                                          2006038047

Contents

Introduction

*The Open Conspiracy is the awaking of mankind
from the nightmare, an infantile nightmare, of the
struggle for existence and the inevitability of war.
The light of day thrusts between our eyelids, and
the multitudinous sounds of morning clamour in
our ears. A time will come when men will sit with
history before them or with some old newspaper
before them and ask incredulously, "Was there ever
such a world?"*

—H.G. Wells, *The Open Conspiracy*

This book is a collection of thoughts and researches about secret societies. It is going to take you on many journeys, but
whether you arrive or where you arrive will be your decision. I
need to make a simple point before you proceed to "bite the
apple": Clear your mind of anything you have been told. I care
not whether you are Christian, Muslim, Buddhist, communist,
capitalist, Freemason, or Boy Scout. I care not whether you see
yourself as just an ordinary man or woman. It is not for me to care.
I care for the truth, because it is, as the Bible paradoxically stated,
the one thing that can set you free.

In the years that I have been researching and writing, I have
been approached by thousands of people asking for help. One
woman, an American multi-millionaire, asked me to write down
10 things she could do to help herself. She offered to give me several thousand dollars just to do this simple thing. The money means

nothing at all. What this lady needed was what we all need—to find herself. You will hear many people say this and then feed you some garbled message of faith or freedom, enticing you into their little club. They will give you 10 good points to set you free. My message to this wealthy woman was to seek herself. I refused to give her what she wanted because she was simply using her wealth to find the easy route, without knowing that such a route leads in circles. The true path to who you are is not easy, and if it were, then it would not be right. The path leads through your own past. Everything you have learned, every emotion that has formed you, every problem, every joy, every piece of so-called knowledge, all these things are what you think you are. But they are not. All these things are external influences, they are what the Buddhists term "phenomena" because they are *not real*. All these things are now electrical impulses in your mind and nothing more. Just because you were taught that Jesus was the son of God in Sunday school or that Santa Claus brought you Christmas presents, does not make them real. These are tales, stories, and fables of other people's creation to explain emotional attachments and evolutionary desires. What is the real you remains inside, crushed by the weight of the world's fables. Only by erasing the subtle mind manipulating of religion or even modern day marketing, can we begin to see who we are beneath, and reveal the true intuition.

This will never be easy, because by the time we come to realize that we need to find out who we really are, we are already loaded down with the phenomena of the world. In fact, the paradox of the situation is that until we are so heavily burdened by the weight of the world's nonsense, we will not realize that it is all wrong. My wealthy millionaire friend had gone through her entire life accumulating wealth, altering her features with plastic surgery, and buying friends. It was only when she sat down and listened to what I call "noise" that she realized all her "things" meant nothing and brought her no more happiness than a fried egg. She realized, in her own heart, that she had become a perpetuator of "noise." She was screwing people for money, power, and real estate, and her intuition or conscience was pushed further and further down until it never saw the light of day. Her real self ended up in darkness.

Only by uncovering this real self could she ever be "enlightened" again.

The articles in this compendium are collated to form an eye-opener. To talk to the parts of you that know there is hidden truth. When this part of ourselves is spoken to, it enlivens something inside of us. That something is the real you, the real me. Listen to it. This real you knows that the world is full of manipulations and yearns to be set free. It is time to give it the knowledge and strength it deserves. It is time to inspire the true self to question!

But what of groups, societies, organizations? What of the collective nature of mankind as he forms beasts of formality? Is it dangerous?

> Dupes of their own disordered imagination, dupes of whoever wishes to make use of their mania for their own diverse purposes, these men have constantly been as a nursery of adepts for secret societies...these societies are a malady which eats into the social body in its noblest parts, the evil had already thrust out deep and extended roots; if Governments do not take efficacious measures... Europe runs the risk of succumbing to attacks upon it ceaselessly repeated by these associations... absolute monarchies, constitutional monarchies, republics, all are threatened by the Levellers. (From a memoire on secret societies sent by Prince de Metternich of Austria to the Emperor Alexander of Russia in 1822)

Mankind has always been forming himself into groups. There is strength in numbers and, as feeble humans, the only possible way to succeed and be the strongest and fittest species on the planet was to use ingenuity and the strength of the crowd. In time these groupings take on religious significance—enhancing the "spirit" of the assembled people with a belief system. Weak people are ejected, and strong, intelligent ones sought after. This evolved through time and today we know these groups often as secret societies. We are led to believe that within the orders and lodges of these organizations there are great secrets about ourselves and our gods. It's time to find out.

PART I

Mythology and Related Mysteries

1

What Is a Secret Society?

In this book we will concentrate mostly on the origin of secret societies and what lies behind the beliefs and rituals of many of the world's religions. In the beginning, this will lead us through seemingly unrelated material, such as electromagnetism and cyclic phenomena, but all will become apparent as we discover that this natural world relates entirely to our belief systems. These belief systems are similar the world over and are the basis of the esoteric side of secret societies.

However, we need to understand the language of secret societies and exactly what a secret society is. This is a hotly debated subject and is open to various interpretations, as we shall discover.

There are tales of secret societies throughout history. The first question we have to ask is why they had to remain secret. According to popular belief, it is because those meeting in secret were "men of renown" or "standing" and were plotting to change civilization—whether this be through destroying the Church or the royalty or through defending the same.

According to this popular belief, one of the original secret societies was called the Brotherhood of the Snake (or "dragon" or "serpent"). Although no real historical records of an ancient Brotherhood of the Snake, first mentioned by Madame Blavatsky, is in existence, it is a fact that the rituals and beliefs of this supposed secret organization are similar to many that do exist and are strangely related to the serpent. This is no surprise to me, of course, as one of the so-called experts of ophiolatraea (serpent worship). In

Secrets of the Serpent I discovered that there had been an ancient and worldwide serpent religion. Merged with solar, lunar, and cosmic belief systems, this ancient faith did, indeed, take on a worldwide aspect, utilizing the serpent on many levels. Eventually, these beliefs crept in to secret cults and societies and became hidden.

Almost in every instance these secret societies are playing a religious role—contacting god or the gods in ways that the state religion cannot or will not.

This, in itself, gives us a good insight. It is a stark fact that religion or beliefs are excellent ways of drawing in members and utilizing a heightened state in the individual for their own ends—whatever they may be. As with most religions, the members of secret societies are chosen ones, members of the few. A clear example of this is the way that Christians say—without knowing the real meaning of these phrases—that the way is narrow, or that it is easier to pass through the eye of a needle than to enter the kingdom of God. This, in turn, makes the initiate feel more important when accepted—even though precious few are turned down at the initiate stage. This chosen way is universal, and not just the remit of secret societies or religion. It is also found in normal everyday clubs and organizations where you still have to pass tests that are blatantly measured to allow everybody to enter, but at different levels. The idea of there being different levels then moves the process on and ensures that the new initiate strives to become an adherent or full member by learning the ways of the club or society—and thus the initiate becomes fully engulfed in the world of the society.

Secret societies take this membership a step further by including certain devices within the "knowledge bank" that the initiate must learn. These devices include secret handshakes and words, special days of the year known only to the few, and insights into standard texts. All this, and more, makes the initiate feel ever more important. In all instances, the ultimate enlightenment experience seems to be kept back for the very highest levels of initiation—lower levels of illumination are permitted and used for the lower degrees.

There is also a build-up of comradeship through regular meetings. This allows the member to feel part of a wider family and thus more important. Speak to any serving military personnel and you will find that one of the major factors in the success of their unit is credited to camaraderie. This leads the member down a path into the secret society of such emotional depth that to leave would feel like losing a member of the family. The comfort zone the initiate finds himself in is such that he does not wish to leave.

The initiation of any institute is the most important part. Generally, it involves a ritual built around a seemingly impossible-to-understand myth. There are levels to the initiation, just as there are in any religion. It actually starts earlier than most people would understand, with just being chosen or selected to join. This selection process appears to have a plan, and the fact that the word "chosen" is used implies that not all can enter. In fact, from studies of societies, the process is almost random, the true selection coming much later. Those not selected for the higher levels are still members and do the bidding of higher members without actually knowing it, and without knowing that they are often on a lower level.

During the initial stages of any initiation, the new member is cleaned, or cleared, of any thinking that would not benefit the society or religion. This can be seen in the world in general with the military, learning especially from this psychological battle of wills. By breaking down the spirit of the recruit, the army is clearing him or her of any preconceived ideas and allowing the full mind-bending techniques to appear unsullied in the mind of the new soldier.

The same is true of secret societies as the new recruits are told to leave the world behind, including family and friends, who are called distractions or are of the world or devil. The initiates are then given as a replacement the new family of the church or society—who, at this stage of the process, are always forthcoming with help and love to such an extent that the recruit is overwhelmed with joy. This remains in the new recruit's mind, deeply entrenched due to the cleaning process previously carried out.

This process inspires loyalty and a desire for more. The church and society alike supply the demand with mystical insights that can only be supplied to those who pass tests. These tests are created to deepen the bonds of the initiate further. With each new learning process the adherent feels more and more special and is, indeed, given special status.

There are tests put in place to determine whether the initiate has the ability to move further. The deeper aspects of these organizations are as ever more and more secret, and at the highest level they have to be, as this is where the true secret or purpose of the society or religion lies.

The Knights Templar tested the initiate with spitting on the cross. The reason is simple and has nothing to do with the irreverence spoken of by the Church. On one level, if the initiate fails to spit upon the cross as requested, he is rewarded for his true faith with membership, and believes he has made it. On the other level, if he does spit upon the cross, then he has shown true discipline and will be led by the masters' authority wherever that may take him—this initiate will move further up the scale that is hidden to the first who failed to follow the command.

> As soon as the proselyte arrived at the ninth degree he was ripe to serve as blind instrument to all passions, and above all to a limitless ambition for domination....We thus see those who should have been protectors of humanity abandoned to an insatiable ambition, buried under the ruins of thrones and altars in the midst of the horrors of anarchy, after having brought misfortune upon nations, and deserving the curse of mankind. (Von Hammer quoted in *The Trail of the Serpent*)

The effects of the ways of the society are seen to the outside world as strange and unusual. However, these can eventually become the norm and accepted by the general population. Take for instance Christianity: In the early years of its existence, it was classed as a cult or secret organization due to having to remain underground. The reason being that the state religion believed itself far removed from the Christian cult's creeds, when in reality they were the same solar beliefs. Roman philosophies were then what we now class as Pagan, but were followed by the majority. Even Pagans had been underground at one point in their existence. Eventually this underground stream of Christianity grew and grew, with members in positions of "state authority" joining. This, in turn, made it more and more acceptable. Yes, there was a lot of "state" hatred for this cult on the surface because of its secret ways and its threat to the state religions. Christianity had secret signs, secret handshakes, special myths, and rituals, just as any secret organization. And this is the nub of the "secret society" question—it has to remain secret because of the state that makes it a secret society. Eventually, Christianity ruled the majority of the globe and was then fighting against other underground streams, which retained the mysteries of ancient myth, as we shall discover.

Amazingly, exactly the same can be said of Islam, Judaism, Buddhism, and even communism—all of which began as secret and clandestine organizations seemingly against the state. Just like the secret society of the Nazis in the 1930s, all these now standard organizations or religions began within secrecy and ended up taking power—a goal mocked by anti-conspiracy theorists across the globe. The fact remains that history has shown, in every generation, that secret societies have gained power and become church and state—as was their goal.

Today we have secret societies across the world in each country—all with their own goal and all being watched, as ever, by the state. The Arabs and some Christians believe that the Jews

Mary the Mother of God or copy of Isis

are in charge of worldwide conspiracies to take over the world. The Druze and Yezidis in Syria and elsewhere are seen as threats to the norm. The fabled Illuminati are seen as a hidden league of gentlemen by many and are believed to be at the heart of Christian American power. The Christian community believes that global terrorism is funded and carried out by worldwide networks of Islamic secret organizations.

What history has shown is that eventually these underground streams do alter the power balance of the world. Just look at September 11 and the disgusting attacks on America—they were carried out by clandestine organizations and did indeed alter the world. Another example was the revolt in America against the British Empire, which was backed, led, and inspired by the secret society of the Freemasons. In Russia and France, the revolutions were similarly created by secret organizations.

This does not mean that every attempt by every secret society will work, and history is littered with hundreds of such failed attempts. Others have managed to claim power only fleetingly.

Another interesting point to note, and something that relates to our understanding of secret societies, is that many of the greatest minds the world has ever come to know were members of secret organizations. Plato was an initiate into the mysteries of Eluesis and he even tells us in his writings how he was initiated. He claimed that he was placed in a pyramid for three days where he died symbolically, was reborn, and was then given the secrets of the mysteries. There is no wonder that the Great Pyramid was claimed to be part and parcel of the mysteries—the names given to it—Ikhet and khuti—meant "glorious light" or "shining."

So what is a secret society? It is simply a group of individuals, basing their origin in the mists of time or in the celestial and solar dance of the cyclic universe, who come together to affect change. Sometimes they are successful, sometimes they are not, but in most cases, they affect some kind of change in society at large. They are, on the whole, spiritually based, and there is a major thread running through those who have been successful, and that thread is illumination, which gave rise to the name "The Shining Ones."

In 1863 Le Couteulx de Canteleu writing in *Les Sectes et Societes Secretes* said:

> All secret societies have almost analogous initiations, from the Egyptian to the Illuminati, and most of them form a chain and give rise to others.

A Secret Language

History is a lie. History is, as Justice Holmes said, "what the people who won say it is." It has been warped over vast periods of time to fit with each generation's idea of what is fact and what is truth. Without the existence of the secret societies, our history would have been totally different.

The history of mankind is like a vast jigsaw puzzle. Only when all the pieces are laid down in the correct order can we see the bigger picture. The result is quite startling. We will see a grand and enlightening picture of how mysteries of the ancient and not-so-ancient world can now be solved, from megalithic standing stones, the Holy Grail, and alchemy, to the truth behind religion and our present political systems. The story of secret societies hides the real history of mankind.

In much the same way that modern day genetic research is showing how recently interlinked we are as a human race, the research and subsequent conclusions set out in this book will show how our own political and religious belief systems are from the same source.[1] There is, after all, nothing new under the sun. New religious systems are just renewed elder religions with different names and different settings—the underlying beliefs are the same.

We can learn from this history and understand the cyclical patterns of human behavior, which will help us to predict the future more easily—or so we are told. We will look at the existence of life and consciousness; trace where it came from and where it is going. We will move over millennia of mysteries to reason an actual history based upon fact and evidence. We will see whether there actually is a worldwide conspiracy, and, if so, where it is leading us. We shall establish motives, seek out new data, view existing documents in a new light to gain an overview of vast periods of time and civilizations, and finally come to grips with the mysteries of faith.

One of the most disturbing aspects of secret societies comes from the clear understanding that we have been lied to for centuries by one historian after another. Yet we must not lose sight of the fact that these professionals are responsible for piecing together huge amounts of information and giving supposedly factual accounts based on their own belief systems, which are influenced by the time and location in which they lived or are living. Without the hard work of these historians, a book such as this would have been impossible to write, even though its conclusions are in stark contrast to the accepted view. We must remember: many of the history books we read today were written, or at the very least researched, during a Victorian age of high Christianity—a time when every theory and fact was bent towards a Christian viewpoint. For instance, when it was discovered that there were ancient crucified gods that predated Christ, these were hushed, destroyed, or even purported to be the God-given knowledge of the future crucifixion of Christ. This is, of course, utter rubbish, coming from a religion that itself was a creation of ancient cults—as we shall see.

We must also understand that many historians, artists, builders, politicians, religionists, and laypeople wanted to pass the truth on but could not. So they devised ciphers, codes, and symbolism for their own kind and future generations to decipher. The beauty of many of these symbols was that most were already known and already held orthodox significances and, therefore, the hidden meaning could easily be cloaked in mainstream religiosity.

Symbols are hidden all around us like a trail of clues leading toward treasure. We come into contact with them everywhere we go—from the symbolic architecture and stained-glass windows of medieval churches, to, for example, the logo on a company van. My own company logo was symbolic of Phase Transition, the changing of one substance into another. For a marketing company, this was ideal. Only people who knew about such things would be able to see this, however. Others would just see an arrow with a wavy line. I had hidden a symbolic device within an otherwise ordinary-looking company logo.

Mankind has used this subtle language for thousands of years. Through each generation, this alternative form of communication has developed and grown increasingly complex, making it more difficult to decipher. The only way to discover the secrets of symbolism is to break down each and every painting, building, or text into every possible meaning, and consider both the people who created these artifacts and the time in which they lived. These finds must then be weighed against known historical data, such as archaeological information.

One of the greatest works of symbolism on every level is the Bible. To the scholar who knows the alternative meanings of some of the apocalyptic texts it has been obvious, for a long time, that there is truth hidden away. To many more the underlying principle of the whole book is astrotheological—Jesus as the sun, Mary the moon, and all 12 apostles are therefore members of the Zodiac. But there are so many hidden layers that show that any number of meanings are possible, and we must remember that lies are also hidden in code. Of course, to add to this, there are hundreds of texts and so-called Gospels, written at the same time as the Bible, that simply never passed the test of the early Christian propagandists and were discarded from liturgy. These are equally valid now to the history of man, or we shall again be susceptible to the manipulation of those who chose the contents of the Bible in the first place.

We must also be careful not to read too much into texts, as we could be in danger of perceiving them in the light of our own modern society. There have been many recent examples of books in which ancient structures and texts are being taken as evidence of "extraterrestrial visitations." Regardless of any other more Earthly interpretation and a huge lack of understanding of the religious and cultural traditions of the time, this evidence is abused for a predetermined idea or theory.

Another example of this is how modern-day evangelists use the Biblical book of Revelation as "proof" of the Lord's imminent return. They point to hidden meanings regarding nuclear war and Middle Eastern dictators as if they have had some kind of divine revelation themselves. The truth is, as any historian will tell you, that every generation since the writing of *Revelation* has claimed the end was very close. That is partly the point of the solar cyclical Gospel, misinterpreted completely, as usual. All of these false interpretations make it more difficult to break the code down into facts.

We shall begin by taking a look at our origins. The origin of life has always been a fundamental part of religion. The age of enlightenment, of Darwin and his contemporaries, drastically altered the religious outlook of the world. If we look at the truth behind the origin of mankind, we will see that Darwin was only "discovering" what was already known—that this age of enlightenment was planned, and that it had to happen for the required changes to occur. We will see how ancient man and his religious beliefs were perfectly parallel to our current scientific beliefs—the difference being only in the terms used. Take the following pattern, which has been simplified but is common to the majority of the world's religions:

1. Only the God exists. He is supreme and is alone.

2. The heavens and earth are formless. Everything is darkness and/or covered by primeval waters.

3. Then there is light.

4. Heaven and earth are split apart.

5. The land is separated from the waters. Day and night are created with the new sun.

6. The land brings forth vegetation and eventually creatures.

7. Birds and animals are created.

8. Man appears.[2]

As you will note, this pattern is also common to the current theories regarding the origin of species without the acceptance of the existence of God. It is completely in line with the so-called big bang theory and yet seems to have emerged thousands of years ago. These patterns were especially notable in ancient Egypt, one of the mysterious forerunners of the world's faiths.

Previously, religion was responsible for informing us of our origins. Now scientists tell us to look for facts about our origins rather than philosophize about them, while at the same time they create new theories, which are sometimes prejudiced and do not take into account all of our knowledge.

New facts come to light with every passing day. New ideas regarding mathematical equations of the laws of physics are proving some theories to be fact. We need to understand these facts and theories and must not be afraid to alter our own personal viewpoint once these new facts emerge. Our own personal truths must change or we risk becoming stale, inert religious fanatics. It is unfortunate that religious fervor in all disciplines (including science) can stop us from seeing these marvelous breakthroughs, and prevents us from moving on and even evolving.

So many facts are hidden from us because of generations of prejudice and intolerance that some of them will be startling. No one will remain unaffected by the evidence presented here. Everyone who reads this book will have his or her own belief system or personal prejudice challenged and will not want to accept everything as fact. Much of the evidence here can be taken in a number of ways, and, where this is known, each alternative viewpoint has been given. Where other views are required, these have been sought from original sources. I include in this all religious factions, whether classed as cult, occult, or mainstream.

In our search for the truth, we will examine everything that could possibly fit into one book. We will start from Adam and Eve and move through to modern science. We will then go on to see how our belief systems began and where some of the more paranormal explanations originated. There will be factual evidence of how our belief systems have been used, abused, and manipulated

The glory of religion—gold

by a secret and deadly group of individuals who have a history going back thousands of years. They had a name, they had a power base, and they had a secret, locked away within their initiated few, which had major implications for the future of mankind. We will discover the secret and reveal it.

There are thousands of best-selling books out there, which support mysteries that simply do not exist. This book will dispel those mysteries and put us back on the straight path. Why, in this supposedly enlightened age, do we still believe and feed off the controlling lies of those in positions of authority? The answer is simple. Knowledge is power—therefore if you keep the knowledge for yourself, you keep the power.

When we come to leave old religions behind we are simply given a new one, more relevant to our age and to the political aims of the power brokers. Do we need the opium of religion or can we survive without it? Do we need the repackaged "New Age" religions, or the pseudo-scientific cults that look towards UFOs for the meaning of life? This book will show how even the new belief systems are based upon the same old lies and the secret knowledge that we are supposedly "too simple" to understand.

The Shining Ones, under different names, have manipulated us over the centuries by many means, including psychology. Utilizing the story of our origins, they played on our desire to know who we are and where we came from, and controlled our belief systems from the start. They also understood some of the very basic and fundamental ways in which our brains work and are influenced. They discovered that we were influenced not only by people, but also by the world around us in more ways than we today can even comprehend.

If you are ready for the truth, if you can honestly say you have an open mind and are prepared to let go of misconceptions, then read on. Forget the false interpretations of myth and religion you have heard so many times, and know them for what they really are: the secret language of the Shining Ones.

2

Heavenly Bodies: The Gods of the Ancients

To further our quest in the understanding of secret societies we need to fully understand their background, both in belief and in history. Because so many of today's secret societies express imagery and symbolism that revolves around the beliefs of our pre-Christian ancestors, we would do well to try and comprehend how and why these beliefs started and what the symbols that we see really mean. To this end, we need to investigate the realm of the "heavenly bodies"—the planets in the night sky.

I am always overjoyed when I visit a remote location, where the light from street lamps doesn't pollute and poison our vision of our heavenly partners. To stand and stare on a crystal clear night at the twinkling stars and to be in awe at the incredible number of lights that reach our eyes is an experience everybody should have. Today we understand what these stars are—they are distant and sometimes long-dead suns. Our ancestors, without the orange glare of a suburban street, were unaware of the science behind the wonder. For them these were the myriad eyes of the gods in heaven—the great Shining Ones in the sky. The father sun and the mother moon were dominant due to their size and the seeming relationship they held to the very hormonal nature of man and woman—they literally controlled our lives. There is little wonder that the tales of these heavenly twinkling gods should remain with us in our religious fables, myths, and folklore.

Similar to the Pagan god Pan, whose name means "All," the Bible says that "Christ is all and in all." Did the early Christians and Gnostics understand man's relationship with the hidden forces of the larger universe? One thing is sure, this understanding has been held like a baby in arms by the secret societies we shall soon discuss.

The questions of whether early man understood and utilized the effects of cyclic patterns, electromagnetic forces, and the closeness of his nature with plants and animals may be answered in the signs of the reverence he paid to these elements; his worship and ritualistic behavior surrounding some of these basic and fundamental parts of the "supernature."

Cyclic patterns and rhythms dominate our lives, from the day to night patterns to the seasonal changes and their effects upon us. If we look at a few of the cycles that have become important to man, we can see how they affect us.

The solar system in balance

Day/night cycles are different in other parts of the world. Some have longer nights and shorter days, for example, and their nature has adapted accordingly. Seasonal Affective Disorder (SAD) is purely the result of long nights. On the equator, where the sun is stronger and is out for longer periods, SAD does not exist and is indeed refuted.

In several parts of the world, we have four seasons. Elsewhere, the seasons are different. Tropical regions have two seasons: wet and dry. Monsoon areas have three: cold, hot, and rainy. In polar regions, the temperature change from summer to winter is abrupt.

Man, animal, and plant life have adapted remarkably well to the different seasons they experience, and so too has their mythology.

The pineal gland actually measures the seasons and length of day. This is how we adapt to the various seasons around the globe. Many species, including some types of bird, can accurately predict the weather to help them plan migratory patterns. The Orange Ladybird insect in the United Kingdom has never been wrong in its long-term winter predictions.

The Moon

The moon plays an important part in all the religions of the world and is hidden deeply in the secret societies. Lunar cycles and human experience are intrinsically linked. The tidal flow of the world's oceans corresponds to the waxing and waning of the moon, as does the menstrual cycle, which has had a profound effect upon our early and later religious beliefs.

Menstruation (moon-struation) occurs only during the fertile years and had symbolic meaning amongst early cultures. The menstrual blood of women is considered with awe and fear and may have much to do with the use of Red Ochre by ancient man. This blood is also derided and called unclean (even today, the women of Judaism go through a purification bath seven days after the end of the menstruation), a poisoning of woman for her sins by the great gods, although this appeared to be a much later addition as a result of the subtle battle of the religious sexes, as the earlier cults seem to have revered the blood, even to the point of drinking it.

Menstruating women were often kept away from the other members of their tribe or village. This may be why the witches' Sabbath took place specifically on the day when the moon took rest, and was associated with evil. Ishtar, one of the Moon Goddess's titles, was said to be menstruating on this day. The menstruating woman is also seen as a symbol of fertility, and in some African cultures she is led around the home of one who wishes to become pregnant and asked to touch everything. The onset of menstruation marks the move from child to woman and was celebrated with Earth Goddess or Mother Goddess rituals and, much later, within the taking of blood in the Eucharist.

The Sabbath (Heart-rest of the moon), the moon's day of rest, the seventh day, was later taken over by the Jews, who turned it into their day of rest and laid waste to the maternal, lunar religions, and inaugurated their paternal "sun god." Christians took this further, moving the day of rest to the Mithraic Sun-day—the original moon day being Monday.[1]

The sidereal lunar month is 27.32 days and the synodic lunar month is 29.53 days. Both have different paths and different meanings dependent upon your culture. In the sidereal lunar year there are 13 months per year. This is a matriarchal structure and is more than 3,000 years old.

The instillation of a 12-month period seems to have been an attempt by the solar patriarchal cultures to gain dominance, and thus we now have 12 months per year. The months are, in effect, symbols of the Zodiac houses. Each "house" or "mansion" of the Zodiac is approximately 30 degrees, so the sun passes through each "mansion" every 30 degrees. Jesus, of course, as the symbol of the sun came of age at 30 and claimed that his Father's mansion had many rooms. All of this was what is known as astrotheology—the theology of the stars—and all of this crept slowly into the hidden chambers of the secret orders.

The elimination of the 13-month period has come down to us today with the persecution of the witches' coven, which has 13 members, the number 13 being considered unlucky in the West, but more importantly the fact that Jesus had 12 disciples, therefore making up 13 in total, the hidden number of Mother Earth. Indeed the very concept of Christianity is built around a celestial and solar worship: Christ is the sun, which dies for three days in midwinter and is resurrected three days later; Mary being linked both in myth and etymology to the moon; and the 12 disciples representing the 12 star-signs.

The moon is tied up in many of our early cultures. The names of its associated deities vary due to locality, language, and ethnic differences, but are all essentially of the same: Aphrodite, Astarte, Badb, Brigit, Ch'ang O, Demeter, Persephone, Hecate, Inanna, Isis, Ishtar, Maja Jotma, Tsuki-Yomi, and all emerging as the Gnostic Sophia or wisdom. Some of these designations have been carried on, kept alive behind the scenes by the secret cults while they were subtly battling or even creating the front lines of the new or growing solar and male-oriented popular gods such as Mithras and Yahweh. They are all literal elements of a very real internal symbolism—the balance of the male and female sides of our own mind.

The terms "lunatic" ("moon-struck") and "mental" are both taken from the moon, under the impression that such effects are brought on by the lunar periods, usually the full moon. It is not surprising that the moon was denounced as the "mad" moon when we consider the patriarchal and matriarchal battles being fought across the continents. The idea was put forward that the electrical energy of the body became drained at this time of the month, and caused the person to lose his or her faculties. Just 200 years ago, Lunacy was even covered by English law. Kleptomania, arson, and dangerous driving have been shown scientifically to increase at times of the full moon, so there may be some scientific reason for this matriarchal lost battle.

The Jewish Passover is celebrated on the lunar calendar; the Christian Easter (Eoster was the Anglo-Saxon goddess of spring) is calculated from the full moon after the vernal equinox. The full moon at the autumnal equinox is celebrated as the harvest moon. The Jews had moon festivals, such as New Moon and Full Moon (see Num. 28,11:14). The eclipse of the moon is considered by many cultures to be the union of the Sun God and Moon Goddess.

There were 500,000 births measured in New York in 1948/57. The results revealed that more births occurred during a waning moon and the maximum after a full moon. In the North Sea coast of Germany, most births occurred at high tides as the moon passed overhead. More children are born in the Northern Hemisphere in May and June than in November and December, and vice versa in the Southern Hemisphere. Size of offspring has also been mapped and shows a noticeable pattern dependent upon time of year. In the 1960s, Eugen Jonas understood the lunar aspect of ovulation and successfully increased the effectiveness of contraception to 98 percent. When he was presented with the birth charts of 250 newborn children he successfully identified the sex of 87 percent of the babies from planetary information alone.

Frank Brown of Northwestern University, Illinois, found that oysters in his laboratory, 1,000 miles from their Connecticut shore, opened at the same time as their home shores' high tide, which, in turn, is related to the moon's orbital pattern. Brown also proved that potatoes, rats, and fiddler crabs are all governed by lunar periods. Within laboratories, the metabolisms of various creatures fluctuated in response to lunar patterns and geomagnetic factors. Now, years later, research is proving that all known sea creatures, when taken from their natural homes, still obey the same lunar cycles. At the time, many scientists thought Brown to be dealing with the paranormal sciences and ignored his research. What it does show (and scientifically) is the effect of cycles and electromagnetic energy on the natural inhabitants of this planet—including humans. It is no wonder the ancients saw in these planetary bodies the gods who controlled their lives.

The Sun

The Shining One, "great light of the world," is venerated all over the globe as the light of life, the giver of heat, and the most important cyclic symbol of all time. Our ancestors knew that it meant life or death. It was essential for the sun to return every day, for its strength to be renewed again each Easter. We say the sun is wise, and therefore in mystery plays around the world, light equates to wisdom. The strength of the sun gave rise to its being considered the most powerful of the deities. In the early developed civilizations the sun is always there. In Egyptian culture, and according to the Heliopolis cult, the sun was Atum, Ra, Re, Atum-Ra, or Ra-Atum. In the Memphis cult, the sun was known as Amun, or Amun-Re. The scarab beetle is often used to portray the sun in some aspects, a symbol of self-regeneration and the early ideas of reincarnation. The sun is generally male and outwits the lunar female goddess as well as mates with her.

We sacrifice, dance (almost always, significantly, in circles or cycles), travel hundreds of miles, and sing to the great light. We humanize it and give it names such as Apollo, and include him in dramas. This, of course, hides a deeper and more symbolic understanding that the initiated, the ancient Shining Priesthood of the sun knew how to decipher. The cyclic pattern and life-giving nature of the sun is key to the secrets of the ancient Shining Ones.

The movements of the sun have inspired tales of where the sun god goes and why he comes back, of battles fought and death overcome. This last idea of overcoming death gives us the first hint at how man has used the sun god fables and mysteries to hide the secret ideas of how we could be reincarnated. Thousands of years of begging the sun to return each day and be reborn each spring led ancient man to develop his own rebirth rituals and ideas of how to accomplish it. Now, with thousands of years of additional mystery and symbolism, we find it almost impossible to decipher the magic secret.

Everyday we rise with the sun. Our bodies release hormones, which waken, revive, and regenerate us. In summer, our endocrine glands release more hormones that bring a sense of well-being. By late afternoon we feel more relaxed as the sun's strength wanes. The secret police of many countries often choose this time of day to arrest people, as they are more easily subdued. If today we understand how to utilize the power of the sun with the regenerative effects of holidays and by the dealings of the secret police, what did our ancient and supposedly less complicated ancestors do?

Sunspot activity affects our biorhythms directly in ways we do not understand. Evidence shows that it can be an irritant to our bodily functions and mental attitude. The Foundation for the Study of Cycles has produced some interesting results with their long-term research, including some of the following: There is a 3.86 year cycle in lemming suicides and North American lumber pine growth; an 11.1 year cycle of sun spot activity and serious upsurge in war and unrest. The Black Death and the Great Plague coincided with this solar turbulence. There is also an increase in traffic accidents every 11.1 years, a rise and fall in hemlines, and an increase of volcanic and earthquake activity. This last point will not be lost on those who already know that Yahweh was in fact a volcanic and solar god—an ancient linking of the two cyclic phenomena.

The Stars

The myriad Shining Ones also have an effect on us. Michel Gauquelin, a French psychologist, placed the hypothesis that we are affected by the position of the planets at our time of birth firmly on the doorstep of science. He showed that the position of the stars had some indication as to what line of work one may enter later in life. This was not related to the practice of astrology or the horoscopes in the daily newspapers, but a serious, scientific data analysis. The psychologist Hans Eysenck said, "How ever much it may go against the grain, I think we must admit that there is something here that requires explanation." His results, however, only showed the astronomically aligned tendencies within the higher professionals, as the same response was not achieved with unskilled workers.

The study of the stars goes back thousands of years. Some say 4,000 B.C. Sumeria was the first to do so. Others put this even earlier and say that ancient man was studying the stars 32,000 years ago.[2] Their evidence is an engraved antler from Abri Blanchard, France, with a strange pattern of notches or calendrical phases of the moon.

With all the evidence on patterns, rhythms, and electromagnetism that affect our bodies, it is no wonder that modern science has taken another look at the ancient art of astrology, which has been neglected because of the widespread misuse of generic horoscopes.

Natal astrology deals with planetary positions at the time of our birth. Astrometeorology concerns the prediction of major earthquakes, climatic changes, and volcanic eruptions. There is much evidence to suggest that certain animals, which can predict such occurrences, are born at a specific time of year that corresponds to certain astrological predictions, and the reason is simple. The movements of the planets cause changes in the subtle electromagnetic energy of the galaxy, and with such organs as the pineal gland, animals can indeed "read" this information. In my other work (*The Serpent Grail*), I have shown how this energy is indeed real and can, in fact, even be picked up by humans, when they revert back to their own superconscious.

Cosmobiology is the study of the balance between cyclic behavior, biological patterns, radiation, and gravitational effects upon us, and as any good scientist will tell you, gravitation is a wave and can affect our psyche.

Ancient peoples must have understood the precise mappings of these newly named sciences when they too predicted such things by the stars. It may be that ancient man was using both his "hidden powers," and the tools of the Earth around him. It may also be that the ideas and symbolism of alchemy were just a few more steps along this path.

The Indian sage, Parasar (circa. 3000 B.C.) used natal astrology in his work. Megalithic structures have many astrological and Earth alignments. The Pyramids map the stars, obeying the Hermetic lore of "as above so below." Ziggurats, temples, floor paintings, carvings, and 40-mile-long lines etched into the ground all convey the ancient and global belief in astrological predictions.

The very earliest almanacs contained weather forecasts based upon astrological predictions. In the countries of Arabia, the position of the stars was consistent with the weather. The ancient priesthood would have appeared to be in the know all the time, and, therefore, would appear holy and godlike; it was little wonder that they became incorporated into the symbolic format and titles of the stars.

The term *zodiac* has a meaning pertaining to animals, possibly "animal map" or "circle of animals." This is seen more precisely in the ancient Chinese chart on which every star sign has an animal name. The Zodiac is the belt of the gods, which lies nine degrees to either side of the ecliptic plane, and contains the orbits of the moon and the major planets. Each Zodiac is 30 degrees apart. The sun originally traversed these minor gods on a regular path and the various signs of the zodiac were blessed with his arrival. All the god-man stories, from Jesus to Horus, can be shown quite easily to be this very progression of the sun through the heavens.

That the word *zodiac* pertains to animals explains why it contains animal symbols, such as the ram and fish. These ancient anthropomorphic beliefs were included into the sky, in the same way that Pagan gods were taken on as saints by the Christian Church. Later on, the saints received their own stars and were painted with them in ecclesiastical fervor—they even took on the symbols of the animals, as they were nothing more than a Christian creation developed from astrotheological origins. This concept has been concealed from the general population, as Acharya S tells us in *The Christ Conspiracy*:

> The cosmology or celestial mythos has in reality been hidden from the masses for many centuries for the purpose of enriching and empowering the ruling elite. Its conspiring priest-kings have ruled empires in full knowledge of it since time immemorial and have 'lorded' it over the heads of the serfs.

Here yet again we have other authors discovering the idea that since time "immemorial" the people of the world have been lied to for power.

In some of the world's zodiacs, such as the Chinese version, there is even a tree at the center representing the Earth's polar axis—and this is the real location of Eden, in the sky.

The Babylonians, and especially people in the Middle East, studied the stars mathematically and attempted, even as long as 5,000 years ago, to scientifically log the reactions and effects of the stars. They produced a calendar and perfect measures of time, essential for a people without clocks. Carl Jung suggested that the Zodiac was an archetypal component of the psyche of mankind, and he linked it with the theory of the "collective unconscious."

The patterns and rhythms of the stars, with their gravitational and radiation activity, have enormous effects upon our universe, but could they also affect us individually and collectively?

The cosmic radiation hitting and passing through our planet is millions of years old. It comes in cycles, as does the solar wind. The cycles increase and decrease, but nevertheless there is a pattern. Our species has been on this planet, and life has been part of the vast universe, long enough for there to be some marked and observable effect.

There are a vast number of other cycles in which we are involved, such as urinary cycles, sexual cycles, stock market crashes, epidemics, and a host of other minor cycles. A study of history will show how generations experience the same mistakes, and successes, all in a cyclic pattern. Stock market crashes themselves make a profound analogy. Those in the know and with the power or money can predict these things, so they can also increase their power and money exponentially. Those with the knowledge maintain the power—the knowledge of cycles.

The Buddhist Wheel of Life reflects the understanding the ancients had of this cyclic life of ours. The Wheel culminates in the 12 links in the chain of causation on the search for truth, and it depicts, amongst others, creatures of passion, stupidity, and hatred, and shows how we endlessly repeat the same things. These repeating patterns of life events, circumstances, and our thoughts and emotions that come round again and again, are just like the planets that orbit the sun at different rates of orbital frequency.

We could say that the orbiting movement of the planets in our solar system represent—and at the same time reflect—the same patterns that are going on within a person's internal dialogue, as if what is going on in outer-space reflects what is going on within our inner-space, and within the inner depths of our own psyche.

The Hindus also make a connection with reincarnation, as the life-death cycle is just another cycle of repeating patterns they believe are due to karma not yet worked out, and broken. It is said that the ultimate goal is to stop or break the Wheel of Karma.

If this is true, then every person's astrological chart will contain information about the present life and maybe even previous lives—that is, the "program" that each person holds within his or her own consciousness—and that an individual's chart or horoscope will also show the strengths and weaknesses of that person, and also those circumstances and events that are both rewarding and challenging. It will also show the stumbling blocks that we each have to overcome in order to move on.

If we are intelligent enough to study the cycle of the heavens and understand this, then it's possible that our own personal horoscope will, more or less, reveal to us the same patterns locked up in our DNA, being the path of our own life, and also the challenges that are set before us, which we are being encouraged to try and break. It may even be possible to break the program or pattern entirely!

It has now been determined that the information one gets from a personal horoscope is usually about 75 to 80 percent correct, depending of course on the skill of the astrologer—adding that this statistic really stems from the fact that, in general, man has only a limited knowledge about astrology—as much knowledge as he has about everything else, if you take things to the highest level that man can understand at this present stage in his evolution.

Lack of knowledge about astrology is really due to certain prejudices people have in regard to the superficial and over-generalized version of astrology that is deemed acceptable both for and by society.

The astrology that we read in the newspapers and magazines and can learn from the books on the shelves in the Mind, Body, and Spirit section is the astrology familiar to society, and which has become too generalized and commercialized to be of any real use. The planets themselves—and more importantly the position of the planets in the solar system at any one time—will give a different meaning for each individual. The different vibrational influences that radiate from each planet, and especially the changing vibrations that result from the changing positions of each planet in relation to the others in the solar system, are very subtle as to be hardly noticeable or measurable. However, because of the continuous bombardment of these vibrations on the Earth, they are also deeply effective and far-reaching with regard to the consciousness of each individual on this planet, and so the meanings that can be read from them is based on the position of the planets at the exact time of every individual's conception or birth. Seeing that most of us are conceived and born at different times this creates a wide variety of different beliefs, experiences, and outlooks. All this is reflected in the positions of the planets in the cyclonic, cycling motion of our solar system, which acts as a giant cosmic clock, containing within all its biorhythmic-like cycles the "blueprint" for each individual life on this planet. So then, in a nutshell, an individual's astrological chart is a picture of that individual's life, and each planet (and the interactions between the planets) charts the repeating patterns in that life—the frequencies of the planets, creating the vibrational patterns that had been imprinted on the central nervous system while the fetus of the individual was growing in the womb. The patterns of events that take years to repeat are linked to the larger, slower, outer planets—such as Jupiter, Saturn, and Uranus. One's horoscope is really a representation of one's picture of reality, and the internal dialogue that creates this particular picture.

I am certain the ancients understood this, and this may have been one of the reasons why great emphasis was placed on the positions of the stars and the movements of the sun, moon, and planets.

The web that man has spread across the many thousands of years is complex and cluttered. Historians would have us believe that various human achievements sprang up spontaneously and simultaneously across the continents. Mathematically, this is in error. There are too many coincidences, too many simultaneous eruptions of human culture and achievement, from the buildings that share a common purpose as solar and astral temples to the emergence of the ancient cross as a symbol—all of this is related to the resonant energy of the universe and is deeply entrenched in the emerging scientific idea of quantum entanglement. This new theory, backed by scientists from Beijing University, actually shows how telepathy is possible and likely when the particles/waves of two individuals are entangled. The same effect occurs with any energy wave/particle. Through meditation the individual comes closer and closer to consciously understanding this energy—an amazing thought, and an amazing deception that this information has been kept from us.

Remember that there is no easy way to show everything that is linked, there is simply too much information and much is hidden in secret societies.

In 1957, Tom Lethbridge wrote a book called *Gogmagog*. He claimed that Druidism and Brahmanism were linked and shared a common origin. Lethbridge believed that their ancient religion was somehow related to and existed for the Earth Goddess, also associated with the Moon Goddess and often cross-linked. This is true in that She was one of the deities worshipped by the ancient priesthood, to whom the Brahmins and Druids were related. The Earth/Moon Goddess, or Mother, had many names, Gaia or Ge, Isis, Astarte, and eventually culminating in the Virgin Mary (Mother of God) or even Mary Magdalene, and leading to the cult of the Black Virgin, which itself seems to be related more to Mary Magdalene than the Mother of God. In essence they are all built around the same energy, the same very human and even universal pattern that is built into each and every one of us.

Lethbridge was so upset by the reaction to his hypothesis that he "retired" to Devon and took up dowsing, itself uniquely linked to the ancient Shining Ones' culture and to the idea of earth energy. Unfortunately, the effect of this was to fuel his adversaries' opinions of him, even though he discovered some remarkable facts, which to this day are highly regarded by dowsers.

Lethbridge showed that different substances or items produce different swing rates of the pendulum. The pendulum is well known for being the most accurate dowsing implement, and in Lethbridge's case this proved to be true. He found that the age of items gave a different rate, as did the surrounding emotions. A pebble thrown violently reacted differently from one thrown in a less aggressive manner. Work carried out by other dowsers has shown that while the rates differ between dowsers, the principle remains the same. This difference may be due to the rate at which the dowser absorbs the emitted energy, but it is hard to understand why the rates are uniformly different. If there had been a pattern of irregular rates this would be sufficient evidence to ignore the practice; as it is, we have evidence enough to require further investigation.

Although some of the conclusions drawn by Lethbridge are open to debate, we are left wondering whether there is any evidence for humans being able to pick up energy. And I was to find there was. (See author's other work or *www.serpentgrail.com*.)

As we have seen, electromagnetism is in all things and we are open to its power, as are animals. The theory is that we transfer this energy to the implements used in dowsing. This may explain why some dowsers have different rates, but still keep the same proportions as Lethbridge's work. In the Vietnam War and World War I, dowsers were used to help the Army find unexploded shells and locate mines. Modern oil companies use the skills of the dowsers to locate oil.

There is much evidence to show that ancient man practiced dowsing, or radiesthesia, in one form or another. In the Tassili-n-Ajjer caves in the Sahara of southeastern Algeria, there are ancient pictoglyphs, approximately 8,000 years old, which show what appears to be dowsing. Thoth, the Egyptian god of wisdom and writing, and the Greek Daedalus, both closely associated, are credited with its invention.

The Chinese, the masters of Feng Shui, have also been credited with the invention of dowsing from the 3rd millennium B.C. In the Bible we find that Moses (the patriarch who, according to Acts, had all the knowledge of Egypt and whose name is linked to the sun and the snake) was adept at finding water with his rod. The writers of the Bible vehemently opposed the tradition of dowsing. This was because just about any layperson could dowse and therefore could take the secret knowledge away from the priesthood and reduce their power.

Later, the Inquisition of the Catholic Church found it necessary to stamp out dowsing once again, while many abbots continued the practice in secret and even wrote extensively on the subject, albeit symbolically. What would be the reaction of the Church if its people were to find out that their own prophets, including the supposed Savior, practiced divination?

Among the other forms of divination to look out for is Bath-Kol: divination by means of the heavenly, divine voice. By interpreting this sound, the ancient Jewish prophets could announce the Will of God to the people. If ever there was a tool to keep the sacredness of God within the elite, then this is it. This practice appears to be worldwide in all cultures but is carried out only by the initiated few. That is not to say that those individuals were not in some way and through some form of formulated ritual actually getting involved in the quantum entanglement of the universal collective.

Necromancy, the art of raising spirits from the dead to discover answers, is another form of divination that has strong links with the Bible. The Witch of Endor, in 1 Samuel 28, summoned the spirit of Samuel for Saul to question. Saul paid the price for this sin, but this demonstrates the existence of this ancient practice, which stretches back to beliefs in the Underworld or place of the ancestors; a belief and a divination accomplished all over the globe. Was this a practice common to the ancient priesthood who may have traveled the world? The period fits well. But it is also part and parcel of the Shining Ones' attempt to contact those who have passed into the Duat or Underworld. The ancient priests actually believed that they could contact the spirits of the dead through meditation, drug-induced states, or even physical actions such as Dervish.

Astrology is a form of divination relating to the stars. This too was practiced globally at the same time as necromancy.[3]

The interpretation of dreams, oneiromancy, is a worldwide custom and one which also appears within the pages of the Bible, as well as many other holy books from just about every other religion and culture from our ancient past. Sometimes the dreamer would choose a specific location and take a hallucinogenic substance to bring on a dream, which only the priest could interpret. In the Bible, the one with the ability to interpret the dream was the chosen one of God—the Shining One, a special person or priest.

Scrying is the method of using a crystal or shining ball, mirror, or, more correctly and more ancient, a shining stone. Only a priest, or latterly clairvoyant, could read the message received. This art goes back to and even further than the Egyptians. Gypsies (the word is derived from "Egyptians") still use the crystal ball today. Hebrew tradition has it that Adam received wisdom from a shining stone, and Nostradamus used a bowl of water, as did Zeus.

Geomancy is the ancient from of reading messages from the earth. The word comes from the Greek word for Mother Earth, Ge or Gaia, and *mancy* or *magos*, meaning knowledge. Ancient Greek, Latin, and Arab writers tell us about geomancy. This divination technique is also global and is referred to in the Bible, in some remarkable places, as we will see in later chapters. The timescale of the spread of geomancy across the globe is much debated. There is, however, no doubt that it was universally used and shows the link of mankind to beliefs within the Mother Goddess, right through into Christianity—a survival of ancient traditions.

In geomancy, the earth is drawn upon by hand or with sticks and a response read. Special codes or symbols are used, which are known only by the initiated. The symbols are usually lines, dots, or stars. The final symbol is probably the one we should remember, as this includes the symbol of the fish, although not in modern geomancy techniques. The Arabs used random marks and read these. In other parts of the world, earth was thrown into the air and the shapes it formed as it fell on the ground it were interpreted.

In China, the most complex form of geomancy was Feng Shui (literally, "wind and water"), the interpretation of the Earth energies (known as "Dragon Paths") and the use of this reading to discover where best to place tombs or temples. The Chinese use a similar technique on humans in acupuncture, a very popular and reportedly effective alternative medicine.

The Chinese called the powers of the Earth "Yin" (female, negative) and "Yang" (male, positive). As we know, everything, including energy, matter, and magnetism, has a positive and a negative, so once again, our ancestors were there before us. Modern-day dowsing has shown that sites such as Stonehenge, Glastonbury, Newgrange, the pyramids of Egypt, and the ziggurats of South America are all situated on these so-called ancient energy lines. This is yet another example of the global aspect of these ancient beliefs, which spread through cultures without altering the ethnicity of the population, but fitting in with it. This ancient priesthood did not change or improve the lifestyles of the general population, which is why it has been so difficult for archaeologists to discover their existence; instead, they simply passed on knowledge, sharing the power amongst themselves and the few who were chosen to become Shining Ones.

There are subtle hints, missed by orthodox history, which are beginning to reveal the patterns of an antiquated hierarchy of special priests. Once we are alerted to their existence, it becomes obvious that they were there all along. If we read any part of the Bible again and replace the words "Lord" or "God" with the "Shining Ones," it will become apparent how deeply rooted into our culture this priesthood really is.

There are many belief systems in the world, but they all come from one basic and undeniable core, invented and evolved separately by the Shining Ones. The same term is used across the globe due to the same enlightened aspect or illumination achieved and sustained by them, and a worship of the same solar globe seen everywhere. These priests were the experts of self-mind-control—manipulating their own minds into the Shining world of the universe through energy cycles and magnetism. With the use of drugs and physical and mental effort, they achieved the Holy Grail of existence. With the benefits to themselves being good health and knowledge of the world around them, they found the Elixir.

Instead of looking for great migrations of civilizations such as Atlantis, we should be looking toward the faith makers, the illuminated ones who spread throughout the peoples of the world and became gods among men.

3

The Truth Inside Your Skull

The Ancient Mystery of the Skull Cup

For some reason, many of us just seem to know that the answer to all our searching questions about time, the universe, and life after death could be answered by our own minds, and this almost paradoxical situation has been with mankind for thousands of years. Man searched within himself for the answers and I believe man found them. Here, in this short piece, I hope to relay some of the amazing symbols of that searching and reveal the hidden meanings behind some of the most enigmatic objects and images of history. This chapter will concentrate on one of the most profound of symbols utilized by secret societies—the skull. But before I move forward into the skull I must concentrate on the energy that is supposedly raised towards it and which was and is believed to infuse it with power—the kundalini.

The kundalini, in one form or another, is found in almost all secret societies—whether they know it or not. It is the core basis of the energy and centered self that they speak of. Without this "energy" they would have no wise masters seeing visions or entering trance states. There would be no "mystical" enlightenment. This kundalini is the serpent energy within, the hidden power inside each of us—or so we are told.

> She, the subtlest of the subtle, holds within herself
> the Mystery of creation, and by her radiance, it is
> said, the universe is illumined, eternal knowledge

awakened and liberation attained. She maintains all beings of the world by means of inspiration and expiration. (*Serpent Power*, Arthur Avalon, 1919)

The kundalini must be roused by one with a powerful, willful, and controlled mind. He or she must be a skilled craftsman—this, like Masonry, is the ability to unify the physical with the mental. A true adept can master this art and raise the feminine coiled serpent into the mind—the cerebral center. And this is how the skull becomes important and why certain skull cups became the Grail of all Grails.

We too must now follow the path of the ancients and search within the skull. We shall begin with one of the most recondite of images—the Tantric Skull Cup.

Skull Cups

In Sanskrit, skull cups are known as kapala (hence "cap" and "cup"), and they are generally formed from the oval section of the upper cranium. They served as libation vessels for large numbers

Baptism in the Grail, Cyprus

of deities, which were mostly wrathful. However, these skull cups are not always associated with wrathful deities; they are also seen with gods such as Padmasambhava, who holds the "skull cup," which is described as holding an ocean of nectar (Elixir) that floats in the longevity vase. So, almost immediately we have a clue to the contents of this receptacle and its real purpose—the Elixir. This Elixir was at the heart of many secret orders and was one of the carrots used to entice people to join.

But it was more than the contents that were of importance. The selection of the right skull was paramount, and the users were looking for Tantric powers or energy. Therefore a violent death would always be better, such as decapitation. The symbolism of the Tantric Skull Cups is very similar to that of the Holy Grail in that they are symbolic of immortality. Even some western alchemical writings advise the use of skull cups in the process of the "great work," which is of course the search for the Elixir of Life. We find again and again that the "energy" spoken of in relation to these skull cups is exactly the same as the "serpent energy" or "fire" that secret societies across the world search for and claim to be able to manipulate.

The Tantric Skull Cups are said to parallel the clay pots of the Vedic sacrifices and the begging bowl of Buddha, which I found in at least one myth contained the serpent.[1] The skulls are said to serve as a constant reminder of death. The contents of the skulls are often blood, but also the blood of Rudra—the "Lord of wild animals" similar to Cernunnos.

Rudra's etymological origins are uncertain. It could mean "the red one" or "the weeper," or derive from the Syrian "Rhad" meaning serpent. In other areas it also means the "removal of pain" or "healer." Rudra is identified with Siva, and he is the divine healer.

Mahadeva, one of Siva's names, is often represented with a snake entwined around his neck, arms, and hair. His consort, Parvati, is likewise represented. Bhairava, the Avatar of Siva, sits upon the coils of a serpent, whose "head rises above that of the gods."

Also, according to Hyde Clarke and C. Staniland Wake in *Serpent and Siva Worship,* Siva is the same as Rudra, the healer, and is called the King of Serpents. He is depicted with a garland of skulls, symbolizing time measured in years, the changing of ages. He is called sometimes Nagabhushana Vyalakalpa or "having serpents round his neck" and Nagaharadhrik or "wearing serpent-necklaces" and also Nagaendra. Nagesha or "king of Nagas" is also known as Nakula, the "mongoose" which means one who is immune from the venom of the snake.

Siva is also seen as a "horned god" and is connected with the serpent worship in many ways. Both Siva and "Siva in the form of Rudra" are seen in their dynamic aspect as being entwined with serpents. These are serpent deities of old and are connected here with the cup of the head, bringing several disparate elements together—the skull, the grail, the mind, the snake, and time or immortality. They are regenerative serpent deities offering longevity via their blood within a cup. In essence, what we have here is the serpent, which resides within the mind and therefore skull, which gives us all those things that Grail is said to give.

But can any of this relate further away in time and space and arrive in Europe, the supposed true home of the Holy Grail?

Livy in *Historae* mentions a similar Celtic operation from the 3rd century A.D., which simply must be connected to the Indian skull cups. Apparently when the Boii tribe got hold of a victim, they "cut off the head, and carried their spoils in triumph to the most hallowed of their temples. There they cleaned out the head, as is their custom, and gilded the skull, which thereafter served them as a holy vessel to pour libations from and as a drinking cup for the priest and the temple attendants."

The sacred water used in the skull cups was often taken from a holy well, which, as I have established elsewhere,[2] were places linked intrinsically with the worship of the ancient serpent. The idea here is that this ritual practice goes back beyond even the total memory recall of the Celts to a time when the cups employed the real power of the serpent, not just symbolic water. In essence, the water, whether of wells, lakes, pools, or seas, was seen by man across the globe as an entryway or portal into the Otherworld. Taking this otherworldly water in a sacred cup fuses a special power into the water—no different to the Holy Water taken from the font in any Christian church.

The etymology of the skull gives some interesting insights.

In Old German it is *Scala*, which is also a seashell; the symbol used by pilgrims on their way to the shrine of St. James in Spain—a symbol of life. Old Norse it is *Skel*, which means "to have scales" or be "scale-like." The word *skoal*, now a fairly common drinking cry, is also closely related and means to "toast from a skull." This etymology alone shows the deep-seated element of the skull in Western Europe and its use as a drinking vessel. Remarkably, *skoal* was also used to refer to a chalice! (The Ukranian word *Cherep* refers both to skull and chalice.)

We must not forget the Christian Messiah was also crucified at the "place of the skull," Golgotha. That is, his sacrificial blood was spilled into the skull!

But there is more to this than meets the eye.

This place, Golgotha, is also connected to the sign Capricorn—the half-goat, half-fish, or serpent. Capri is from Latin, meaning "goat" or "head," and corn is "horn." This then, is the "horn of the head" or "goat"—the Golgotha.

Christ crucified at Golgotha, Kykkoss Monastery, Cyprus

So Jesus spilled his blood into the secret Grail on that fateful day—the secret Grail being the horn or cup of the skull.

Just as the serpent blood is found in the skull cups, so too is the blood of Jesus.

Now we can see why the Templars' infamous Baphomet head[3] was seen as a skull *and* a goat; it was a hidden mystery—a mystery which has been misunderstood ever since. The Brazen Serpent, the healing snake of Moses now seen as Christ in the New Testament, was lifted up at the place of the skull and his offering of blood[4] was collected—the ultimate sacrifice on the tree of life for the ultimate prize of immortality. But truly, if Christ is all and in all, as we are told by the Bible, then we can all obtain this immortality of the one, the shaman deity or Jesus, who visited the Otherworld. Jesus went down into hell for us, we are told; the shaman would enter a trance, drink from the skull cup, and visit the Otherworld for us; the priests of Egypt, South America, and the Celtic lands would do the same. This then is a universal experience expressed in symbolic form via the skull. The reason is clear, because the mind resides within the skull; the Tantric power and the perceived wisdom of the united serpent energies all act within the skull. No wonder it was cut off, turned upside down, and gilded. But is there any more evidence showing this remarkable symbolism?

There is a Naga[5] myth that relates to the place of the skull. It is about Padmasambhava (Guru Rinpoche) or simply Padma. He is revered in many places, and in Tibet held alongside Buddha; indeed, many see him as the "second coming" of Buddha. He is inseparable from the primordial Buddha. He was "in the beginning," the way Jesus was "the Word."

He received the wish-fulfilling jewel from the daughter of a Naga king and used it to restore sight and make riches. He is said to have transformed himself into a demon by tying a snake into his hair, and practiced a secret language to enable the Nagas to assist him. He spoke to those who had ears to hear; Arjuna (John) taught him astrology and he learned all about medicine from Jivakakumara.

While Padma was practicing his skills in a cemetery, Garab Dorje was born to a *virgin* daughter of King Dharmasoka. Now, please don't try this at home, but she had no use for the bastard son and so tossed him into a burning pit; but the child survived. Then she remembered a dream in which she gave birth to a celestial being, so she pulled him from the pit after seven days[6] and, finding him alive, called him Rolang Dewa.

During the child's early years he learned many wise things and debated against 500 great pandits who all said he was the Buddha.

Padma then came, as a wise man and (very much as John the Baptist did to Jesus) taught Garab Tantras. Padma then went on to seek the secret of longevity and was directed to Kungamo, who dwelt in the palace of skulls.

Kungamo turned Padma into a syllable, like Jesus as the word, and swallowed him. Inside the stomach he found the secrets he was searching for.

Padma is often seen holding a cup filled with the divine liquor, which he offers to his disciples—saying "drink of this to attain liberation."

Padma then is linked to the Naga serpent cult, to healing, to the Elixir via the palace of skulls. He is the word; the teacher of the Christ, like Garab who was born of a virgin; and he gives the Eucharist cup to his disciples. All of this is a symbolic representation of the almost exact process an initiate into the mysteries of secret societies must go through. It is a parable of the pathway.

In all respects, this wonderful stylized Indian tale has all the elements we could possibly require to show that the Christian and medieval Grail stories are nothing more than a retelling of much more ancient concepts, and that these concepts revolve around a universal and archetypal truth. This truth is that our own immortality and our own salvation lies within our own minds. Secret orders that teach these processes remain in the world today. Some teach the truths through Eastern methods and others have Westernized them, but all speak of the truth that is inside our own skulls. Now you know the truth; will it set you free?

4

The Secret of the Holy Grail and the Discovery of the Elixir of Life

In the last chapter, we saw how the Eastern concepts of the skull cups held the secret of the power within our own mind, and how this concept became Westernized. In this chapter we will take a quick look at that Western concept and how it has trickled into our culture through medieval texts that sought to hide the truths from an oppressive Catholic Church.

What Is the Grail?

In truth, the Grail did not emerge strongly into the popular culture until around the 12th and 13th centuries with the familiar poems and stories written by Chretien de Troyes, Wolfram von Eschenbach, and others, but traces of its idea in Celtic cauldrons and various legends can and have been found.

It is believed basically and originally to be the cup that caught the blood of Christ as he hung from the cross, or was even used by him at the last supper. The most recent beliefs are in stark contrast to this and yet still back up the Christ mythos and even various royalist and secret society propaganda, as we shall see.

Ever since the publication of *The Holy Blood and The Holy Grail* by the authors, Baigent, Leigh, and Lincoln in the early 1980s we have had a constant barrage of "bloodline" theories thrown at us, culminating in the *Da Vinci Code* hysteria we see today.

This recent concept gives us the idea that the original word or words used for the Grail, *san graal*, in reality means "Holy Blood."

However, Walter Skeat (A.D. 1835–1912) was one of the greatest investigators of the roots of the English language, and in his *English Etymology,* he points out that the etymology of the Holy Grail:

> ...was very early *falsified* by an intentional change from San Greal (Holy Dish) to Sang Real (Royal Blood).

Skeat claims that the word was a corruption of the Low Latin, *cratella,* a "small bowl," or "crater," which actually and originally meant a *bowl in which things were mixed,* from the Greek *kpa*— "I mix."

Of course, before the evidence in *The Serpent Grail* is understood, this etymology makes little or no sense. But, as we shall see, all shall become clear.

There was more than the actual etymology of the 1980s theory that I needed to look at, in order to prove it to be incorrect, as I believed it was. In the first place and most strongly, I have shown that Christ, as a literal man, and in all likelihood all those surrounding him, may never have in fact existed and were created

St. John's chalice with dragon

elements of a much older mystical language of enlightenment. Therefore, both existing theories on the Holy Grail would fall: There can be no chalice used by Christ at the Last Supper, or a vessel that caught his blood. There can also be no "children" of Christ spawning the Merovingian lineage. There is no bloodline at all and Christ is, in reality, an ancient serpent archetypal deity, as too are St. John, Horus, Aesculapius, and a thousand others.

In order to disprove the bloodline theory, we also have to look at the infamous Priory of Sion nonsense. For those who know nothing of this priory, it is simply a recreation of a supposed secret organization said to protect the bloodline of Christ by the fraudster Pierre Plantard. Indeed, I even got hold of his early "newsletters" and found that they were nothing more than a kind of "neighborhood watch."

Three Levels of Our Grail Reanalysis

So, with all this in mind I needed to completely reappraise the whole mythos of the Grail, and what I was to find was startling.

There is the obvious tradition that the Grail is a journey, a method of self-improvement, and I looked into all the texts I could find with this Gnostic viewpoint in mind. I found that this was completely correct and that Grail literature was hiding the Gnostic traditions of the "mixing of the opposites." These Gnostics were nothing more than an early Christian secret society—stamped out by the Catholic Church and so going underground to avoid detection. The original Gnostics were known as Ophites, meaning simply "serpent worshippers." They worshipped the wisdom of the serpents and had wonderful symbolism that remains with us today of the uniting twin serpent energies, symbolizing the union of the opposites.

This is where the split personalities of the "mind" are rejoined, repetitively, in order to "make the perfect man"—symbolized by alchemists as the Androgyne or Hermaphrodite (Hermes and Aphrodite, man and woman united within us). The process is much deeper than this and would take too long to explain in full. Suffice it to say that this mixing procedure occurred in the "brain" and therefore the skull, and was envisaged symbolically in colors as red and white.

This brain or skull location became apparent in other cultures from where the European Gnostic ideas had also risen, one of these being the Tantric Skull Cups of India and even in the story of Christ as he spills his sacrificial blood at Golgotha—the place of the skull.

In essence, the whole mystical process was virtually the same the world over and is commonly known today in India as the kundalini. This is an Eastern tradition of attaining enlightenment and means coiled serpent. It is the method of raising up twin serpents through a specific psychological process until one is completely illuminated—obtaining the Grail. In each case, from around the world, this process related to the serpent, snake, or dragon, each one being for this mythical purpose the same thing. It can be seen clearly today in the infamous image of the Caduceus upon medical insignia, ambulances, hospitals, and elsewhere. It can also be seen in the powerful representation of the Uraeus serpent, which emerges from the forehead of the Egyptian pharaohs. It can also be found in almost all secret societies.

Now what I discovered during the course of my research was the amazing occurrence of the serpent in myth, folklore, and religion across the entire world and in every period.

We can see its origins even as far back as ancient Africa, where even today the serpent is pinned to a tree or cross as a sacrifice for the community. This is a continuance of a system, which stretches back in time for thousands of years. It is a symbolic element, but it also has a practical level, as we shall see. Even as late as the 16th century there were German coins called Thalers with Christ on the cross on one side and a snake on a cross on the reverse. The image was said to depict the "all-healer."

We can also see the serpent influence in the Bible as early as Adam and Eve. Believe it or not, Eve actually means "female serpent," coming from the root *hawwah* or *hevviah*, and is derived from, amongst others, the goddess Ninlil, the Sumerian serpent deity also associated with the goddess Asherah, who was seen in the Temple of Jerusalem as a tree entwined with serpents. Even the constellation "serpens" was called "little eve" by certain Arabs.

Adam was fabled to be the father of Seth, who was called the "Son of Serpents."

The serpent was not bringing mankind down at all—he was making Adam and Eve like "God," he was bestowing the ultimate knowledge. This is secret Gnostic language for the very knowledge to be found within oneself via the union of the male and female opposites and a whole process of psychological growth.

We even see the ultimate image of Godhead or enlightenment in the aura or halo seen around the heads of saints. This image I revealed derived from the hooded cobra of India as a symbol of immortality and divine serpentine wisdom.

In Malta, I uncovered elongated skulls of certain priests dating back to the Temple-building era. These skulls were created using planks of wood on the heads of babies, in order to make the individual appear serpent-headed, with long drawn eyes and stretched skin. These people were known as serpent priests, and the elongation of the skulls made the glands in the brain secrete certain psychotic hormones, beneficial to the enlightenment experience and altered states of consciousness. The original serpent priests were an elite, kept apart and secret from the main group— the original shining serpent secret society!

Of course Malta itself is overrun with serpent folklore, the latest being that of St. Paul. This is a story created in the 13th century whereby St. Paul is said to have shipwrecked on Malta and subdued the vicious serpents, and then to have gone on and healed people with his newfound serpentine power. Of course none of this happened, but you can't knock the Christians for their marketing skills.

Having now, I believe, sufficiently proven the fact of worldwide serpent worship, and basically reinforced what certain Victorian scholars had failed to bring full weight to because of Christian fear, I moved on and into each and every one of these traditions, for in these traditions were the origins of the serpent worshipped by the Freemasons, the Assassins, the Rosicrucians, the Templars, and many more.

In each case, the serpent or snake was a symbol of wisdom, energy, and immortality.

The wisdom and energy element of the serpent could now be explained via the "awakening" of the "coiled serpent" or kundalini process, but this did not entirely explain the immortality aspect of the serpent symbolism. For an explanation of this I had to turn to science, and it was really here that the whole process had started in the first place, and it was here that I would find the secret Elixir protected by secret societies for generations and hidden within the arcane language of the alchemists.

The Elixir

Before I had ever thought about writing a book on the Grail, Elixir, or Philosopher's Stone, I had released *The Shining Ones* and had just finished doing lots of publicity and radio. I was now, at this stage, looking around for something else to have a go at. Well, one night I lay in bed reading some fusty old book about alchemy.

It was about 1 a.m. and I was having a cup of tea, when my wife, who was reading her medical journals, said something about snake venom and T-cells. It didn't make any sense so I asked her to elucidate.

She explained that scientists had found that certain elements of snake venom had been recently found to help T-cell replication. T-cells, she said, were the things that helped our immune system—keeping us alive.

Well, my mind went into overdrive as I already, even at this stage, knew a lot about serpents, dragons, and their symbolic elements in the legends of Arthur and others. I instantly knew or was "enlightened" to the fact that this was a physical side of the symbolic immortality of the snake, and so began two years of research into the snake, its myths, and now its science.

What I found following much scientific research and cross-checking was that the unique proteins, peptides, polypeptides, and enzymes found within snake venom had, in fact, been used by ancient man for thousands of years in all kinds of medical applications and that it was even amazingly mixed with the snake's or a host's blood. This was the red and white mixing to aid the health and boost the life of the individual. We amazingly found that this was mixed within a "mixing bowl" or skull and then drunk as an Elixir of Life, and that this had then come down to us as one of the elements of the Holy Grail.

Snake venom was also made into a "stone" or pill. We also found that snake venom has *psychoactive* properties, which induce altered states of consciousness and mystical experiences, much akin to those needed for the true enlightenment experience. It was therefore seen physically as a method of meeting with the "gods."

In both ways then, as a serious vitamin pill and as a key to the mystical world, the venom of the snake was a unique product.

To add to this I then found that the same "Christ" who it was said provided the blood of "everlasting life" in the chalice, was seen originally in early Christian and Gnostic cults, such as the Ophites or snake worshippers, as nothing more than a serpent himself!

"Just as Moses lifted up the brazen serpent in the wilderness, so too must Christ be lifted up"—says the Bible, and so he was.

Early Christians even had a Eucharist of the Agathodemon or "good serpent," enacted with live snakes and a special chalice, and this became the fabled Holy Grail we all know so well today. In the early years of Christianity, Jesus was even imaged as a snake on a Tau cross.

Going back to ancient Africa though, I noted the similarity even here of the crucified Christ and the serpent pinned to the tree. But what I also found was that these same people were then actually taking the various parts of the snake and using them for healing, with the saliva- or venom-producing glands being the most treasured.

Another side effect of taking the snake venom is genetic malformations created by the huge amounts of protein, and one of these malformations is cranial—thereby elongating the skull, just as those we found on Malta.

Conclusion

Although I do not have the space to explain the Philosopher's Stone in this short chapter, I did find that it truly represented both the Gnostic and duality aspect of the wisdom side of the serpent, and also was used as a cover for the true mixing of the venom and blood within alchemical texts. As the infamous Grail author Wolfram von Eschenbach himself claimed that the stone and the grail were one and the same, I found this to be the case.

Basically then, the whole modern Grail mythos is wrong. Not just the latest "bloodline" theory, but also the original concept of it being the literal cup that caught the blood of Christ. In fact this element of the myth is symbolic and should remain as such, for Christ as the good serpent did provide his true Elixir of eternal life, in both Gnostic psychological concepts such as the Kundalini, and also in the literal venom and blood of the snake. An indication of Christ as the serpent was also found in the sloughing of skin. Snakes regularly slough their skin, and the ancients saw this as a rebirth. This was copied with Christ entering the cave and *sloughing* his shroud.

Arthur, as a literary figure, was chosen as the modern "savior" to rediscover this chalice because he was the *Pen*dragon. *Pen* means "head," and therefore Arthur is the head dragon or serpent, just as Jesus was.

What we also find is that every single royal lineage on the globe has claimed descent from the serpent. Whether it be the Merovingians or the Chinese dragon emperors—they are all claiming to be descended from the "bloodline" of the serpent! And this is how it has become so easy for David Icke and those like him to claim that the royal family are really shape-shifting reptiles, because their own mythological history claims descent from the wise serpent—the same wise serpent that lies at the heart of the world's secret societies.

The history of the world is certainly not as we once thought.

5

The Watchers

We must now move on to one of the earliest of all origins of secret societies from which is derived much of the terminology and symbolism still used today by the Freemasons, Rosicrucians, and many others—the Watchers—otherwise known as the "sons of God" and in Hebrew as Eyrim (Irim). In doing so we shall be taking a look at the very origins of the first secret societies and the influences of astrotheology and serpent worship upon them.

Zecharia Sitchin in *The Stairway to Heaven*, states:

> The Akkadians called their predecessors Shumerians, and spoke of the Land of Shumer. It was in fact the biblical Land of Shin'ar. It was the land whose name—Shumer—literally meant the Land of the Watchers. It was indeed the Egyptian Ta Neter—Land of the Watchers, the land from which gods had come to Egypt.

So, Sumeria could mean "Land of the Watchers," and it is from this land that the Elohim or Shining Ones, who governed the Watchers, also came. In *The Origin of Consciousness in the Breakdown of the Bicameral Mind*, Julian Jaynes tells us something interesting about these governing gods:

> Throughout Mesopotamia, from the earliest times of Sumer and Akkad, all lands were owned by gods and men were their slaves. Of this, the cuneiform texts leave no doubt whatever. Each city-state had

its principal god, and the king was described in the very earliest written documents that we have as "the tenant farmer of the god."

Let's just take a look at these Elohim for a moment to find out who these "gods" were that supposedly enslaved men and were in charge of the Watchers.

Elohim

This is the term used often in the Old Testament (and other texts outside of it, as in the Muslim Allah = Elah) for the Lord; an incorrect usage, as the term is plural and means "Shining Ones."

We can see this plurality in the text from Genesis 1:26: "And God said, Let us make man in our image, after our likeness." And again in Genesis 6:2: "The sons of god saw the daughters of men that they were fair." This term "sons of god" is literally "sons of gods" and comes from ben ha-elohim, "sons of the shining ones."

The Sumerian EL means simply bright or shining; the Old Irish Aillil means shining; Old Cornish EL means shining; Elf means shining—hence Elves as tall/mysterious angelic beings; Inca Illa is bright or to shine; Babylonian Ellu is to shine—to name just a few that have sprung up worldwide from the same Sumerian source.

Baal, the deity often spoken of as the "Lord" in the Bible, is also seen as a shining one in the Old Testament and is called the Owner. At that time there were many "Owners" or shining ones; in fact, there was one for each village.

To these Hebrews the Elohim were nature divinities from ancient Sumerian times. According to General Albert Pike, the famous Masonic historian, in *Morals and Dogma*, the Elohim were the "host of heaven," ascending and descending to pass messages to and from god or leader (Yahweh). The host of heaven were of course the stars in the night sky humanized.

Some of the shining ones were termed Watchers and are akin to the angels of the Lord. Yahweh Elohim means simply "leader of the shining ones."

So now we have these plural Elohim or shining ones as gods, being above even the kings, and supplying Watchers—to watch over man, and as Sitchin pointed out, they were also in Egypt.

This Ta Neter that Sitchin mentions resembles the Egyptian Ntr, a name for Ptah and other gods, which means guardian or watcher. Ta Neter is also the name for the Red Sea straits, which connected Mesopotamia and Egypt and is known as the place of the gods. The Neter or Ntr word means and is derived from the concept of neutrality and is simply the place between, the path between the pillars or the place between awake and asleep that we spoke of earlier in this chapter.

These Watchers were also known as Urshu and were classed as being less divine than the gods, although in this instance, as Graham Hancock points out in *Fingerprint of the Gods*, the Urshu speak of the Neteru (Ntr) as if it were they who were the gods and the Urshu the Watchers. Whatever the truth in this matter, it is no wonder that confusion has arisen over so many thousands of years. The fact remains though, that the ancients spoke of a time when there were gods or shining ones who ruled up and down Sumeria and Egypt and who employed watchers over the ordinary folk. In the same way a Pharaoh of Egypt was a god-on-Earth, so too priests of the Elohim (stars) were stars-on-Earth.

The Egyptian Book of the Dead calls these Watchers:

> Anubis and Horus in the form of Horus the sightless. Others, however, say that they are the Tchatcha, who bring to nought the operations of their knives; and others say that they are the chiefs of the Sheniu chamber.

So, even in ancient Egypt, by the time of the writing of the Book of the Dead, there was confusion. According Sitchin in the *Wars of Gods and Men*:

> They had come to Egypt, the Egyptians wrote, from Ta-Ur, the "Far/Foreign Land," whose name Ur meant "oldest" but could also have been the actual place name—a place well known from Mesopotamian and biblical records: the ancient city of Ur.

We should note at this point that this Ur is the same place that the father of the world's three great religions, Abraham, is also said to have trained.

According to The Legend of Votan (note similarity with the Nordic Wotan who is said to have come from across the sea) from Mesoamerica, this Votan was the serpent who was a descendent of the race of Can and was called a guardian or watcher, amazingly similar to Canaan, as such people as Zelia Nuttal in *Papers of the Peabody Museum* has suggested.

These Canaanites are implicated in many places revolving around the Shining Ones and the original serpent priests— another name for the Shining Ones.[1] The serpent was known in the language of Canaan variously as Aub, Ab; Oub, Ob; Oph, Op; Eph, Ev. In the Mayan language "Can" also means serpent, as in Cuculcan the bird serpent, and just as in the ancient Sumerian Acan and the Scottish Can for serpent (which is where we get the word "canny" like the wise snake). Vulcan (sounding like Votan and Wotan), the Roman god of fire, comes from the Babylonian Can for serpent and Vul for fire, showing an etymological link across thousands of miles and oceans and meaning, therefore, that Vulcan is the shining serpent. Indeed even the very center of the Christian world, the Vatican, comes from the words "vatis" for prophet and "can" for serpent, making the Vatican a place of serpent prophecy.

The Hebrews termed these Watchers as nun resh'ayin, meaning "those who watch." In the Greek this is translated as gigantes or giants, a race that even the 907 B.C. writer Hesiod featured as being monstrous (due to their serpentine aspect no doubt). Now we can understand the role of the giants[2] seen across the world of folklore as the presence of the Watchers.

Enoch in 1 Enoch 20:1-8 even gives us the names of these Watchers, and I noted that they were all subtitled Shining Ones with the ending:

> And these are the names of the holy angels who watch. Uriel, one of the holy angels, who is over the world and over Tartarus. Raphael, one of the holy angels, who is over the spirits of men. Raguel, one of the holy angels who takes vengeance on the world of the luminaries. Michael, one of the holy angels, to wit, he that is set over the best part of mankind and over chaos. Saraqael, one of the holy angels, who is

set over the spirits, who sin in spirit. Gabriel, one of the holy angels, who is over Paradise and the serpents and the Cherubim. Remiel, one of the holy angels, whom God set over those who rise.

Note that Gabriel, the messenger who told of the birth of Jesus and who passed on wisdom to Mohammed, is in charge of the serpents. Remiel is over those who rise—those seeking enlightenment.

In the Testament of Amram (manuscript B) we have a remarkable insight into the aspect of these shining Watchers:

> I asked them, "Who are you, that you are thus empowered over me?" They answered me, "We have been empowered and rule over all mankind." They said to me, "Which of us do you choose to rule you?"I raised my eyes and looked. One of them was terrifying in his appearance, like a serpent, his cloak many colored yet very dark. And I looked again, and in his appearance, his visage like a viper, and wearing exceedingly, and all his eyes....I replied to him, "This Watcher, so is he?" He answered me, "This Watcher....and his three names are Belial and Prince of darkness and King of Evil."

The Mosaic Book of Jubilees was originally called the Apocalypse of Moses as it was supposedly written by Moses while on Mount Sinai and dictated by a Watcher or angel. This book was intended as a history of the days of old and reveals the purpose of the Watchers:

> For in his days the angels of the Lord [Elohim—Shining Ones] descended upon the earth [came down from their mountain stronghold]—those who are named Watchers—that they should instruct the children of men, that they should do judgment and uprightness upon the earth.

These Watchers, according to the Book of Jubilees, are the sons of god spoken of in Genesis, sent from their heavenly abode to instruct men. What seems to have occurred is that they fell from grace by mating with the daughters of men and were thus outcast—giving us the fallen angels we are familiar with today.

However, according to *A Dictionary of Angels*, not all these Watchers descended from the heavenly abode, and those that did not were termed holy Watchers, residing in the fifth heaven. As Enoch himself had testified against these fallen Watchers he was protected by the ruling Shining Ones and transported to the Garden of Eden (Eden means plateau and is therefore a specific place):

> And I Enoch was blessing the Lord of majesty and the King of the ages, and lo! The Watchers called me—Enoch the scribe—and said to me: "Enoch, thou scribe of righteousness, go, declare to the Watchers of the heaven who have left the high heaven, the holy eternal place, and have defiled themselves with women, and have done as the children of the earth do, and have taken unto themselves wives: Ye have wrought great destruction on the earth: And ye shall have no peace nor forgiveness of sin: and inasmuch as they delight themselves in their children, The murder of their beloved ones shall they see, and over the destruction of their children shall they lament, and shall make supplication unto eternity, but mercy and peace shall ye not attain." (1 Enoch 10:3–8)

According to Andrew Collins in *From the Ashes of Angels: The Forbidden Legacy of a Fallen Race*, the fallen Watchers swear an oath and bind themselves together. The place of this action is called Ardis, the fabled summit of Mount Hermon, which derives from the Hebrew word for *curse* (harem). Following these actions of the fallen Watchers, the Shining Ones called down a great flood upon the Earth to destroy the offspring, and Noah is warned to build a great ship to escape the impending doom. There was obviously some great battle between the dissenters and the Shining Ones and the loyal Watchers, which allowed Michael, Gabriel, and the others to slay the remaining fallen Watchers. The flood is the symbolic idea of the later cleansing of the land (and mind) and the restarting of the human race (or self) on track with the Shining Ones' ideals—a probable merging of a folk memory of some great catastrophe and the actual event. There were other catastrophes written up as being the judgment of the remaining Watchers, which must simply be folk memories of actual catastrophes that occurred and were blamed upon the transgressions of the fallen Watchers. Indeed, even the spirits of these fallen Watchers are blamed for future evils, as Enoch points out:

> And the spirits of the giants afflict, oppress, destroy, attack, do battle, and work destruction on the earth, and cause trouble: they take no food, but nevertheless hunger and thirst, and cause offenses. And these spirits shall rise up against the children of men and against the women, because they have proceeded them. (1 Enoch 12)

St. Michael and St. George—angelic watchers

Notable revelations admitted by the Watchers to the sons of man were knowledge of the signs of the earth: writing, meteorology, geography, and geodesy—all implying that these Shining Ones understood the energy and power of the Earth and its electromagnetism, not to mention the movements of the planets. There

are many fables of these times from across the world of great builders, architects, and magicians all relating entirely back to these
Shining Ones' origins. We can see the similarity in the structures
of Europe (and elsewhere) of the burial mounds with the fact that
one of the fallen Watchers, Azazel, was cast into the desert where
they placed upon him rough and jagged rocks.

Much of this myth of the Watchers is found to be within the
tales of wars and merging of peoples across the Middle East—
between Canaanites, Egyptians, Sumerians, and even Asian civilizations. But the underlying current is a belief in the Shining
Ones as leaders, with Watchers doing their bidding—evolving into
God with his Angelic beings.

All of this so far is exactly what we have been saying about the
secret societies, that they were in charge and maintained authority from a religious standpoint. We know that mankind deified
the "men of renown," the same Anunnaki/Anakim to whom this
refers, and therefore we know that these Shining Ones were mere
men—the difference being that the hypnagogic state (the place
between awake and asleep) had set them apart. The terms
Anunnaki, Anakim, and even Nephilim mean "those who came
down to Earth from heaven" and is a reference to their position
and location on the plateau of Eden (Eden means plateau). They
looked down on the people below—watched. They represented
the sun, moon, and planets, on Earth. It does not, as some would
have us believe, imply that they came from the stars, but were
representatives of the celestial deities.

The truth of the story of the Shining Ones and their Watchers
has been the subject of a purging by many Jewish authorities, who
were understandably concerned that the myths of these angels
and their worship would distract people from the worship of the
one god. To this end, the book of Enoch and the book of Jubilees,
mentioned previously, were stricken from the accepted list and
are now known as Apocrypha or pseudepigrapha. What we do know
though, is that these Watchers continued in what has been described as the underground stream and were called egregors.

> The Kabbalah names 72...national angelic regents,
> which the Hebrews call Elohim [Shining Ones]; the
> metaphysical technical term Egregors is also used

for them. Derived from the Greek word egreoros, it means "watcher" or "guardian." The office of a Watcher is to protect from outside pressures a region or ethnic group assigned to its care. The region is always measured off from another posing a threat of some sort to it. A given group of persons (the group of those being protected) is "tied" to a certain area of jurisdiction....Here, too, we meet the "riddle of the founding of cities and states...." What is more, both the ancient Romans, and quite recently the Chinese, have recognized the existence of guardian spirits set over cities. Indeed, one author reports as follows on the occult war waged on enemy cities by ancient Rome: "The Romans, when besieging a city, made a habit of carefully enquiring the name of the city and of its guardian spirit. When they knew these, they would summon the guardian spirit of the city and its inhabitants, and conquer it." (Willy Schrodter, *Commentaries on the Occult Philosophy of Agrippa*) .

Egregor

This term is Greek and means "to rouse from sleep," "be excited by passion," "to be awake," or "to watch"—incredibly etymologically linked to the enlightenment experience of the awakening or the place between awake and asleep. The root of the word appears to be the Syrian ir or er, and reverts to Watcher and is also related to Ur, the home of Abraham.

It also became a Gnostic and mystic term thought to mean "collective unconsciousness" but linked with the Watchers by M. Denning and O. Phillips in *The Magical Philosophy*.

Eliphas Levi (19th century magician and mystic) speaks of these egregors on numerous occasions, and even links them to the giants or Watchers spoken of in the book of Enoch, saying that they "take shape and have appeared in the guise of giants: these are the egregors of the *Book of Enoch*....Termed the celestial watchers or egregors, by the ancients."

Levi also calls these egregors the Anakim (Shining Ones, men of renown, giants) of the Bible, and that they are expressed in the myths of various cultures—just as we have been finding.

It therefore appears that Levi (and others) knew of these egregors or Watchers from the recently translated and widely (in mystic circles) available book of Enoch. Levi was well known to have Rosicrucian tendencies, and this movement too was aware of the meaning of the word. In fact, they believed that the egregors were still in existence and were in the background. There are a whole host of 16th and 17th century mystics, including Dr. John Dee, who were also aware of the Book of Enoch and plagiarized it extensively. Dee has been implicated as one of the founders of the Rosicrucians as well as being a spy of the realm under Queen Elizabeth. Dee's official number in court spying circles was 007 and Elizabeth was M. Like the later Illuminati, the Rosicrucians were a supposed response to the activities of the Jesuits. All of this brings to mind the texts taken down by Dee and his cohort, Edward Kelly, that were dictated by angels! These texts surprisingly deal with the "old ones." Some of the texts came into Dee's possession (and were therefore not given by angels) whilst he was in the service of Rudolph II in Prague.

Amazingly, the infamous Necronomicon tells us about a "fabulous city of Irem." Irem of the Pillars is part of Arabian magical lore and was built by the Jinn or angels and were possibly also Watch Towers—"towers of the Watchers." The Hebrew Erim means to awaken.

The Pillars were built on the instructions of the Lord of the tribe of Ad (meaning eternity), who are referred to in Hebrew terms as Nephilim—the giants or Watchers of the Shining Ones, and referred to in the book of Enoch as Irim. According to Arabian legend this Irem is located in Rub al Khali, which means the empty quarter or the void. The void could be a real barren location or a term for the "space between" that we have been discussing. Archaeologists have identified the very spot of this infamous Irem as being the lost city of Ubar.

One further link with Enoch to the mysteries of the modern alchemists, mystics, and seers is seen in the 13th century texts of A. Bar Hebraeus, who spent many years investigating the ancient texts at the Library of Maragha and gives us this unique insight:

The ancient Greeks say that Enoch is Harmis Trismaghistos. (*The Chronography of Bar Hebraeus*, translated by E.W. Budge 1932)

This is none other than Hermes Trismegistus,[3] the thrice great Hermes, whom all mystics hold in high esteem as having passed down ancient and profound secrets and who is seen as the father of almost all Western secret orders. We also have here evidence that the book of Enoch was understood as far back and as late as the 13th century.

Whether or not the actual Shining Ones, Watchers, or egregor were actually physically around during this vast expanse of time is the subject debate still, but what this does show is that the ancient influence of the Shining Ones was certainly still in existence.

Even the *Thesaurus Temporum* translated into Latin in the mid 17th century gives us a chronology of events surrounding these egregors.

In 1000 B.C. they descended (primus egregorum descensus), and by 1487 B.C. they had taken Enoch to Paradise (Enoch transferatur in paradisum) due to the dissent of the fallen Watchers.

It seems then that the extremely ancient concept and story of the Shining Ones was still very much alive and being propagated secretly by the mystics of the last few hundred years. These were part and parcel of their hidden secrets. The question arises, why did they feel the need to hide such secrets?

Today the egregor is seen in occult circles as an energy form— akin to the kundalini! According to the Rosicrucian Website:

Quickly, from the mystical point of view, Egregor(e) (a word of Latin origin) is the set of thoughtforms produced by a group of individuals on the Astral plane. The Egregor(e) may change over time, according to the quality of the group's members. Each group has a distinct Egregor(e). Any group which has the ability to get in synchronisation with a specific Egregor(e) may claim authenticity and continuation from earlier groups which used or developed this egregor(e).

And the Martinist Order of the Knights of Christ, who claim to be heirs to the Rosicrucians and others, say:

> Its goal is to set the human being free from the hold of the Prince of this World and of achieving the Mystical Union of the self-aware personality (conscience) with the individual profundity (super-conscience). Its members strive to have access to mastery by reuniting with the "Kingdom of the Center," propitious with the descent of the Paraclet, sent by Christ, in addition to the assistance rendered by the attachment, on the side of the Initiator with the Egregore, protector of the Secret Chain.

"An apostalic succession of power," suggests John Michael Greer in *Inside a Magical Lodge*, is "a basic function of the egregor.

> "'Worship me!" cries the Egregora. "I am the son of God; you are nothing but a worthless and sinful creature, damned from birth and destined to hell were it not for my sacrifice; and without me you will never reach heaven!" (Marcelo Ramos Motta, *Letter to a Brazilian Mason Unexpurgated*)

> The egregore is a group spirit that serves to remind the initiate of his or her goals. It informs and guides the individual and it protects the living chain of brotherhood. The living chain of brotherhood is entered into when a Setian performs a rite of their own creation intended to protect and enhance the Temple of Set. The egregore protects the brotherhood by letting them know their enemies are there. A symbolic representation of the egregore is used to maintain a link to the Prince of Darkness. (Sir Ormsond IV, *Saturnian Principles*)

> The Sufi Saint, Mansour Al-Hallaj, is almost identical to the Masonic egregor, Hiram Abif, in respect to the circumstances of his death....In masonry, the Two-Headed Eagle is a cognate of Baphomet, a chimera-like composite animal that represents the

Universal Force of matter. In some Gnostic Systems this would be the Demiurgios, or "Lord of this World." (Malgwyn, from *Yesidism, Zoroastrianism in Western Secret Societies*)

Round Towers and Pyramids

One of the peculiar archaeological evidences we have of ancient "watchers" are the round towers. What was being watched is a matter of some debate. It may have been the people or it may have been the stars. Indeed, it is highly likely they were built for both, as well as for the search for aggressors.

In symbolism, the round tower was the internal psychological ascent, the axis mundi (axis of the world), and has the symbolism of the ladder or gateway to heaven—just as does the cord[4] or rope said by Enoch to have been carried and used by the Watchers. Because these places and this internal process were inaccessible to many, the term "Ivory Tower" emerged. The pyramid, as the Mountain of Heaven, was just the same as the round tower and the stupas of India—which themselves originated from the Kurgan mound builders of Nordic origin.

Both myself and others have found that the Great Pyramid of Giza was seen as a gateway for the mind/soul. In his paper "The Great Pyramid Texts," Clesson Harvey points out that in the pyramids of Saqqara there are more than 3,000 columns of texts from the 5th and 6th dynasties, which he believes holds the secret to the pyramids use. These texts include incantations and magical formulae that used to be invoked in certain locations around the pyramid but in the "upper passage, chamber, gallery and shaft...is an incredibly old, unmistakable megalithic glyph." This glyph or phrase translates remarkably into "sar door" and "tunnel opening gate."

Because glyphs are sadly lacking from most pyramids, this information is a startling discovery; indeed, there was probably more information that has now been destroyed, such as when Herodotus was said to have visited Egypt in the 5th century B.C.—the outer casing of the pyramid was awash with writing.

Egyptologists claim that the "star" is mythological and leave it at that. I will not, however, and I say that this "tunnel" and "star door" is the entrance to the trance state—as "star" and "shining" are intimately linked in meaning, having emerged from the enlightenment state, which was seen as the connection point to the gods—the stars.

We already know that the Egyptians called Giza "Rostau" (*ros* in etymology means either "head" or "hros," which is horse; *ros tau* is therefore the "tau of the head" and *tau* means "hidden treasure"). Rostau also means "Gateway to the Other World."

But, I wondered, how did the pyramid work in this respect and in relation to the trance theory we have been discussing? And more than this, were there any further buildings or structures in the world that related to all of this? It was now time to take an alternative look at the possible science behind the earth structures.

Back in the 1970s and '80s, a scientist named Joe Parr decided it was time to take a look at the Great Pyramid, and pyramid shapes in general, and what he discovered is completely amazing.

In his experiments, Joe set up an aligned pyramid north-south and east-west, with flat coils placed on the north and south. A blown, 1 microfarad capacitor was sparked across the gap using a battery, resistor, and chart recorder. This was to simulate the electromagnetic energy of the Earth passing over the pyramid. The scientists registered the changes on a daily basis, recording the state of an energy bubble that surrounded the pyramid.

Strangely, the energy actually stopped all kinds of radiation, and the bubble showed attenuation to beta emitters, ion sources, and magnetic sources when in the bubble. Feeding negative ions into the bubble actually intensified the energy. The energy was also found to alter over the course of the year, and 13 years of experimentation gave good results. Most peculiar was the effect upon gravity, which is linked intrinsically to electromagnetic radiation. It appeared that the bubble actually blocked out the force of gravity as well as electromagnetic energy, showing a 113,000 times increase in kinetic energy, leading the researchers to theorize that the pyramid actually moved in time and space—a place known to theoretical physicists as h-space. Incredibly, when negative ions were fed into the bubble, the pyramid was drawn to the moon (positive ions moved it away) an amazing correlation with the feminine and, therefore, spiritually negative aspect of lunar worship.

But what relevance could this have on our work here? Well, if, as it appears, many secret societies point toward the Great Pyramid, then there has to be a reason (or two). I have stated my belief that the Pyramid was an entrance to the trance state, or Duat, and the pyramid texts as well as much more Egyptology evidence actually proves this point. The effect caused within the brain, which releases the hormones required for the trance state, is basically electromagnetic and is affected by all manner of ion activity. I am firmly of the opinion that the ancient serpent cult or Shining Ones were on to this in their own way, perceiving energy as the serpent wave and worshipping this invisible god as a snake. Eventually, gathering sufficient knowledge of this serpent energy, they erected buildings that conducted the energy into a controlling element. With the effect of the "plugs" in the air vents having a resonant effect also upon the electromagnetic energy, we can see how it was honed specifically to create the effect.

But there must be more evidence of ancient buildings with this peculiar in-built design—and there was.

One peculiar and little-written-about structure is the round tower. These are worldwide in the hundreds, and strangely are linked to the serpent in almost every instance.

Tall, elegant, round structures, built by cultures as diverse as the Irish Celts and early Christians, to the Hopi Indians and Egyptians—all of which are linked with serpent worship. Even the Dead Sea Scrolls refer to "towers" protected by angels or Watchers. In the famous Qumran Community of the Dead Sea Scroll, the war between the Sons of Light (the Qumranites) and the Sons of Darkness (all those outside the sect) "is to be conducted with acute awareness of the place of the angelic world in it...."

The Qumran War Scroll (1QM 9.10–16) even gives us details on the battle formations, which involve four "towers" ("Migdalot") that are units of soldiers with specifically long spears and shields. On each of their shields is written the name of one of the four archangels. This links the round towers or watch towers to the Watchers or the giants.

In Ireland there are over 65 round towers, many more than 100 feet tall, and claimed by academics to be no more than 1,000 years old.

However, as with most Christian buildings, they are generally built upon much more ancient religious ground, and, indeed, many of them can be proven to be older than first believed. Some even have churches built onto them, as if to attach the church to the ancient shining-serpent worship physically. In fact, I have already shown in the *Serpent Grail*, how St. Patrick "kicked" out the serpents from Ireland, and that these serpents were indeed an ancient serpent worshipping cult—the whole story being symbolic of the Christian Church taking over.

Gradwell, writing in the 19th century pointed out that:

> St Patrick and his followers almost invariably selected those sacred sites of paganism, and built their wooden churches under the shadow of the Round Towers, then as mysterious and inscrutable as they are to-day.

Some claim these structures were fire temples dedicated to sun worship, and it is easy to see why, when we discover that sun worship is connected to serpent worship and the enlightenment experience. Others claim them to be "watch towers," which would relate nicely to the ancient term for the serpent cult as "Watchers." In fact, Hargrave Jennings, author of *Ophiolatraea*, relates them to the obelisk, that ancient serpent-derived pillar to the heavens.

The towers are also found close to rivers, streams, and holy wells. Again, this was something we discovered in the *Serpent Grail* to be closely and intimately connected with the worship of the healing serpent. The water was the subterranean home of the serpent race and was the "entrance" to the Otherworld—which is where the enlightenment experience was intending to take you. But it is this association with water that seems to be important to such structures in terms of earth electromagnetic energy.

There may be an important link between round towers and the Phoenicians, who had similar structures dedicated to their rain and water deity Baal. There are thousands of these towers scattered across Sardinia, just north of the Phoenician city of Carthage, dating to at least 2,000 years before Christ.

But, as Ralph Ellis pointed out in his *Jesus, Last of the Pharaohs* book, the round towers are remarkably similar to the Benben tower to be found in the Temple at Heliopolis, which links to the Phoenicians, as their very name comes from the Benben bird, or better-known Phoenix. The Phoenicians would then, in our modern age, become infamous for spreading beliefs across the world via their many trade routes. They were one of the most proficient sea peoples ever to have lived.

The round tower has also been related to the djed pillar or backbone of Osiris. This is the pillar or backbone up which the kundalini or serpent energy was to rise in India and is perfectly in line with the enlightenment concepts leading to "shining."

There are also those who believe that these towers served as astronomical tools, similar to Stonehenge, and this may be the case also. The tower in Iran called Radkan (rhad = serpent) is thought to be one of these, and like the European towers of a much later date, it has a conical cap.

In the Naga or serpent homeland of India the round tower became the stupa and in China the pagoda—both other forms of round tower. In Feng Shui, we get a glimpse of the real use of the towers—the pagoda and indeed the stupa are thought to trap negative energy or chi (dragon/serpent energy), what we would call negative ions. Remember that these negative ions in the Parr pyramid experiments were thought to cause antigravity and anti-electromagnetic effects. The very tale of Lady White Snake is popular all over the world, and is ultimately due to this electromagnetic energy. It is the Lady White Snake or lunar snake that is trapped in the pagoda for a thousand years.

The Giant's Tower of Gozo near Malta has also been related strongly by many historians to the tower 20th century historian Captain Oliver said:

> It may be conjectured, that these loculi [small holes] may have been intended to hold the small idols, whose trunks [headless], made of stone or clay, are not dissimilar to the conventional female figures of Hindoo representations, on the numerous large and small rudely shaped conical stones (possibly sacred symbols, analogous to the larger stone cones, on which female mammæ are found engraved in the

ruined nuragghi of Sardinia) which are found in those ruins. Somewhat similar small pyramidal cones, which by some have been supposed to represent the sun's rays, are to be seen in the hands of priests kneeling before the sacred serpent god in Egyptian paintings.

Further round towers can be found as far away as southern America, New Mexico, Colorado, Utah, Chichén Itzá, Africa, and many more. All are related to the serpent energy and serpent cult, and many have the same astronomical alignments.

Indeed the Hopi snake tribe actually refer to them as "snake houses." The Hopi god of death and the Underworld is Masau'u, and he has to explain to the snake mother why her children cannot live in the house:

> And Masau said, "No, the snakes have no houses; because they have bitten and killed Hopi they should never again have a house, but should live under rocks and in holes in the ground." But he also said the snake houses [the round towers] which were built for them should never again be destroyed and that all coming generations of people should know the snake's doom, never again to have a house. (Alexander M. Stephen, *The Journal of American Folklore*)

Could this be an indication of the death of the snake cult? Could this be the Hopi version of St. Patrick's story? And if so, then it relates back to Ireland, where, again, there are hundreds of round towers connected with the serpent!

Remember that Baal was implicated earlier. Baal, being the Canaanite rain god, can also be related here, as the Hopi have a word for water—paal (they have no b and therefore it resolves into p. Paal also means broth and wonder).

If it is the case that these round towers or snake houses are seen across the Atlantic with the same religious and cultural grounding, then it is also true to state that the Anakim are also related in some way. Anak means "long neck" or "necklaces." The Hopi too have a similar word, *anaaq*, meaning "necklace" or "earring"—it is also an expression used when in pain from snakebite!

But what about the science of the round towers? Is there anything that can be related to the energy discussed with the pyramids?

In the book *Ancient Mysteries, Modern Visions*, Professor Callahan relays his research, which amazingly shows that the round towers may have been designed as huge resonant systems for collecting and storing meter-long wavelengths of magnetic and electromagnetic energy. Sound fanciful? It did to me, so I looked deeper.

Basing the hypothesis of his work on insect antennae and the capacity to resonate electromagnetic waves, Callahan hypothesized that the tall round towers were made to be "earth antennas," and that similar buildings or structures around the globe could have been made for the same reason. He believed (before his time, I might add) that this energy would be passed on to those meditating at the site. It is my contention that this is true and that it spurs along the trance state and brings one closer to "god." Full evidence of this is outlined in my book *Gateway to the Otherworld*.

Of the towers tested in Ireland, Callahan found that the iron-rich rock that they were made from indeed helped this effect along. The towers made from other materials, such as limestone and granite, were still "paramagnetic." Callahan goes on to show how the rubble within these towers, which has baffled people for decades, was truly there as a "tuning" implement, in much the same way I say the "plugs" in the "air vents" of the Great Pyramid are tuning plugs.

It is my opinion that further research should be carried out at all the round tower sites in Ireland and elsewhere before the ravages of time are allowed to destroy what could be a remarkable insight into the practices of the ancient serpent cult.

What we can see here is the extent of the influence of the first origins of secret societies, both in culture and texts, but also in the many fascinating and mysterious archaeological remains of the world. These Shining Ones are the first on paper. They have a structure and a basis of authority. They rule over man and are all-wise, having their "Watchers" to ensure that their instructions are carried out. Either the Shining Ones are still in power now, generations later, or the secret societies of the globe have copied the methods, structure, and symbols of these first few. The great religions of the world have all been created by some secret method. The early Christians met in secrecy and spread the word of "Christ" far and wide whilst the orthodox religions and powers of the day struggled to rout them out. The same is true of Islam. Power then is derived from control of the masses, and here in Sumeria control was formed by those who possessed great knowledge, wisdom, and a seeming ability to access God. This has always been the lure of the secret orders and also that of orthodox religion. One is open, one is not.

6

The Serpent Sword

When I was first invited to join a certain secret society—one that shall not be found on the Internet—I was amazed at the imagery and symbolism that surrounded me. On the night of initiation, one particular device set itself apart from all else—the sword.

I was in a long hall that looked like an old chapel, with wooden beams and high windows. The lower parts of the windows were now boarded with finely painted oak—murals depicting the trials and tribulations of a medieval warrior monk. At the end of the hall were large satin curtains of deep red. On either side of me stood a line of men all dressed in white robes, holding aloft gleaming silver swords, and at the end the Grand Master beckoned me "come." As I walked, the swords fell behind me and were placed zig-zag fashion across the floor so that my path behind was no longer one I could walk. This is a symbolic device, a truth we all must learn—attempting to rewalk the path we have already trodden is pointless.

Eventually, I reached the Grand Master and we followed a ritual that can be dated back many hundreds of years. I bowed low and accepted my pledge as the Master's sword symbolically killed my old self so that I might be born anew.

The sword here is used as a device to bring to life the symbolic aspects of a hidden Gnostic truth and a psychology as relevant today as ever. It has been this way for an awfully long time, and it is interesting, therefore, to discover that King Arthur himself, a symbol of so many things, also held the sword of truth, energy, and wisdom.

In *The Quest of the Holy Grail*, a uniquely alchemical tale created by secret orders, the sword is seen as a fiery serpent, symbolic of energy. It is the sword of King David or made by the wise Solomon with a pommel stone of all the colors of the Earth and two rib hilts, one made from the fish of the Euphrates, and the other, the serpent.

It is said to resemble the sword of Arthur, which itself is said to be serpentine in the *Dream of Rhonabwy*. When Arthur's sword is drawn it was said that two flames of fire burst out of the jaws of the two serpents, and so wonderful was the sword that it was hard for anyone to gaze at it. It is necessary for Arthur to maintain ownership of the sword, whether it is the sword from the stone or Excalibur, as it ensures his victory and his life. Malory indicates again the brightness of the sword and its fiery aspect, writing: "but it was so bright in his enemies' eyes, that it gave light like thirty torches." But the sword in the stone does not last long, and the Lady of the Lake gives Arthur his Excalibur, and also a serpent scabbard, which ensures eternal life. Malory states quite clearly, "...for whiles ye have the scabbard upon you, ye shall never lose no blood, be ye never so sore wounded; therefore keep well the scabbard always with you." It is only when Arthur's half sister Morgan le Fay steals the scabbard and replaces it that Arthur becomes susceptible to the deadly blows of Mordred. The once-prized sword is then returned to the water, the home of the Lady of the Lake—the serpent spirit.

There is a remarkable resemblance between the tales of Arthur's sword and Chinese legend. A hero from the 6th century B.C. named Wu Tzu-hsu threw his sword into a river.

> It shot forth like a spirit-glow, sparkling brightly as it thrice sank and thrice came to the surface with a great gush and then hovered above the water. The god of the river...heard the swords roar...he rolled in the waters in a great and frothing frenzy.... Dragons raced along the waves and leaped out of

the water. The river god held the sword in his hand
and, frightened, told Wu Tzu-hsu to take it back.
(Mair 1983, 141 and 286)

This story, related in the 8th century A.D., simply cannot differ
from Malory's tale of the sword. In China there were tales of great
swords such as Dragon Spring and others that leap into waters
surrounded by dragons, which churn up the water. Wu Tzu-hsu's
sword is also called Dragon Spring.

But is there any archaeological evidence for the existence of a
real sword or swords that were seen as serpents? Well, I just so
happened to find such evidence in the *Catalogue of The Fourteenth
Park Lane Arms Fair*. Lee A. Jones authored a fascinating article
titled, "The Serpent in the Sword: Pattern-Welding in Early Medieval Swords," which immediately made the hairs on the back of my
neck tingle. (*www.vikingsword.com / serpent.html*)

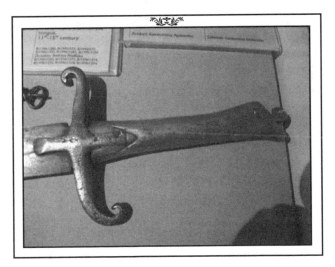

Medieval snake sword

The sword first appeared around 4,000 years ago and immediately became the preeminent weapon, preferred by the warrior
class. Recent metallurgical studies have shown how complex piled
structures or layers improved the sword from as early as 500 B.C.
in Celtic artifacts. Little wonder that the smithy was an important part of legend and folklore, as the skill implied in the making

of these swords is substantial: Several rods are welded together down the length of the blade, joining the various levels of metal together. It was then heated and pounded into shape. Sword-making was an awesome task. Smaller rods that were carburized (improved carbon) were introduced to increase the hardness. This formed steel, an alloy of iron with small amounts of carbon, was introduced into the edges of the blade because it was stronger and more effective.

Through the 5th to 10th centuries A.D.—the approximate period of King Arthur—sword smiths actually managed to manipulate this piled structure to create wonderful designs within the blade. The method remained virtually unchanged even into the 20th century, as can be seen with the daggers of the Nazis, who utilized it extensively.

The patterns are seen via the varying degrees of trace elements within the different rods, showing alternating shades. The rods are invariably twisted down the shaft, forming a spiral effect. These "twisted" swords are seen as early as the 1st century B.C. in the La Tene period, although more effectively used from the 3rd and 5th centuries—the exact early period of Arthur. Cassiodorus was a secretary of Theodoric, and in A.D. 520 he wrote to a northern Germanic tribe regarding a gift of words praising their skills, especially the shadows and colors seen in the blades, which he likened to "tiny snakes." The 10th century Kormaks Saga says this concerning the sword Skofnung:

> ...a covering goes with it and thou shall leave it quiet; the sun must not shine on the upper guard, nor shall thou comest to the fighting place, sit alone, and there draw it. Hold up the blade and blow on it; then a small snake will creep from under the guard; incline the blade and make it easier for it to creep back under the guard.

It is the considered opinion of some scientists that this implies that the dew would reveal the pattern of the serpent upon the sword, giving the impression that a serpent is emerging from the sheath.

This inclusion of the serpent in the blade was eventually replaced with iron inlaid letters and symbols, and Christian phrases such as In Nomine Domini ("In the name of the Lord"). The remarkable archaeological fact of serpents appearing in the designs of 5th century swords links perfectly with the time of Arthur. As the Pendragon or Head/Chief Dragon Lord, he would certainly have been seen with such a device, and in the stories mentioned previously, there are textual links in the legend. Could it be that the tales of Arthur and his serpentine or dragon swords were based upon reality?

And so, coming full circle, I am drawn back to that first initiation years ago and the sword that was bestowed upon me and which is now back with the order. It stood nearly 5 feet with a gold pommel of writhing dragons. The silver sheen of the blade when turned in the light would reveal a beautiful pattern of two entwined serpents, heads coming closer together as they raced toward the tip.

The sword, as a fighting tool, has been with man for more than 4,000 years, and as such it has crept into the comradeship of the warrior elite that could afford its luxury. Symbolism of wisdom, energy, and illumination has been melded in with the steel structure in the same way that the sword has been melded into the myths and tales that were themselves stories of inner light. The shining sword is symbolically utilized throughout secret societies today and has been so for hundreds of years—creating a bond between man today and man yesterday.

7

The Secret History of King Arthur and Robin Hood

King Arthur

In the last few chapters, we have often come across King Arthur and tales of the Grail. What we have to understand is that these tales hide secrets. These hidden depths were placed there by various secret organizations that were too afraid to place the truth openly before the public for fear of Catholic inquisitions and Christian intolerance. In the search for the truth about the secrets of secret societies, we need to understand what they were trying to tell us and what links these tales might have to the history and lineage of secret societies. We have already learned that religion and the Ophite, or serpent worship of wisdom, are at the core of the world's secret societies. Will we discover the same in the tales of Arthur and his literary-related character of Robin Hood?

Most historians place the Arthurian period in the 5th century A.D., and so this is where I began my historical journey to find the "real Arthur" and the real "truth."

In about A.D. 402, Stilicho, the Vandal Regent of Rome, needed the remainder of his troops back in Rome to defend the homeland against the invading Goths. This left Britain militarily vulnerable and weak, and by 410 the Anglo-Saxons were mounting a terrible invasion that set the countryside alight. But why did the Saxons delay their invasion? The answer lies within the extremely clever way the Romans had previously cleared the country of what they called "arbarians"—that is, those people who would have either utilized inside intelligence to assist any invading force, or who would have undermined the existing rule. The Romans were using secret service methods of infiltrating and undermining the existing power base.

> Britain was near to death until Stilicho arrived, and that with the Saxons defeated, the seas were safer and the Picts were broken, thereby making Britain secure.

So wrote the early Christian poet and historian, Claudian, in A.D. 399. Even the Welsh monk Gildas (c.504–570) described how "the legions came into close contact with the cruel enemies and slew great numbers of them. All of them were driven beyond the borders and the humiliated natives rescued from the bloody savagery which awaited them."

For eight years, between the Romans leaving and the Saxons invading, it appears that Britain enjoyed a brief time of relative peace. This peace was shattered violently as the Saxons instigated their bloody onslaught in the summer of 410. By winter, the British "civitates" had simply had enough of their Roman pretender, Constantine III, and the old Roman system, and so they decided to go it alone. However, the British message to the Emperor Honorius left open a small inroad, just in case they were making a mistake. Britain wanted to stay in the Roman Empire, not as subjects, but as allies aiding each other with trade and defense. So Britain became an autonomous state within the Empire, especially after the sacking of Rome by Alaric's Goths in 410.

This balance of power continued, and in A.D. 417 the units of Comes Brittaniarum partially reoccupied the Saxon forts along the southeast coast. This British force comprised six units of cavalry and three of infantry, a unique mobile field army whose method of fighting was influenced by the Scythian warrior-élite who had been brought to Britain by the Romans. These Scythians also brought many of the serpent-related traditions we have found associated with Arthur—including the worship of Uther/Zeus and the plunging of the blood-soaked sword into and out of the ground as an offering.

Following the death of Honorius, Rome suffered badly at the hands of usurpers, and the final remnants of the Roman army vanished from Britain. The exact date of their departure is not known, although Nennius, the 8th century Christian historian, tells us that Vortigern had become king of Britain by A.D. 425. This probably referred to the southern regions and those parts of Britain previously held by the Romans. Vortigern, it seems, filled the gaping hole that Rome left behind.

Whether there is any truth in it or not, the *Historia Brittonium* states that it was Vortigern who invited Hengist and Horsa, the Norse warriors, to settle in Kent, only to later argue and fight against them. The old system of Roman rule finally began to crumble.

Vortigern's answer was to invite yet more foreigners to settle in the country, creating for them settlements called foederati. Was this wise council on Vortigern's part? It may just have been his only answer, and a Roman answer at that, for the Romans had utilized this settlement procedure themselves. The Romans had also been powerful enough to keep these settlements under control, and had more incentives to offer them in exchange for their loyalty, whereas Vortigern had no other choice. Word had reached him that the Picts and Scots were massing on the borders, and he simply did not have the power to repel them. His tactic was Roman: bring in other Barbarians and get them to fight each other—a classic Roman and later secret service tactic. It seems, however, that rather than settling warrior Barbarians on his coastlines in order to protect Britain, Vortigern opened the floodgates to the land-hungry Saxons. Vortigern was defeated by Hengist in 455, the lowlands were put to the fire, and the Britons fled the country, heading for Spain and Armorica. The economy collapsed, and by 461 Vortigern the Great was dead.

There was a recovery of British fortunes a decade or so later, when Ambrosius Aurelianus (thought to be the son of a Roman consul) fought against the Saxons. On Marlborough Downs in Wiltshire there is a huge earthwork built by a British chieftain between 2900–2500 B.C., and later used by the Romans and Saxons. Archaeological evidence of battles from this period on this reused fort clearly shows that the Saxons were being repulsed.

It was then the turn of Arthur, who upheld the pride of the British nation through various documented battles. Many historians state that the true Arthur is elusive in the texts of the time, but there are hundreds of Welsh texts that refer to Arthur, which have not yet been translated into English. Not being a Welsh scholar, I, unfortunately, have to leave this task to them, but we should remember that there is more yet to learn.

This history of the 5th century Britons is interesting, but only partially of interest in our search for the secrets' depths. The Romans had brought the Scythians to Britain, and the Scythians brought along their cultural belief systems. They fought well, and in all probability, aided the Britons with training in their warrior ways.

The memory of these cultural additions seeped into the British consciousness and became British, Celtic, and eventually "New Age." This very real struggle for power and for the defense of the realm was an ideal backdrop to the mystery that is now called the "Arthurian cycle."

There probably was an Ambrosius, an Arthur, and a Vortigern, and they doubtless fought great battles and overcame terrible troubles. But would they have understood the idea of the Grail as the "serpent people" would have understood it? I doubt it. Of course, they would have been familiar with stories of a legendary "magical substance" that could help soldiers recover, heal battle wounds, and "resurrect" them in great numbers. This understanding would have come from what they had picked up from the myths that had been encoded with the wisdom of the shamanic "serpent people," otherwise known as the Shining Ones.

This magical substance was "mixed" in the sacred mixing bowl, and Britain in the 5th century was itself a great and wondrous "mixing bowl." Cultures from across the known world traveled to it. Exports of British copper, lead, tin, and much more were shipped across Europe and the Mediterranean. There is even evidence that the ancient Egyptians visited her shores and that a Pharaoh's daughter may well have settled in Ireland. Folklore tradition also tells us that Joseph of Arimathea visited these shores, and owned tin mines in Cornwall—although this I seriously doubt. If traditions such as these are far from truth, I had to ask myself, then why were these strange tales invented?

If, as it seems, Britain was an important place, or even just as important as, say, Gaul, then why could Britain not also be the new home to the secret of the Grail? As I have shown in the *Serpent*

Grail, the Grail on the "first level" or venom, is not place-specific. It is a secret held by all the civilizations of the globe, called many things, but essentially the same substance.

Robin Hood

Etymologically, Robin comes from the Norman "Robert," a form of the Germanic Hrodebert, and it originally meant "famous" or "bright"—possibly "shining."

Robin Hood is therefore the "Bright Hood," a similar name to the Naga with their illuminated serpent or cobra hoods. As many have previously stated there are strong links between the origin of Robin Hood and the Green Man, who is also the ancient Egyptian god Osiris and the Greek-Roman god Dionysus/Bacchus, and so we should hope to find something of interest in the many stories surrounding this enigmatic character.

It's no surprise to also discover that the Templars are very much associated with Robin, and many of the tales of Robin also match in format those of King Arthur. In the popular retelling by Henry Gilbert (*Robin Hood*, 1912) we find mention of a pig-like serpent. Robin wants to know who the hermit of Fountains Dale is and how the one named as "Peter the Doctor" managed to cure people:

> "Oh," said Nick with a smile, "I meant no ill-will to Peter. Often hath his pills cured our villeins when they ate too much pork, and my mother—rest her soul—said that naught under the sun was like his lectuary of Saint Evremond."
>
> Peter the Doctor speaks, "I deserve well of all my patients, but"—and his eyes flashed—"that great swinehead oaf of a hermit monk—Tuck by name, and would that I could tuck him in the deepest, darkest hole in Windleswisp marsh!— That great ox-brained beguiled me into telling him of all my good specifics. With his eyes as wide and soft as a cow's he looked as innocent as a mawkin, and asked me this and that about the cures which I had made, and ever he seemed the more to marvel and to gape at my wisdom and my power. The porcine serpent! He did but spin his web the closer about me to my own undoing and destruction. When I had

told him all, and was hopeful that he would buy a phial of serpent's oil of Jasper—a sure and certain specific, my good freemen, against ague and stiffness."

So, Friar Tuck is like a snake-pig and Peter the Doctor hopes to sell him "serpent oil." It is likely that Gilbert used the "serpent oil" in the early 19th century, as this peculiar substance was quite fashionable at the time, and no matter how hard I searched I could not find Gilbert's source material.

There are elements of the Robin Hood myth that relate to other legends. The "Tree of Life" is seen as "Robin's Larder Tree," supplying all that could be required, similar to the "Horn of Plenty" or the "cauldron" of Celtic folklore.

Robin's link with the Horned God is also telling, as he is lord and master over the human "animals" of the Forest and they are guardians of their stolen treasure, similar to the hoarding, serpent Nagas of Hinduism. They do good deeds for those who deserve them and dastardly deeds to those who do not. In the connected tales of Robin Goodfellow, the "trickster of the woods" also known as Puck, there is also the link of Sib, the fairy who lives in the hillside and is linked as being a "serpent spirit" of healing. Robin falls in love with his lady of the waters or Queen of Heaven, later to be known as the Maid Marion (Mer = Sea/water, Marion = Mary) and in many ways is undermining the new Christian world that forced itself upon this ancient mixture of Paganism. Robin Hood and Robin Goodfellow are therefore secret tales of an oppressed culture, just as are the letters and gospels of the Christian cult.

Puck, incidentally, is thought to have a much older pedigree, being traced back to an Irish Pan-like deity known as Pouka. Indeed, Robin Goodfellow is said to be born of a human mother and a god-like father in the form of Oberon (king of the fairies; *Ob* meaning "serpent"). He is also green like the "Green Man," which is the special healing color attributed to many things surrounding the serpent cult—such as the Emerald Tablet, the color of initiation into Gnostic mysteries, associated with the Masons and the Green Glass of the Grail.

It is believed by many that the crescent shape of the bow recalls the crescent moon and horns of the Pagan "Horned God," as does the horn Robin uses to call his people together. Even Little

John in the tale of "Robin Hood and Sir Guy de Gisborne" is tied to a tree, being saved at the last minute by Robin disguised as Sir Guy. As with most folklore there is symbolism, myth, legend, and probably some element of a real origin.

Robin Hood may well have some aspects of his personality and acts from real historical figures, but most historians would steer away from stating anything as fact.

As Fran and Geoff Doel point out in their book, *Robin Hood: Outlaw or Greenwood Myth*, "the origin of Robin Hood was obscure…suggests a mythological or folklore origin."

What we also find, however, in some of the earlier tales is that Robin Hood and Little John—like Jesus and John the Baptist—were equals. In the 15th century, Walter Bower said that Robin Hood together with Little John and their companies rose to prominence. This in itself points out that both Robin and John were seen to each have their own followers very much like Jesus and John. They are therefore the "twins" of Gnosticism, like Castor and Pollux—the duality and balance.

Other elements of Robin's life and especially his death show an ancient link:

> Curiously the ballad of Robin Hood's Death also has a ritualistic element, with foreknowledge and ritual 'banning' and a death by bleeding, which is suspiciously close to the ritualistic dismemberment of other European and Asiatic Springtime gods and heroes such as Tammuz, Adonis and Osiris. The cognitive connections between the outlaw and Robin the bird may be coincidental, but the possibilities of a Greenwood myth underlying the later outlaw traditions needs to be examined. (Doel, *Robin Hood: Outlaw or Greenwood Myth*)

Tammuz, Adonis, and Osiris are vegetation gods of greenness. Indeed Osiris himself in the Pyramid Texts at Saqqara is called the "Great Green" and often appears green-skinned as a symbol of "resurrection and life." The battle between Osiris and Set seems all the more familiar now in the struggle that ensues between Robin and his arch-rival the Sheriff of Nottingham. Osiris becomes Horus when resurrected, and we find that it is Horus who is protected by the Wadjet snake—the green snake.

Even in the way he dies there are links with older mysteries. Robin is ritualistically bled to death like the ancient Pagan sacrifices. The deed is done by the Abbess of Kirklees, who acts as the priestess in some ancient Pagan ritual. Could it be that the tales of Robin are more ancient than previously believed? Could they really be tales of ancient Egypt and even Sumeria? Passed down over millennia and altered by time? One thing is true: These tales were written up by clerics of the Church and members of secret orders. The Arthurian tales had influence from the white robed Cistercians and the Knights Templar—indeed it was the Templars who were protectors of the Grail itself, guardians of the secret knowledge.

Author in Roman tombs or Gateways for the dead, Cyprus

The fact remains that Christianity was stomping all over old Pagan beliefs, rewriting tales that had existed for hundreds of years. But, as the Christians were destroying cultural history, there were those who defended it. The Masons of the period in which Robin Hood grew to popularity were hiding their symbols and Pagan ideas in the framework and masonry of churches across Europe. Green Men sprang up in every sacred Christian place. Strange characters seen hiding in foliage peeped out like messengers from the past. Grails, beheaded victims, pillars of foliage, and images of serpents were placed everywhere and often at the behest of the same Cistercians and Templars—not to mention the myriad other orders and groups that were maintaining the hidden Gnosis which was to emerge in later times within the ranks of the so-called modern secret societies.

These peculiar and somewhat disturbing images are none other than the characters from the Pagan past—gods and deities such as Herne the Horned God and many other images of Mother Goddesses. The truth to the past of man's religious upbringing can still be seen in the stonework of Christian churches and cathedrals, in places such as Rosslyn Chapel and Lichfield Cathedral. But not just in the stone.

We must also look to the legends, for as we can see, the tales of Robin Hood are not only linked to the ancient past; they are also linked inextricably to the tales of Arthur and his search for the Holy Grail with instances such as those of the knight Gawain decapitating the Green Giant, and mysterious images of a Green Knight. It is seen clearly in the fact that the "plays" of old, enacted by local people and paraded through streets, have changed titles across time and location. From the St. George play to the Robin Hood and Green Jack, from Wildman to Green George, the basic story is the same.

These tales, as we have seen, can be traced backward across time to India and Sumeria, Egypt and Persia. They formed the basis of secret priestly orders many thousands of years ago and they still do today.

8

Here Be Dragons

The Sacred Places of Ancient Secret Societies

The secret societies of the globe from ancient times down to today all had many things in common. Not the least of which was the need for a place to meet. But what was the origin of the symbolism of a temple or a lodge? Why is this place a stairway to heaven? A gateway to another world? And why is the serpent or dragon often involved? If we go back across the mists of time to the original meeting places of the serpent cults and shining secret orders, will we discover the secrets of the mysterious landscape that now surrounds us?

Over the course of many years and with more air-miles than I care to remember, I have journeyed on a quest to uncover the secrets of the ancient serpent cults that I reveal in my books. Each time I journey, I discover something new. There truly is a whole new world opening up before our eyes. Suddenly, and often without warning, I am faced with a reinterpretation of history that I am simply not looking for.

In another twist in the tale of the serpent, I am about to uncover before your eyes one of the ancient truths about dragons, remembering that, in myth and in ancient history, dragons and serpents are intertwined like the coils of a pit viper.

I shall to begin in America of all places, for two reasons. Firstly, that this is the last place I would even consider looking for dragons, and, secondly, because the evidence is most profound here in archaeological terms.

The evidence of serpent worship in the Americas can largely be shown by the many serpent mounds that appear across the continent. The most famous by a long way is the "Serpent Mound" of Ohio, Adams County. According to some,[1] this marvelous mound is related to Stonehenge, and it is the "Dragon Guardian" of the East to Stonehenge's Secret of the West. Indeed, it is thought that the two ancient structures actually do share the same timeline and may very well have a relationship to each other—if ancient man shared the same beliefs and traveled extensively, as is the growing belief of many scholars. Of course, Stonehenge is also directly north of that infamous serpent temple, Avebury.

Dragon at Cistercian monastery

Avebury is a huge British temple and stone monument erected around 2000 B.C. in the shape of a serpent when seen from the sky. Once known as Abury which, according to Deane,[2] is evidently Abiri or Ab-ir (after the Abiri people or Cabiri who were serpent worshippers). Abir means the solar snake or fire snake.

Although some have argued whether Avebury was ever Abury or Aubury (serpent sun), the fact remains that even as far back as the 17th century there was a Mr. Aubury who said that it should be pronounced and spelled Aubury (found in the ledger book of Malmesbury Abbey).

Of course even as Ave Bury, the "Ave" reverts back to the root of "Eve" which I know means "female serpent." The pathway of Avebury passes through a large circular temple of the sun, emerging, and then winding again and ending with an oddly, not quite circular head—directly in line with "Snakes Head Hill" (Hackpen).

The central circle is symbolic of the sun, which is the male principle in the creative process and is symbolized elsewhere as a bull or lion. Once the serpent has passed through or around this sun circle it is recharged for new life.

In Egyptian hieroglyphs, we can see similar imagery with the symbol of the snake going over the solar disc, emerging with its head erect. Overlaid onto Avebury it is the same image! Adding to this, that the snake is often depicted with the ancient Egyptian ankh symbol dangling from its emergent neck—the Ankh being a symbol of new life—the great circle of Avebury simply has to be the "solar disk," and the pathway is the snake—thus illustrating in a painfully labor-intensive way, the ritualistic path of the serpent worshipper toward new life.

The circular aspect of the stone circles of Europe are strangely reminiscent of the temples of Quetzalcoatl, which were "circular, and the one dedicated to his worship in Mexico, was entered by a door like unto the mouth of a serpent"[3]—a very similar ritualistic inference to those based around Avebury and other stone circles.

In his book the *Worship of the Serpent Traced Throughout the World*, John Bathurst Deane explains, "A third description of temples consecrated to the service of the Ophites' god remains to be considered: and these were not only the most rare, the most characteristic, and the most magnificent; but, probably, the most sacred of them all. These were erected in the form of the Ophite hierogram, the serpent passing through a circle."

This hierogram is the symbol of the serpent, a circle with a snake passing through it, like a needle and thread. He continues, "They were composed, like the circular temples, of a number of Baitulia, or amber stones, so arranged as to describe the mystic circle, through which the still more mystic serpent trailed his majestic form."

And this is the truth of the Stone Circles and physical hierograms: that they were rebirthing circles (a being born again through the spirit, through the circle). I can even make a remarkable deduction from the strange word "baitulia" mentioned previously by Deane—these are betyl stones or serpents' eggs. In Wales, the serpents were said to emerge and congregate on Midsummer's Eve to blow into the Serpent Stone-Eggs or Glain Neidr, which is reminiscent of the Roman historian Pliny's tale of this activity among the Gauls. These serpent stones were said to be colored pebbles, which gave "second sight" and healing. Midsummer's Eve was the night when the serpents would role themselves into hissing balls and create the glain egg, also known as "snake stone" or "Druid's egg." In Welsh myth, even Merlin himself went in search of them.

The egg, Cosmic Egg, or Cosmogenic Egg is universally seen with the serpent—as in the symbol of the Orphic Egg shown with a snake wrapped around it. From the serpent mound of Ohio to Mithras and Cneph, the egg is associated with serpent worship. Why? According to most scholars, it is the emblem of the mundane elements coming from the creating god. Therefore, it is a symbol of the elements of the universe. Surely there is also another reason, a reason that would relate to early man more than such complex ideas sprung into the mind of modern scientists and scholars.

What is an egg? Simply an "entry portal" into this world. A device to give life. And what animal is seen in relation to this unique device and portal? It is the snake. Again, it is the snake—a symbol of the life force—that creates the device, which gives life.

Megalithic hole from the serpent island of Gozo

The Egyptian creator deity, Cneph, was represented as a serpent with an egg thrusting from his mouth, similar to the Ohio Serpent Mound and other places. From this egg proceeded the deity Ptah, or Phtha—the creative power and "father god" who is the same as the Indian Brahma. These Brahma have been related by scholars to the Jewish Essene community and also to Mithra I. Mithra was encircled by serpents and can be equated in many ways to Jesus, being a solar divinity and reborn on the 25th of December, like the sun. There is little wonder that a Persian god, such as Mithra, and a Judaic semi-deity, such as Jesus, would be linked when one understands that the folds of the ancient serpent cult were so all-encompassing that they encircled the globe like a Leviathan. We can even see elements of this when Jesus is equated to the Brazen Serpent of Moses when we are told to be wise as serpents and that he even shed his shroud or skin once crucified upon the cross. Incidentally, snakes are still, to this day, nailed to trees in certain parts of Africa as a sacrifice for our sins and for healing remedies.

And so we have circular monuments and serpent mounds associated with the egg, which from all the evidence simply gives us the conclusion that these were places of rebirth. One would push through the symbolic circle, or out of the egg, or slough off the old skin, but there is more evidence yet to be unearthed and which reveals this sloughing of the skin to be linked with these ancient sites.

The classical Greeks frequently depicted a serpent squeezing between two upright stones, which they called Petrae Ambrosiae (stone or rock ambrosia), noting that Ambrosia is the nectar and Elixir of the gods. According to the 19th century archaeologist, Bryant, Stonehenge was seen as amber stones, with nearby Amesbury—previously Ambrosbury—as proof. In this way, the healing abilities of the megalithic stones are attributed to the serpent. In fact, we do still find traces of this in many stories about dragons, who protect, serve, and heal those ancient *people of the stones.*

The antiquarian and stone circle-spotter extraordinaire William Stukely also found two other "serpent temples"—one at Shap in Westmorland and the other at Classerness in the island of Lewis.

Stukely thought that the Greek legend of Cadmus sowing dragons' teeth alluded to his building a serpentine temple. Cadmus was turned into a serpent (or followed the serpent cult), and stone temples were erected in his and Harmonia's honor. Pausanius helps us along and points out that "In the road between Thebes and Gilsas, you may see a place encircled by select stones, which the Thebans call The Serpent's Head."[4] So, ancient tales may be clues to the real identities of the serpents and dragons of fable, and these real identities may in fact be literal places and monuments. Places where, perhaps, snakes were held in high esteem by the ancient Ophites or serpent worshippers of the world.

There are many more texts mentioning dragons and serpents, such as the one that Taxiles showed to Alexander the Great, which was sacred to Dionysus. It was said to be of enormous size, walled around, and resided in a low, deep place. It is my conjecture that such places, similar to Stonehenge, were "portals" or "gateways" to the "land of the serpents"—places of mystery and rebirth, where offerings and sacrifices must be made to the serpent benefactor.

Indeed, there is plenty of evidence now from people such as Paul Devereux that shows such places were also great resonance boosters. That is, they amplified sound in peculiar ways, thus creating the booming sound of the dragon. Such scholars even go as far as saying that the resonance creates spiral and serpent wavelike shapes from the dust and smoke, as the sound wave carries the particles along its serpentine path. The serpent could truly have been seen to rise and heard to roar.

However, most people are not aware that similar mounds and monuments also appear elsewhere and often associated with the serpent or dragon in similar ways.

In 1871, at the meeting of the British Association in Edinburgh, a certain Mr. Phene gave an account of his discovery in Argyllshire of a similar mound, "several hundred feet long, 15 feet high, and 30 feet broad."

The tail tapered away, and a circular cairn, which he presumed to be the solar disk above the head of the "Egyptian uraeus," surmounted the head.

This amazingly is not the only instance of huge serpentine images upon the ground. In the Zend Avesta of the Zoroastrians, one of the heroes takes a rest on what he thinks is a bank—only to find out that it was a green snake!

Iphicrates related that in Mauritania "there were dragons of such extent that grass grew up on their backs," thus showing the highly likely chance that tales of massive dragons in far-off lands could easily be serpent mounds.

Other instances of serpent mounds, however, are to be found mentioned by Strabo (Lib xv. P.1022), in which two dragons are said to have resided in the mountains of India, one 80 cubits long and the other 140. Posidonius also tells of one in Syria, which was so large that horse riders on either side could not see each other. Each "scale" was as big as a shield, so that a man "might ride into his mouth." Bryant concurs with the belief that these must be ruins of Ophite temples.

And for what were these temples used?

In ancient Egyptian papyri and in the Mesoamerican codex borgia, there are instances or tales of the king entering the serpent and going through it in order to be resurrected—much like those I find in the myth of Osiris. This is exactly the same process that lodges and temples today are used for in modern secret societies. In Freemasonic rituals, the initiate must be hung, placed in a coffin, and then called forth like Lazarus in the Bible. In my own ritual, I was ritually slaughtered and then brought back to life by the symbolic energy of the snake.

A book said to have been written by Votan (Quetzalcoatl) in the language of the Quiches and thought to have been in the possession of Núñez de la Vega, the Bishop of Chiapas, also has some revealing elements. So revealing that the Bishop tried to burn it. Votan says he left Valum Chivim[5] and came to the New World to apportion land among seven families who came with him and were said to be *culebra* or of "serpent origin." Passing the "land of 13 snakes" he arrived in Valum Votan, founding the city of Nachan (City of Snakes), thought to be modern day Palenque, possibly around 15 B.C. or even earlier. Votan is said to have made four trips to the east and even to have visited Solomon.

An interesting aspect of serpent mounds is the description of a subterranean passage, which is said to terminate at the root of "heaven." This was called a "snake's hole" and Votan was only allowed in because he was the son of a snake. Surely this can only mean that Votan was an initiate in the serpent cult and that there was a ritualized serpent mound or pyramid which led to snake heaven or Patala.

The Fenian heroes of ancient Ireland are recorded orally in song, and one of them, Fionn, was their "dragon slayer." One of the legends tells us that:

> It resembles a great mound, its jaws were yawning wide;
> There might lie concealed, though great its fury,
> A hundred champions in its eye-pits.
> Taller in height than eight men,
> Was its tail, which was erect above its back;
> Thicker was the most slender part of its tail,
> Than the forest oak which was sunk by the flood.

Fionn asked where this great monster had come from and was told, "From Greece, to demand battle from the Fenians." It seems that the serpent worshippers had come to Ireland from Greece, and had fought the ancient inhabitants, leaving behind such terror of them that they became symbolized as this great "dragon mound." Fionn, it is said, opened the side of the dragon and released the men, going on to kill it. It may be that there is a mixture of wartime fact built in with ritualistic truth in this legend. Emerging from the side of the dragon, as in other myths, gives new life.

The rituals of the secret societies date back thousands of years and have their origin, yet again, in the worship of the serpent. With the oncoming of orthodox Christianity, Islam, and Judaism, this serpent worship was eradicated and went underground—emerging it seems in the guise of secret societies. Here we have archaeological and textual evidence that the ancient mounds of the world were rebirthing places for these ancient cults that were wiped out, adapted, or swallowed up by the dominant cults (Christianity, and so on). Obviously the lodges and temples themselves would take on many more symbolic devices as time passed by—such as symbolism from the Temple of Solomon.

9

Do You Want to Know a Secret?

Solomon's Temple Revealed

In the last chapter, we discovered the serpent secret of the cult centers of our globe and their influence on the modern meeting places of religions and secret societies. Perhaps the most important of all influences on the most powerful secret society—the Freemasons—is the Temple of Solomon. But there is a deep psychology held within the walls of this temple, one that has permeated secret societies for millennia. It's time to take a look at this secret.

There is a journey that we all must take. It is called life. There is no escaping this journey. We cannot pay somebody to take it for us or to take the pain and sorrow that frequents our path. Without our mother and father there would be no help at all from the very start. We would be helpless and we would, in all likelihood, die.

We are born with no knowledge whatsoever other than some minor genetic memories, and many of us simply follow the patterns that life, evolution, and our peers throw at us. We subconsciously assume we must do as our forefathers; we must follow in their footsteps; we must marry, have children, get a job, and step onto the roller-coaster of commercialism and the greed-oriented rat race we know as capitalism or even communism. There is seemingly no way out of this life, and anyway, most of us are enthused by the chase—for we truly know no different.

All of this is perfectly natural. We are, after all, apes with less hair. We strive to be the alpha male and female; to be top dog; to fit in with the society or "tribe" that surrounds us and support the same football team as our friends. And often that society is just a larger version of our selves; it is created by groups of selves.

In the times gone by, our ancestors saw through all of this and recognized that there was another way. They discovered that in order for man to elevate himself above the level of the brown earth upon which he scrambled, he needed to alter his internal dialogue. Man needed to understand himself and the forces that drive him.

This unique understanding—that there could be a higher goal for mankind, whether collectively or individually—evolved into what we now know as Gnosticism. Of course, this is a massive oversimplification and we should always take into account the mystics—those who have experienced what we would call otherworldly emotions or visions. Also, regardless of popular perception, the Christians were not the only Gnostics and mystics. Gnostic comes from the Greek word *gignoskein* meaning, simply, to know. It was applied to "one sect of so-called philosopher's in the first ages of Christianity."[1]

However, the term is now being used more loosely, and I personally see the term slightly differently than others, and probably in a controversial light.

To me, the Greek term implies all-knowledge. This is a kind of knowledge gained much like plugging ones mind into the World Wide Web and being able to download every single piece of data in an instant. In the same way, the true Gnostic, much like the mystic, could supposedly understand all things in a unique way. Whether this is the mind tapping into the collective unconscious, the Akashic records, or any other name given to the process, does not matter for the purpose of this chapter; the fact remains, it was believed. And because of this belief, physical manifestations of the internal belief system emerged the world over. In this way, the temples of man were exactly that—Temples of Man.

Gnosis, then, means knowledge of the most esoteric kind, and this is the story that has been hidden from our eyes for too long. This is the truth of the secret societies that we on the outside are supposedly too worldly to comprehend.

The Temple

So, let us now try our best to comprehend the Temple of Solomon and, in doing so, let us walk upon holy ground, trodden only by the initiated.

In the years of my own searching, there were times when I would be found at the feet of the Magi, sitting and listening to the wise words of the Sufi, joining in the debate at a more enlightened Freemasonic Lodge. I was learning and viewing the process with an open ear and an open eye, and yet also balancing it all with the knowledge of modern science and reductionism. Both worlds, the one of the esoteric and the one of science, are useless apart—both are needed today if we are to truly understand.

So down to the facts about the Temple of Solomon. We are sadly lacking in any archaeological evidence, regardless of what you read on some literal fundamentalist Website. What we are told is that in the 10th century B.C., the wise King Solomon erected a great temple to the Lord. Unfortunately, if any of this is true, then we actually find that it was a temple that encompassed many Pagan religions.

According to Professor James Pritchard, in his book, *Solomon and Sheba*:

> ...the so-called cities of Megiddo, Gezer and Hazor, and Jerusalem itself were in reality more like villages....Within were relatively small public buildings and poorly constructed dwellings with clay floors. The objects reveal a material culture which, even by the standards of the ancient Near East, could not be judged sophisticated or luxurious....The 'magnificence' of the age of Solomon is parochial and decidedly lackluster, but the first book of Kings implies exactly the opposite.[2]

In fact, and in the bright light of day, what we actually have (which most writers are afraid to say) is no evidence whatsoever for Solomon's Temple. We have no evidence for Solomon, other than these peculiar Biblical texts. Nor do we have any evidence for the Queen of Sheba, or any of the other characters involved. Instead, there is more depth than could ever be imagined, more meaning than we would dare to believe.

In *The Temple at Jerusalem: A Revelation*, John Michell gives us an insight to the real meaning:

> Legends of the Temple describe it as the instrument of a mystical, priestly science, a form of alchemy by which oppositely charged elements in the earth and atmosphere were brought together and ritually married. The product of their union was a spirit that blessed and sanctified the people of Israel.

How right Michell is. The Temple is an instrument of mystical and priestly science, or even magic. The secret unravels before our eyes the more we learn. You see the true Gnostic, the true disciple or perfect one, must be a man or woman of balance. He or she must unite the two sides of the mind—the male and female principles, as they are called. We are all both male and female, and the alchemists used this concept of balance and revealed it in their images of the Hermaphrodite (half man and half woman).

Solomon was no real man, and Sheba was no real woman. Instead they were symbols of this internal and often external process. The whole story of Solomon, Sheba, and the Temple, which is the perfectly formed body (both physical and spiritual) is the story of our own psyche. It is an esoteric truth, misunderstood in its exoteric form.

Hiram

Hiram was the son of a Jewish mother and a Phoenician father and is credited with the decoration of the Temple of Solomon. He was said to have been the "son of a widow of the tribe of Naphtali.... He cast two bronze pillars" in 1 Kings 7:13–15.

We must also note something of interest found in 1 Kings 16:

> Then he made two capitals of cast bronze, to set on top of the pillars. The height of one capital was 5 cubits; and the height of the other capital was five cubits. He made a lattice network, with wreaths of chainwork, for the capitals which were on top of the pillars: seven chains for one capital and seven for the other capital. (Masonic Bible, Collins)

These pillars became known as *Joachim*, meaning "he establishes" and *Boaz*, which means "in him is strength," and these are now familiar to most modern Freemasons as central to their own lodge or temple. Copies of these can be clearly seen at the infamous Rosslyn Chapel, as we shall discover.

But what is interesting here is the original text about these pillars. Firstly, bronze is used for the capitals, just as bronze is used for the "Brazen Serpent" of Moses and is indicative of the fiery aspect of the serpent as one of the channels in the kundalini process. Their "heights" were 5 cubits, matching the five hooded cobras seen across India and atop many pillars, although the Bible calls them Lilies, which are symbols of balance anyway.

Leading up to these capitals were "wreaths" of "chainwork"—seven on each pillar. Strangely, these chains were "for the capitals," so we conclude that these seven leveled chains (coils) were pointing towards the head (capital) just as the serpents of the Kundalini do.

There are more real links between Hiram and the serpent. For instance, we noted previously that he was of the tribe of Naphtali. The standard of the tribe of Naphtali, according to Jewish tradition, is a serpent or basilisk, and this could have come from Egyptian origins, as Jewish tradition states that Naphtali was the brother of Joseph, chosen to represent the family to Pharaoh.

> And now I have sent a skillful man, endowed with understanding, Huram [Hiram] my master [father] craftsman, (the son of a woman of the daughters of Dan, and his father was a man of Tyre), skilled to work in gold and silver, bronze and iron, stone and wood, purple and blue, fine linen and crimson, and to make any engraving and to accomplish any plan which may be given to him, with your skilful men and with the skilful men of my lord David your father. (2 Chronicles 2:13–14)

Here, Hiram is said to be a son of the tribe of Dan, which had an emblem—the serpent, this time with a horse.

Incredibly, there is also a hidden truth and repetitive pattern in this little statement about the real skills of this literary character. Follow this pattern:

Hiram is skilled in:

1. gold and silver.

2. bronze and iron.

3. stone and wood.

4. purple and blue.

5. fine linen and crimson.

6. making any engraving.

7. accomplishing any plan that may be given to him.

Note that there are seven "balanced" elements to the skill of the man who will build the Temple! This is a real clue to the Temple's secret indeed.

According to this book of Chronicles, Hiram was a cunning man (a word used for the serpent) endued with understanding, and skillful in the work of gold, silver, brass, stone, and timber. But he was also credited with certain tools, which could pierce stone. Stone, as I show in *Gnosis*, is symbolic of wisdom and foundation. Hiram's tool, therefore, pierced the veil or even the very root of wisdom.

According to the book of Kings, the Temple was built of stone (or wisdom) before it was brought to the site—something similar to a prefabricated building. It was said by tradition that neither hammer, nor axe, nor any tool of iron was used in the building. So how was it built? This in itself is a paradox, which can only be answered by the true secret of the Temple being revealed.

According to Rabbinical teaching, the prefabrication of the Temple was performed by the Shamir, a giant worm or serpent that could cut stones (incidentally, worm means serpent). Not dissimilar to Norse and Celtic beliefs in which Valhalla and Camelot were built with the fire of the dragon, and in China where building is aided by the serpent energy.

This is a universal concept as can be seen in India, where it was the serpentine-linked Nagas of fable who escaped their country and took the architectural wisdom abroad. The architect gods, such as Thoth of Egypt, are linked strongly with the serpent wisdom because they are linked with the building of "Temples of Wisdom" inside our *selves*.

The real you at the center

The Shamir, according to one legend, had even been placed in the hands of the Prince of the Sea,[3] which is symbolic of the Prince of Wisdom.

In essence, what we really have here is the Temple of Wisdom being built by the serpent, and that serpent is none other than that of, or similar to, the internal kundalini, later to be developed into the Kabbalah. This is a psychological training manual, a method of self-improvement, a way for society to become One, a multilayered method of getting closer to the deity that resides in each and every one of us, a deity that the ancients saw as being the same in each of us.

The whole process repeats again and again throughout the Bible. The Temple is reduced (like the alchemical method) and is remade. Then again and again, until finally the Christ *is* the temple tht is reduced (killed) and then rises again for the last time. And now, according to the texts, we can all meet with this Christ and we can all have the knowledge. We just need to understand that the true Christ is all and in all. But this hasn't worked, has it? Man is still, even now in the 21st century, searching for answers, and so the temple is being reduced once again....

I say, we should all take a look at our own "temples" and knock them to the ground. We should then go about rebuilding them in a bigger and better way than before, just the way the Bible states. And more than that, we must keep on doing this until this world of ours has peace and all truly are equal before God....

But we need to beware. All this can sound very wonderful and enticing. In a way, I am playing a trick upon your mind in the same way that secret societies often play games of manipulation. There is truth in the previous statements for sure—but to gasp in awe at the power of the kundalini simply because ancient man found it "enlightening" would be foolish, as we shall now discover.

10

Secret Societies and the Links to the Enlightenment

One of the most profound enigmas of the existence of secret societies is and has always been why people join. Why do people find these groups so interesting? What is being sought?

There are the usual and obvious answers to these questions: We are all searching for enlightenment in our own way, and each person finds it in different ways—hence the need for so many kinds of secret organizations. This has been called a void that we need to somehow fill; an emptiness within each one of us that calls out for a higher being or state of consciousness. Some psychologists believe that this is an evolutionary aspect of our lives, that within us there is a constant urge to improve and a deep-rooted hope. This hope makes us strive for more and, thus, we become the strongest and fittest of the species—hence evolution.

But, there is a truth in this that has missed many. There is a void within us, quite literally. This void is the lack of the true enlightenment experience. There actually is a higher state of consciousness. If it were not so, then the feeling and emotions that drive people towards rediscovering it would not be so strong and so universal. It is not—and I have to state this each time—the kundalini, which is a troubled and yet beautiful human electro-biochemical reaction. To follow this ancient Hindu concept to the letter is, in the first instance, next to impossible because texts do not exist, and secondly it is highly dangerous and can easily lead to psychosis and other forms of mental problems. It is one aspect of the true inner wisdom, but not the only aspect.

Over the millennia, the secret societies, and, indeed, some religions of the globe, have attempted to bring us back to this state of consciousness, but they have, more often than not, utilized it for their own gain—power. How do we know this? A quick study of the secret societies of the globe will show that the enlightenment experience has been used in every single occasion to draw people in and keep them.

From as early as the 11th century, an enigmatic group known erroneously as the Assassins emerged in Persia. They take their name from Hashish (hashish-im, "hashish takers"), a trance inducing drug thought by many to help the leaders control the minds of the subverts. The name was originally an insult.

In one famous apocryphal statement of folklore, Hasan, son of Sabah, the Sheikh of the Mountains and leader of the Assassins said to an official of the emperor's court, "You see that devotee standing guard on yonder turret-top? Watch!"

The sheikh made a signal and immediately the devotee threw himself off the mountaintop precipice to his death. "I have 70,000 men and women throughout Asia, each one of them ready to do my bidding."

In the first instance, this is amazing control over the mind of another individual. In the second, it implies that the Assassins were much older than this early appearance, with 70,000 devotees cast throughout Asia. No society can set up that many devotees over night. It would take many years to cultivate this kind of following, and it would also take a lot of convincing—unless there were an easier method of control, that is!

As if to mimic or follow an older institution, the Assassins went through a cycle of initiation based upon seven levels. This relates entirely to the seven chakra points of initiation in the close-by Hindu tradition—a tradition based around the energy of the serpent. It was at the seventh level that the Assassins reached the "great secret," that all mankind and all of creation were one, and that everything was part of the whole. This great secret included being part of the whole and understanding its creative and destructive elements (order and chaos). The Ismaili (Assassin initiate) could therefore make use of this great power held within him. They firmly believed that the rest of mankind knew nothing of this power, with the exception of the other societies. The power came through the use of the drug hashish and clever ritualistic involvement—making the Ismaili feel part of a greater good, as a "chosen one"—a feeling Adolf Hitler would later use to gain control of the German people. There was, however, an eighth level that was slightly separate, and this taught that all religions and philosophies were false, and that the only thing that mattered was fulfillment of this greater power, which lay within. Contrary to popular belief, the Assassins were not just Muslims; they were not under any category that is currently known other than secret society. It was only later on in their existence that they had to turn to Islam as a means of survival, and even then they granted themselves special privileges that allowed them to alter religion at will.

The Assassins are (rightly) always linked to the Knights Templar. These groups had dealings with eachother and a mutual respect. There are even monetary dealings between the two groups. Could it be that the Templars understood this greater secret and brought this "Holy Grail" of enlightenment back to Europe with them? It appears so, as we saw in the tales of Arthur and Robin Hood.

The whole process certainly relates to the serpent energy or fire of the ancients around the world, which was related to the serpent cults I revealed in the *Serpent Grail*. But there is another piece of evidence that relates to this. The second Grand Master, Buzurg-Umid (Great Promise), situated himself at Alamut, otherwise known as the Viper's Nest. There are further links to the Templars in that Buzurg-Umid actually made a deal with King Baldwin II of Jerusalem, a man closely connected to the Templars. In 1129, the Templars and crusaders actually allied with the Assassins to take Damascus. This is an indication that the Assassins were not just Muslim and were even prepared to take on the cloak of Christianity, should it bring them further power.

The secret rituals of the Templars and the accusations made against them would relate entirely to the cult of the Assassins. The question has to be asked, did the Templars utilize the same mind-controlling techniques as the Assassins? There is evidence to suggest that the Templars, in connection with the Assassins, actually understood the use of drugs, especially for the relief of pain. In his book *Sex and Drugs*, Robert Anton Wilson indicated his belief that the Templars used hashish, and learned the use from the Assassins. This is not an unreasonable assumption, given the links. There are links to be found in the Templar rituals and beliefs with much of the Middle Eastern religions. There is even Sufi influence, with the Golden Head of the Sufi being implicated as the Baphomet of the Templars. This Golden Head, as Idries Shah points out in *The Sufis*, was implicated as the "worship of a mysterious head [which] could well be a reference to the great work of transhumanization that takes place in the aspirant's own head." This was the idea that one's own humanity was transmuted into gold through the enlightenment experience and thus the secret of alchemy is revealed—virtual kundalini.

Also, the initiate ritual of the Sufi involved passing through a doorway of two pillars. This entrance symbolized the portal into a world of illumination, knowledge, and enlightenment. If it is true

The illuminated eye of god set within a triangle. A symbol used later by the Illuminati

that the Freemasons emerged from a font of Templar knowledge, then this could be one of the origins of the twin pillars of the Mason guilds. It is also similar to the twin pillars that pilgrims to Mecca must pass through (Safa and Marwa).

Parsi (Persian Zoroastrianism) influence is also seen in the Kusti ritual. Each day they would tie a sacred cord around their waist. The fact that the Templars were accused of holding a ritual with a sacred cord closely resembling the practice of the Zoroastrian Kusti, indicates a tradition of knowledge going back through thousands of years.

These traditions can also be seen in that great Roman religion of Mithraism, in which the initiate was marked with the sign of the cross on the forehead. This was to signify the sun and the place of illumination, the very same as that of the Hindus, ancient Egyptians, and tribal Americans to name a few.

Much of this ancient and supposedly secret teaching was passed in what is known as Gnosticism. All Gnostics cannot be drawn into one bag, but there is a general theme—that of illumination and enlightenment. The methods are now familiar to us. Many believed that, through a frenzy, they could achieve the ultimate state, and others believed that, by fasting and mediation, they would be drawn closer to God. The results were the same: a deeper understanding of themselves and the belief that they were in touch with God. This ecstasy would invigorate, and, similar to being in a Nexus, the initiate would constantly want to reachieve this state, thus keeping him in the fold. The experience being so very real to the religious mind that they truly believed they were in communion with God. And this is why I constantly draw a line at the kundalini, because it has dangers that its proponents not only refuse to see, but *can't* see because of its very nature!

The various methods used to access this altered state are very ancient. The ritual abstinence from food was as old as man. Practiced in the rituals of Eleusis, of which Plato himself was a member, the initiate would undergo a prolonged period of fasting, followed by a period of waiting. This increased the sense of anticipation and heightened the mind, which would create the event in his mind before it actually occurred. No leader could ask for more. Eventually, the initiate was lead into the temple, where he enjoyed a ritualistic meal and, thus, great effects were produced in the body with increased levels of sugar in the blood, the mind almost in a trance state. There was whirling like the dervish, sleep-inducing drinks, and play-acting by the great and seemingly powerful priests. Sacred objects and sacred words were then, at this point of heightened state, revealed. The age and breadth of this system of indoctrination can be seen in the closing words, "Cansha om pacsha," a Sanskrit term. Indeed, it is accepted by scholars that these rituals emerged in India from the ancient Brahmins. Strangely, these rituals also involved a sevenfold cord that marked the passing of the initiate.

As Aristotle wrote, "Those who are being initiated do not so much learn anything, as experience certain emotions, and are thrown into a special state of mind."

This "special state of mind" was a plasticity of the initiate that the priests could bend and manipulate to their own ends; just as the Old Man of the Mountain manipulated the Assassins. The initiate truly believed he or she had visited other worlds.

All these methods and means of manipulation were passed on through time into all manner of modern secret societies. In the High Priesthood of Thebes, a society first revealed in Germany in the 18th century, it was written of the initiate:

> He was led to two high pillars between which stood a griffin driving a wheel before him. The pillars symbolised east and west, the griffin the sun and the wheel the four spokes of the four seasons. He was taught the use of the level and instructed in geometry and architecture. He received a rod, entwined by serpents and the password Heve (serpent), and was told the story of the fall of man. (Enquire Within, *The Trial of the Serpent*)

The symbols within this initiation are now obvious and ancient.

In the initiations and rituals of witches, similar themes are found. Whirling, dancing, and a general build-up to frenzy would bring the participant into a trance state—known today as catharsis. This was helped along with drugs, such as the "ointment" used by the witches to help them fly and which contained hyoscine. The leader would then guide them through a set-piece ritual of words and incantations leading to complete mind control. With such control, as in many religions, the participant would often give up his or her own family and friends. This is the origin of what we call in modern times a cult, and it can now be realized just how hard it is to break out of a cult.

This awakening of the mind through ecstasy is, on the one hand, a release from the norm and a breakthrough for the mind into a freedom state, but on the other hand it is a dangerous tool, used by many cults, secret societies, and mainstream religion to control and manipulate the masses for their own ends. It may be that some have nothing but good intentions at heart, but history has shown, repeatedly, that greed is all-powerful and can take the soul of many well-meant groups.

The lesson is, be careful in what and whom you believe.

11

Serpent Origins and the Real Origins of Freemasonry

*This mysticism is indeed the great Masonic Secret,
the Supreme Initiation.... It is old as is this world.*
—*La Trahison Spirituelle de la Freemason,*
J. Marques-Rivere

So, at the root of the secret is an electrobiological and chemical reaction inside the mind often termed the kundalini. This we now know to be linked implicitly with the serpent from the internal process and vision, and therefore being spoken of as serpent power. But are there any real links to the world's biggest secret society—the Freemasons? It is clear that the serpent is, and has always been, a symbol of the Freemasons of which they have been perfectly proud. The question is: How many of its members realize what its all about?

Origins

Abraham, the Israelite father of mankind, and Hiram of the Freemasons, are one and the same. Both are based upon serpent worshippers with Indian Naga or serpent deity backgrounds. A grand statement, but one that I am not alone in making.

Flavius Josephus said in his *History of the Jews*:

These Jews are derived from the Indian philosophers; they are named by the Indians Calani.

Megasthenes, sent to India by Seleucus Nicator, also said that the Jews were called "Kalani" and that they were an *Indian tribe*.

Clearchus of Soli said: "The Jews descend from the philosophers of India. The philosophers are called in India Calanians and in Syria Jews. The name of their capital is very difficult to pronounce. It is called Jerusalem."

If Abraham as the father of the Jewish race is therefore a legendary figure of India, then who is he, and did he exist at all? It's time to upset traditionalists.

The obvious person for an Indian Abraham is Brahma (A-Brahma) who just happens to have a consort and sister named Saraisvati[1]— which is amazingly similar to the name of the Biblical Abraham's wife, Sarai. Abraham is said to have learned his trade in Ur, which is very close to the Persian border—being en route to India.

It is also a fact that the name of Brahma spread throughout this entire area—so much so that the Persians even adopted him as one of their deities. So, the very area where Abraham is said to have learned his priestly trade is the very area that the Indian Brahma was being spread and worshipped. What more can we find within this area of the Chaldees?

The Chaldeans were called Kaul-Deva, and they were a priestly caste living in, among other places, Afghanistan, Kashmir, and Pakistan. (Kaul-Deva meaning the Shining Calani, hence these were enlightened Shining Ones, a group going back to ancient Sumeria and outlined in my book *The Shining Ones*.)

So Abraham/Brahma learned his trade among the Chaldeans, who were related to the Indian subcontinent and were the Shining priesthood or enlightened souls. In this respect, then "Abraham" was simply a title given to the high priest or lord of the sect of Brahma. But if, as in ancient Egypt, he needed to duplicate the life of the gods, then he, too, would have needed a wife/sister.

The fact that Saraisvati was both Brahma's consort and sister also relates to the Biblical account of Abraham.

> But indeed she is truly my sister. She is the daughter
> of my father, but not the daughter of my mother; and
> she became my wife. (Genesis 20:12)

This same pattern of hidden Gnosis would later become part of the Mary/Jesus myth. The complex twists and turns that modern writers such as Dan Brown in the *Da Vinci Code* seem to have to create to explain the seemingly peculiar nature of Jesus' relationship with Mary the Mother and Mary Magdalene, are really quite remarkable. It is simple.

In the same way that Sarai is Saraisvati, she is also Isis, the greatest of Egyptian goddesses. Mary too is a duplicate of Isis. You see, Isis was the consort of Osiris, hence the wife part. She was therefore the mother of Horus the Savior—hence the mother of god. But Horus was Osiris reincarnated, so Isis was also his sister. Mary the Mother, Mary Magdalene the lover/consort, and Mary of Bethany the sister are really and truly the hidden aspects of a much older Gnostic tradition that has no literal element at all! The three Marys are in reality three aspects of the one feminine principle—the feminine trinity.

Of course, we could find ourselves in trouble here, as nowhere does it state that Mary of Bethany was the sister of Jesus. However, it does state that Mary of Bethany was the sister of Lazarus, whom Jesus raised from the dead, or more pertinently *was* Jesus, raised from the dead.

You see, in Egyptian mythology it was the role of the son of god and savior, Horus, to raise his father, Osiris, from the dead and in a sense resurrect himself (as Horus was Osiris resurrected).

However, Lazarus and Osiris are distinctly different names and so cannot be related. Still, although there is much debate on the exact etymology, many believe that there *is* a proven link. How?

The ancient Egyptian designation for Osiris was Asar or Azar. Now, when the Egyptians spoke of their gods they indicated them with "the" and so we would have had "the Azar." This term "the" also meant lord or god, like the Greek word for God, *The-os* or *Theos*. One of the Hebrew terms for Lord was *El* and was applied to their many deities, such as El-Shaddai or El-ohim. So when the Hebraic writers included Osiris in their myths, they put him in as El-Azar—the Lord Osiris. This, in the later Latin translation, was changed to El-Azar-us. This use of the "us" was the way that masculine names ended in the Roman language. In fact, in Arabic,

Lazarus is still spelled El-Azir, missing the "us." So we now have El-Azar-us, which reduced further into Lazarus. In this way the Egyptian, or should we say much older mythos, became the literal truth of the biblical record.

Horus, therefore, raised "El-Azar-us" or "El-Osiris" from the dead, just as Christ was to raise "Lazarus." This story is an allegory of the sun god Osiris being reborn, but nevertheless gives us the remarkable fact that Mary of Bethany, as the sister of Lazarus, was in literary and esoteric reality, the sister of Jesus.

And so, as we find that Jesus and Mary were in reality based upon a much older Egyptian mythology, which itself stretches back even further in time to ancient Sumeria, we also find that the story of Abraham and Sarai is no different. In the Koran (6:75), we find that Abraham's father was called Azar (Osiris), and so Abraham was Horus, just as Jesus was Horus. Lo and behold, we also discover (Luke 16: 22–25) that Lazarus himself rested in the bosom of Abraham, just as Osiris, as the crippled god, rested in his resurrecting son's arms.

And it was this Abraham, this Brahma or Osiris, that is said to have spawned the very Children of Israel. Let's take a look at Abraham's sons and see if we can reveal the hidden serpent lineage or serpent secrets that we found elsewhere in *The Serpent Grail*.

Abraham's son Ishmael, by Hagar, his maidservant, also had children who lived in India, or Havilah (land of serpents), as it is in Genesis. Both famous sons of Abraham, Ishmael and Isaac, have names that revert back to the worship of that Hindu serpent deity Siva.[2]

Ishmael is Ish-Maal in Hebrew, and in Sanskrit, Ish-Mahal means "Great Siva." Isaac is Ishaak in Hebrew, and Ishakhu in Sanskrit—which means "Friend of Siva." Most startling of all is the very name of Abraham himself, which could mean that Abraham was nothing other than a Naga King—Ab Ram actually means "exalted snake."

Hiram, the famous Freemasonic and biblical builder of temples, was Ahi-Ram, and it is time to take a look at this mythical character.

Hiram and the Temple

Hiram of Tyre was a member of the Tribe of Naphtali, which had a standard of a serpent or basilisk. He was also said to be a son of the Tribe of Dan, which had an emblem of the serpent and the horse. In *The Woman's Encyclopaedia of Myths and Secrets,* Barbara Walker points out:

> Writers of the Old Testament disliked the Danites, whom they called serpents (Genesis 49:17). Nevertheless, they adopted Dani-El or Daniel, a Phoenician god of divination, and transformed him into a Hebrew prophet. His magic powers were like those of the Danites emanating from the Goddess Dana and her sacred serpents....Daniel was not a personal name but a title, like the Celtic one.

Here we have a distinct conclusion, that Daniel of the Bible is related to the very same Danu or Dana goddess of Celtic Europe, and that this goddess is conclusively related to serpents—in this case, the serpens astrological sign as worshipped by the Danites. We also have confirmation that the Jewish people collected their belief system from those around them. Thus far, as we have gathered, they have melded the beliefs of India, Egypt, and now Phoenicia into their own growing system.

According to the book of Chronicles, Hiram was skillful in the work of gold, silver, brass, timber, and, importantly, stone. According to the book of Kings, the Temple was prepared in stone before it was brought to the site—perhaps prefabricated somewhere else. It was said that neither hammer nor axe, nor any tool of iron was used in the building. So, how was it built?

Well, in Exodus, Moses is told to build an altar to the Lord without tools, lest he should pollute it, and it seems the same symbolism was utilized here in the building of the Temple. According to Rabbinical teaching, the prefabrication was performed by the Shamir, a giant worm or serpent that could cut stones. According to the Islamic accounts of Rashi and Maimonides, the Shamir was a living creature. This is hardly likely, unless we understand this creature to be ourselves. What is more likely is that the idea of the wisdom of the "worm" (which evolved from the *word* worm for serpent anyway) or snake,

Shamir, was used in the construction of the symbolic Temple of man—a Gnostic belief.[3]

It was fabled that serpent-linked Nagas escaped their country and took this deep and seemingly architectural wisdom abroad. This linking of the esoteric and underlying principles of self-illumination, manifested here in architectural symbolism, eventually gave rise to modern Freemasonry.

The "architect gods" such as Thoth or Hermes are linked strongly with the serpent wisdom, as we discovered in *The Serpent Grail*. Other references also link the Shamir to the snake, such as the *Testament of Solomon*, which calls it a "green stone," like the Emerald Tablet,[4] which obviously provides further evidence for the Shamir to have been serpent wisdom.

Returning to Hiram we find that the name Hir-Am actually means "exalted head of the people" (Hir = Head, exalted, Am = people)—and is closely related to Abraham (Ab Hir Am).

However, it also has another and more telling meaning.

Ahi-Ram actually means "exalted snake." So, in either meaning Hiram was the "exalted head" or "snake," both meanings being paramount to the discovery of the thread of the snake cult and religious underlying beliefs—the mixture of the opposites within one's own head as shown in the *Serpent Grail*.

Hiram was also believed by some (according to David Wood in his book, *Genisis*) to be descended from Cain via Tubal-Cain, who was said to be the only survivor of the "superior race" after the flood.

The race is supposed to be called Elohim (people of the "fiery snake") or the "Shining Ones," also known as the "serpent people." This tale is derived from a text known as E or Elohim from around 750 B.C., and also gives rise to the stories of the Dionysiac Architects—also linked with the Freemasons.

It is no wonder that the pillars of Hiram should be related closely to the worship of the snake. Rosslyn, and especially one of its mock temple pillars, is entwined with the symbolism of snakes, not just as a direct relation to the Norse myths of Yggdrassil, with its gnawing serpent, but as symbols of the religious power of the Gnostic serpent.

On the Secret Scroll discovered by Andrew Sinclair, one of the most important images is the sight of a large, coiled serpent beneath the Temple steps, with a crown, a pick, and a shovel, as if pointing towards the excavation of the Temple itself.

There is a legend that may back up Andrew Sinclair's findings:

This Oriental legend tells how the Queen of Sheba was attracted to Hiram and that King Solomon became jealous. So jealous, in fact, that he plotted the death of Hiram. Molten metal used in the casting of a "brazen sea" was going to be used to kill Hiram, but he was saved by the "spirit" of Tubal-Cain—his ancestor—who is linked with serpent worship. He was saved, by the serpent, from death. Hiram threw his "jewel" down a deep well, but was then killed by Solomon's assassins by a blow to the head. It was said that three masters later found the body and venerated it. The jewel was found and placed on a triangular altar, which Solomon then had erected in a secret vault beneath the Temple (Josephus, *Antiquities V111*, 3:4). What was the jewel of this builder, which caused so much veneration? Whatever it was, later crusader knights—under the guise of Knights Templar—were supposedly to dig furiously beneath the Temple to discover it. The Templars are believed to have dug for other items they (and others, such as St. Bernard) thought were located there—such as the Ark of the Covenant. It may be that even this is symbolic and Gnostic language—the eternal search for our own divinity.

Following the dubious excavations, both the Templars and the Cistercians under St. Bernard grew in immense wealth. Great building works were carried out across Europe—all hiding secret symbolism of the snake and all using the architectural skills discovered while on their travels in the Middle East. Greatest of all, however, is the symbolism that was brought back with them, which invaded European culture like a contagious virus, seeping into and onto its buildings and works of art and keeping alive an ancient tradition for us to one day rediscover.

The hollow and nonliteral Brazen Pillars of Hiram became the twin pillars of the later Masons—who, like Moses as the emergent serpent, emerged from the Templars. These pillars were said to be hollow and to contain secret manuscripts—which reminds us of the supposed discovery of ancient and secret manuscripts from

Rennes Le Château, also thought to have been found inside a pillar and made popular by *The Da Vinci Code*. In truth they do hold a secret, but not one that can be held in the hand.

Now it is time to take a look at another exterior source of the modern Freemasons to see if there are any parallel influences at play: the Dionysiac Architects we have just mentioned.

Masonic symbol at Llanfairfechan, Wales

These are said by Masonic historians to be the prime originators of their guilds. A secretive group or secret society with doctrines said by Manly P. Hall (in *Masonic, Hermetic, Quabbalistic & Rosicrucian Symbolical Philosophy*) to be similar to the Freemasons. They are thought to have been great builders, reminiscent of the idea of the great architectural Nagas who escaped India.

It was supposedly this secret society, under Hiram Abiff, who built the Temple of Solomon and erected the great brass pillars now seen as Boaz and Joachim in Masonry. They were also known as the Roman Collegia and were said to have wandered around like the medieval Masons, building such fantastic places as the Temple of Diana at Ephesus (John Weisse, *The Obelisk and Freemasonry*).

Weisse also points out that the Collegia influenced the Islamic building efforts, which were later to become a turning point in

Western European architecture after the crusades and possibly via the Collegia's influence over the Templars, amongst others.

These Collegia were also thought to have been known before the Romans in Greece and were said to have worshipped the serpentine Bacchus. Considering the Masonic fascination with the Druids, there is little wonder that the infamous historian and archaeologist William Stukely believed them to have been the builders of Stonehenge and other ancient monuments. Many Masonic writers love to associate themselves with the Druids and we find that they "had a high veneration for the Serpent. Their great god Hu, was typified by that reptile" (George Oliver, *Signs and Symbols*).

If it is true that the Dionysiac Architects and the Bacchus/ Dionysus-worshipping Greek and Roman Collegia, were among the originators of the Freemasons, then it is highly likely that they were linked also with the serpent-worshipping Druids who were also known as Adders or Snakes. They were all a later showing of the worldwide serpent cult—the same as those in India, Egypt, and elsewhere, who all had fantastic building skills and held secrets of the true and hidden Gnostic traditions. Today we can still see a remnant of this great architectural, serpent-worshipping and secretive cult in the Masons. As George Oliver points out, "The Serpent is universally esteemed a legitimate symbol of Freemasonry," and now we see its history is worldwide, and some would say justifiably kept alive within the initiated Freemasons.

PART II

Secret Societies

12

The Knights Templar

No book exploring the myriad myths and tales of secret societies can leave out the unbelievably popular Knights Templar. There are links between this medieval order of warrior monks and Muslims, Masons, and even heretics, so we need to get a grasp of their darker side.

Whether stars of the Disney film *National Treasure* or pawns of modern-day political and commercial propaganda, the Knights Templar have taken root as one of the world's leading mystery groups. But what is the truth? Did they really have a great secret? Did they really hide treasure? Were they really guardians of the Holy Bloodline? Let's take a look.

Supposedly a group of nine knights (debatable and highly unlikely) were taken from the ruling nobility in the region of France known as Champagne, collected themselves together in Jerusalem around 1118 A.D., and formed the now infamous Knights Templar. All of this cannot be totally proven from the texts—however, it is repeated so often that it *becomes true*. In all likelihood, they had been formed in France years before, although I have new evidence placing their creation further back in time than even I had ever imagined (see *The Ark, the Shroud, and Mary*).

They were pledged, it is said, to commit their lives and work to a strict code of rules and were simply ordained to ensure the safe passage of pilgrims to the Holy Land. The knights request this task of the first King Baldwin of Jerusalem, who refuses. He then dies under mysterious circumstances, to be replaced by

Baldwin II, who almost immediately grants them this privilege. This is the same Baldwin who went on to deal directly with the Assassins.

For the next nine years (there's that number again) the knights excavate beneath the Temple of Solomon (which didn't ever exist) in complete secrecy, and the Grand Master returns to Europe, supposedly with secrets that have been hidden for hundreds of years. Very quickly, the knights achieve a special dispensation from the pope to allow them to charge interest on loans—indicating their swift path to wealth. Soon the great cathedral-building period arrives across Europe with the newfound architectural "secrets" discovered by the crusaders. This newfound knowledge may very well have come from some of the discoveries made by the Templars, especially when we consider that the man responsible for energizing the building program was none other than St. Bernard. Bernard gave the Order of the Knights Templar their rules and was related, by blood, to various members. He was also indicated in the propaganda of the Arthurian and Grail literature we have already learned so much about.

The Templars grew in wealth and power. Their land-holding and banking system made them one of the most powerful and feared groups in Europe. Virtually nobody could match their international strength. According to George F. Tull in *Traces of the Templars*, they were also "well placed to obtain relics," as they held the respect of nobility and had many strategically placed premises across the Holy Land.

Near Loughton-on-Sea in England there are several Templar connected sites. The temple here, Tull continues, was "well provided with liturgical books, plate and vessels of silver, silver gilt, ivory and crystal, vestments, frontals and altar cloths. Among the relics kept there were two crosses containing fragments of the True Cross and a relic of the Holy Blood," whatever that might have been—it was not a bloodline. Tull also tells us of how some of these relics entered Britain:

> Sometimes the hips returned with more specialized cargo, as when in 1247 Br. William de Sonnac, Master of the temple in Jerusalem, sent a distinguished Knight Templar to bring to England and present to King Henry III 'a portion of the Blood of our Lord,

which He shed on the Cross for the salvation of the world, enclosed in a handsome crystalline vessel.'
The relic was authenticated under seal by the Patriarch of Jerusalem, the bishops, abbots and nobles of the Holy Land.

In Surrey, the Templars held land known then as Temple Elfold with 192 acres of arable land. Here again, in 1308 there was mention of a grail and a chalice. It is obvious that part of the wealth of the Templars came from the propaganda tools of the medieval reliquary business, proving their business acumen and their ability to root out those tools. They were also instrumental in spreading the cult of St. George, especially when we consider that they knew of his shrine in Lydda.

But in the early 14th century, King Philip of France organized their downfall, and the supposed secrets and wealth of the Templars disappear.

At their trials, the Templars were not only accused of worshipping the sacred head, but also the *veneration of the serpent*. As Andrew Sinclair points out in *The Secret Scroll*, another Templar emblem was the foliated staff of Moses, the very same staff that turned into a serpent and was emblematic of the serpent religious cult and healing.

The Rosslyn Missal, written by Irish monks in the 12th century, shows Templar crosses with great dragons and sun discs. Upon the Secret Scroll itself is the symbol of the 12 tribes of Israel, the breastplate of Aaron (whose serpent staff is said to be in the Ark) with 12 squares signifying the 12 tribes surmounted by a serpent. The serpent rules the tribes: "...the Serpent as a symbol obtained a prominent place in all the ancient initiations and religions. Among the Egyptians, it was a symbol of Divine Wisdom." (*The Secret Scroll*, Andrew Sinclair, which of course has been dated by scholars to the 16th or even 18th century). Many people believe that quite a few of the Templars and their secrets escaped to Scotland, and the dawning of a new age of Freemasonry emerged in later years—thought to be directly from the Templars.

In the year 1314, King Edward of England invaded Scotland, hoping to bring an end to the border battles. Meeting the Scottish army at Bannock Burn, he was surprised by a force of well-trained men fighting for the Scots. The tide turned and Scotland achieved independence, if only for three years. The standard history has it that these well-trained men that turned the tide against the well-trained English army were nothing more than camp followers and servants. Many, though, now believe that these were the famous Knights Templar, who had taken root in Scotland and hidden away from Catholic tyranny. Strangely, immediately after the battle, Robert the Bruce, the new Scottish king, rewards the Sinclair family with lands near Edinburgh and Pentland, the very same lands associated with hundreds of Templar graves, sites, symbols, and much more, such as Balantrodoch (a temple).

An indication of the popular liking for the Templars is shown in the Peasant's Revolt of Wylam Tyler in A.D. 1381, when a mob marched in protest of the oppressive taxes placed upon them. Strangely, they did not harm the old Templar buildings, but turned their attentions on those of the Catholic Church. In one instance, they actually carried things out of a Templar church in London to burn the items in the street, rather than damage the building. It may be that this uprising was a natural incident, or it may be that it was inspired by the actions of a hidden and now secret society of the Templars—hidden because of the new Catholic hatred towards them. If it is the case that the Templars did indeed inspire this revolt, then, even though they were not successful, they tried again 100 years later, and forced the Reformation. It was around this period (15th century) that the first records of Scottish and York Masonic meetings appear.

Let's take a rather sideways look at the history and symbolism of the Templars.

There are some strange links between Sumerian iconography and Templar symbolism that need to be voiced. The most obvious Templar imagery is that of the two poor knights seated upon a horse, which is very similar to the idea and concept of two riders seen in ancient Sumeria. This was purely a tactical device in warfare—although there may be some truth in believing that it has origin in the "balance" hypothesis of the "twins." The Templar cross is equally seen in many Sumerian images normally associated with an upturned crescent moon. The Fleur de Lys is also a common image, as well as bees, which were common also to the Merovingians. The pentagram is also seen in the images of both, and symbolized the essence of the Merovingians as the "Shining Ones."

Another symbol seen in various forms from Sumeria to France is the Abraxus—a figure with snakes for legs—a symbol used for gods such as Oannes, and, not surprisingly, this later became the symbol of the Grand Master of the Templar Order. What could this mean? That the head of the Order of the Templars saw himself as the chief of the serpents? And what was another name for the head serpent? Pendragon! In essence, the Master of the Templars was therefore not only by literary means including the Templars as the knights who would protect the Grail, but also himself as Arthur and vice versa.

In conjunction with the fact that the Templars also used the serpent symbol of eternity and immortality (the snake eating its own tail), we have a serpent secret being held by the very highest of Christian guardians.

The Cross of Lorraine, a symbol used by the Templars before their usual "Maltese"-style cross, is seen in Sumeria as a symbol for kingship. These influences must have been picked up while the Templars were in the Middle East and utilized later on. We know that they used the sign, because the trials in the early 1300s had the prisoners etching the symbol into the cell walls. What other ancient secrets did they collect?

An article by Boyd Rice titled "The Cross of Lorraine: Emblem of the Royal Secret" mentions that the Cross of Lorraine, apart from being a symbol of poison, was the emblem of heraldry for Rene D'Anjou, said by Charles Peguy to represent the arms of both Christ and Satan and the blood of both. It is also said to incorporate the symbol phi or the Golden Ratio of Sacred Geometry—so very important to the Masons. Rene d'Anjou was keenly aware of and interested in many things occult. He led a search for new (old) hermetic texts. The Cross of Lorraine was taken on by Rene, and, subsequently, by Marie de Guise, the wife of James Stuart V (parents of Mary Queen of Scots), for its occult symbolism. This occult symbolism showed the cross to be representative of poison. Proof of this meaning comes also from the fact that it became an icon used by chemists (originally alchemists) on the bottles of poisonous substances. The idea is hidden in the duality. Why would monarchs and Templars use a sign for poison, if that poison did not have an opposite side? That of cure! Later on in the early 20th century, Aleister Crowley, the arch Magus and self-proclaimed

British Alchemist, would assign this very same symbol as the Sigil of Baphomet—the Templars' own icon of adoration. The Cross of Lorraine is also thought to be a sign of secrets; a sign of the Angelic Race, which came down and posited wisdom and the secrets of immortality upon the Royal Bloodline. According to Boyd Rice it is "a sigil of that Royal Secret, the doctrine of the Forgotten Ones." And for this reason it seems peculiar that in the 1940s Charles de Gaulle should make it the official symbol of the French Resistance. Of course we now know that these "angelic" beings were Elohim/Shining Ones or Watchers, and that the underground stream of knowledge from these, right up to the medieval period and probably beyond, is derived from Sumeria.

Baphomet

This mysterious object was said to have been venerated by the Templars and to have been written about extensively for the past 30 years. It was thought to be a skull, by some.

One possible explanation for the origin of the word could strangely be found in the deserts of Yemen. The people who live here are called the Al-Mahara, and they have developed many ways of combating snake poison. The special snake priests are called Raaboot men, and they are said to have learned the secret from father to son. Their legends state that they have immunity from snakebites.

If somebody is bitten, then a Raaboot man is called upon, who then sits by the patient, along with several others who then chant in a monotone voice, "Bahamoot, Bahamoot." The poison is then vomited up or passed out of the body in the other direction. The Raaboot man then leaves. Again here, as I have pointed out before, the snake is said to have a jewel in its head, indicative of the enlightenment aspect.

Is it not possible that Bahamoot, as a chant for the curing of snakebites, could have made its way through the various cultures and found itself as a word for the "head serpent?"—*The same "head serpent" that the Templars worshipped?*

If nothing else, then the etymology of these two related items is so similar that it again shows, in the language of the serpent cult, a worldwide spread.

Friday the 13th, October 1307, was a terrible day for the Knights Templar as King Philip IV's men descended upon all of the Order's French holdings, seizing property and arresting each of its members. Why? Simply because Philip owed them huge amounts of money and had no way of paying them back. To add to this he had hoped that the infamous Templar treasure would be his.

With the help of his puppet, Pope Clement V, the French king tortured the knights to discover their secrets. Finally, to justify his action, the knights were accused of heresy, homosexual practices, necromancy, and conducting bizarre rituals such as desecrating the cross—as if to show their lack of faith in this Christian icon. This was, however, a method of initiation and not a heretical act.

The most unusual and perplexing evidence they came across was the worship of this idol called Baphomet. This strange "thing"— although sometimes referred to as a "cat" or "goat"—was generally seen as a "severed head." In the *Magic of Obelisks,* Peter Tompkins says:

> Public indignation was aroused...the Templar symbol of Gnostic rites based on phallic worship and the power of directed will. The androgynous figure with a goat's beard and cloven hooves is linked to the horned god of antiquity, the goat of Mendes.

The list of charges used by the Inquisition in 1308 reads:

> Item, that in each province they had idols, namely heads.
> Item, that they adored these idols or that idol, and especially in their great chapters and assemblies.
> Item, that they venerated (them)
> Item, that they venerated them as God.
> Item, that they venerated them as their Savior.
> Item, that they said that the head could save them.
> Item, that it could make riches.
> Item, that it could make the trees flower.
> Item, that it made the land germinate.
> Item, that they surrounded or touched each head of the aforesaid idol with small cords, which they wore around themselves next to the shirt or the flesh.

Some said it was a man's head, but others a woman's head. Some said that it was bearded, others nonbearded. Some presumed that it was made from glass and that it had two faces. This general mixing of ideas shows where the idea of the head could have come from. That it was a man's head or a woman's, indicates its "dual nature"—and much like the ancient Celtic heads, it would incline me to the opinion that it emerged from part of the supposed ancient head cult.

The Celts, it is said, believed, as did the Hindus, that the soul resided in the head. They would decapitate their enemies and keep their heads as talismans. Probably the best-known head in Celtic lore is that of Bran the Blessed, which was buried outside London—some say in Tower Hill—facing towards France. It was put there to see off the plague and disease and to ensure that the land was fertile—the same powers that were attributed to the "Green Man."

"Bearded" and "nonbearded" simply indicates again the dual nature, as does the idea that it was "two-faced," like the god Janus. It was apparently called Caput 58 (*Caput* meaning "Head"), indicating that there may have been possibly hundreds of them. There are also strong links with Islam at this time; links that the Templars should probably not have made in their supposedly Christian world.

It is also said that the name Baphomet was derived from Mahomet—an Old French corruption of the name of the prophet Mohammed. Others claim that it comes from the Arabic word *abufihamet*, which means "Father of Understanding."

In all likelihood, though, Baphomet comes from *baphe* meaning to submerge and *mete* meaning wisdom. The Baphoment being a device for the Gnostic tradition or belief of being "submerged in wisdom," is associated with the concept of the Sophia or wisdom goddess.

The Symbol of the Cross

We now turn to the cross, for there is great depth to its history and mythology that may well reveal more secrets of the Freemasons and Templars.

Today the world is going mad for all things Knights Templar. They have never been so popular. Everywhere you turn there's a new book, poster, T-shirt, and even mug with their infamous red cross on a white background. But this wasn't their only symbol, and I discovered that there was even greater truth to be found behind this enigmatic imagery and, believe it or not, it had nothing at all to do with Dan Brown.

I begin my quest with a familiar symbol to many people: the ankh. Today there are millions of people walking around with this unique and extremely important symbol on chains around their necks, and it is deeply embedded in the secret societies of the world, including the Freemasons, Rosicrucians, and many more. Even Christians adorn themselves with the image, thinking it to be a normal cross. And yet the significance of the symbolism implied by this seemingly unobtrusive little object is very profound.

This enigmatic symbol of Egypt represents "eternal life" and was often found in the names of Pharaohs such as the infamous Tut-ankh-amun. The symbol is often depicted being held by a god to a Pharaoh, giving him life, or held out by a Pharaoh to his people, giving them life—this basically set aside the immortals, from the mortals, for anyone wearing or carrying the ankh had gained or hoped to gain immortality. Those holding the ankh were the great magicians, the ones capable of altering reality. They had the power of the Otherworld through the device, which symbolized

Author at a Templar castle in Portugal

the access to the Otherworld. So, what elements of this ankh give it this special power?

The ankh is technically known as the Crux Ansata. It is a simple T-cross, surmounted by an oval—called the Ru. The Ru is often seen as the portal or gateway to another dimension such as heaven—in essence, the Otherworld. The ankh therefore becomes the symbol of transition from one plane to another. It outlived Egyptian domination and was widely used by the Christians as their first cross, but in this symbol holds a clue to the secret of the serpent.

One character intricately linked with the ankh, and specifically the Tau cross, is Thoth or Taautus—a character no different from the alchemists' and Greeks' Hermes or the biblical Enoch, both of whom were transported to other worlds in ways similar to modern altered states of consciousness, and both of whom are spoken of again and again by the secret societies.

Amazingly, Thoth was said, by Eusebius, to be the originator of serpent worship in Phoenicia, and this will prove to be of worth. Sanchoniathon called him a god and says that he made the first image of Coelus[1] and invented hieroglyphs. This links him with Hermes, whom I mentioned previously. Thoth also consecrated the linked species of dragons and serpents; and the Phoenicians and Egyptians followed him in this superstition.

This Thoth could very well be a memory of the first group who originated the worship of the serpent after the flood or the end of the last ice age approximately 12,000 years ago. Thoth was deified after his death (a time that nobody knows, if he existed) and given the title "the god of health" or "healing." He was the prototype for the serpent-linked healer, Aesculapius, and identified with Mercury, who bore the serpent-entwined caduceus: All healers, all wise, all teachers, all saviors, and all associated with the serpent for their powers. Indeed, it was as the healing god that Thoth was symbolized as the serpent—he was normally represented with the head of an ibis and baboon.

The letter or symbol "Tau" is the first letter of Taautus, Tammuz, and Thoth, and is thought to be the "Mark of Cain," who was called the "son of serpents." In many respects, it is also linked with the ancient swastika, so well-known to us now from Nazi imagery. We shall soon discover that the Nazis themselves began life as a secret society.

Swastika

The ancient symbol of the swastika is simply a stylized spiral, as can be shown from the many depictions across the world of swastikas made up of spirals and snakes. It also shows up in the spiral fashions of the labyrinths and mazes. The word *labyrinth* comes directly from the ancient Minoan Snake Goddess culture of Crete, where the swastika was used as a symbol of the labyrinth and is linked etymologically with the "double headed axe"—which is none other than the Tau cross. Similar labyrinthine swastikas have been found in the ancient city of Harappa from 2000 B.C. As the labyrinth is viewed as a womb of the Mother Goddess, and a symbol of the snake, there is little wonder that these two symbols became fused. However, labyrinths were also seen as places of ancient serpent initiation. In ancient Egypt, the labyrinth was synonymous with what was called the Amenti—the snake-like path taken by the dead to journey from death to resurrection. It was Isis, the serpent queen of heaven, who was to guide the souls through the twists of the Amenti. The path towards the center leads towards treasure.

The snake adorning Athene in ancient Greece is shown with a swastika skirt. The same is true of Astarte or Asherah and Artemis. There is Samarran pottery dating from 5000–4000 B.C. from Mesopotamia showing a female and swastika, on which the female's hair swirls with Medusa-type serpents. The swastika is also shown as two serpents crossing each other.

In Norse myth, the hammer of Thor,[2] Mjollnir, is closely connected with the swastika and is found to be a prominent motif in Scandinavian art from the Bronze Age to the Iron Age. It is found on swords and Anglo-Saxon cremation urns and on numerous Viking items. It was seen as a protector against thieves, reminiscent of the fact that serpents were known to guard treasure. As Thor's hammer was also seen as a Tau cross, it is certainly related to the secrets of the serpent. It was used by Thor to lop off the head of the sacred ox, which he used as bait to catch the Midgard

Serpent, which encircled the globe in the symbol of the Ouroboros, eating its own tail. This was Thor offering a head as sacrifice to the serpent to try to gain immortality in the mead—the drink of the gods. He was using the serpent to catch the serpent. It was the cessation of the constant cycling of the Midgard Serpent that Thor attempted and, in this way, he beat time itself.

Thor's aim was to gain a cauldron big enough to take the mead for the immortals, and he needed to prove his worth by fishing for the serpent. He had power over the serpent as the slayer with the swastika or Tau cross. There is evidence to prove that the myths of these Scandinavians and the Hindus are related, as the story of Thor and the Midgard Serpent closely resemble the battle between Indra and Vritra, showing a common origin.

Vritra is the great serpent, which lies at the source of two rivers (the positive and negative, or male and female), as the Midgard Serpent lies beneath the sea (of the mind). Indra slits open the belly of the serpent to release the waters and therefore fertility back to the land. Both gods (Indra and Thor) are related to the weather, both are warrior gods with a thunderbolt as a weapon, and both slay the dragon. The swastika of the serpent is a common motif in both Hindu and Scandinavian cultures. Eventually, the Christians steal both Pagan myths and place St. Michael and St. George in their place—both having the red serpent cross to replace the swastika.

The cross is also found in the legends of Thoth or Taautus, who was said to have symbolized the four elements with a simple cross, which originated from the oldest Phoenician alphabet as the curling serpent. Indeed Philo adds that the Phoenician letters "are those formed by means of serpents...and adored them as the supreme gods, the rulers of the universe." If Thoth, Hermes, and even Enoch are the supposed inventors of the art of writing, then there is little wonder that they are so closely linked with the serpent.

Victoria de Bunsen in the 19th century thought, "the forms and movements of serpents were employed in the invention of the oldest letters, which represent gods." This symbol of the four elements was altered slightly and became the Egyptian Taut, the same as the Greek Tau, which is where we get the name Tau cross from—a simple T.

The T or Tau cross also gives its name to the bull in the astrological sign of Taurus—note here the two elements of the Tau and the Ru being brought together. The Druids (or "adders," after the snake) venerated the tree and the snake by scrawling the Tau cross into tree bark.

In the Middle Ages, the Tau cross was used in amulets to protect the wearer against disease.

Among the modern Freemasons the Tau has many meanings. Some say that it stands for Templus Hierosolyma or the Temple of Jerusalem. Others say that it signifies hidden treasure or means Clavis ad Thesaurum, "A key to treasure" or Theca ubi res pretiosa, "A place where the precious thing is concealed."

It is especially important in Royal Arch Masonry where it becomes the "Companions Jewel": a serpent as a circle above the cross bar in place of the Ru and forming the ankh with the Hebrew word for "serpent" engraved on the upright, and also including the Triple Tau—a symbol for hidden treasure.

It was also the symbol for St. Anthony—later to become the symbol for the Knights Templar of St. Anthony of Leith in Scotland. St. Anthony lived in the 4th century A.D. and is credited with establishing Monasticism in Egypt, and the story goes that he sold all his possessions after hearing from the Lord and marched off into the wilderness to become a hermit. On his travels, he learned much from various sages in Egypt and grew for himself a large following. He was sorely tempted by the devil in the form of "creeping things" and serpents. In one episode, he follows a trail of gold to a temple, which is infested with serpents, and takes up residence, needing little food for sustenance other than bread and water. He is said to have lived 105 years, and due to this longevity he is credited with protective powers.

The Order of the Hospitalers of St. Anthony, who would later take much of the Templar wealth, brought many of Anthony's relics to France in the 11th century. Previously they were said to have been secretly deposited somewhere in Egypt just after his death and then later to have found their way to Alexandria. All of this is a symbolic representation of the truth. The truth, in fact, is that the secrets of these stories found their way to Alexandria, which was a mixing bowl of the occult, esoteric, Gnostics and

Jewel."

The Taut or Tau symbolizes the four creating elements of the
universe. It is the center of all this creation, it is the spark in the
cycle, the very center of all. Next, the symbol of the solar-serpent
was added: a simple circle or the oval Ru. This loop above the T-
cross created the ankh, the symbol of eternity. The snake in a
circle eating its own tale is symbolic of the sun and immortality.

Eventually, the symbol of the moon was added to this, turning
it into the sign for Hermes or Mercury and showing the Caduceus/
serpent origin. It is no wonder that this, the most perfect and simple
of symbolic devices, became the symbol of the early Christians. It
is also no wonder that, even though there were no cross-beam
crucifixions, Christ was nevertheless symbolically crucified on a
symbol of eternal life, a symbol of the serpent.

This symbol became the mark or sign that would set the be-
liever aside for saving. In Ezekiel, this is the mark that God will
know, the mark on the forehead. As Deane points out, the Ezekiel
passage (9:4) should read, "set a Tau upon their foreheads" or "mark
with the letter Tau the foreheads." The early Christians baptized
with the term "crucis thaumate notare."[3] They baptized with the
symbol of the snake.

Is this the original mark of Cain, which we have found elsewhere, to be of the serpent tribe?

The idea of this sign or mark is widespread once discovered.
In Job 31:35, we read in our modern King James Bibles "I sign now
my defence—let the Almighty answer me," which should properly
read, "Behold, here is my Tau, let the Almighty answer me." He
then goes on to say, "Surely I would take it upon my shoulder, and
bind it as a crown to me."

This remarkable idea of wearing the Tau cross on the shoulder as a sign would later become part and parcel of the crusader
Templars' markings. Also, the Merovingians (said by some to be
descended from Jesus and a sea serpent or fish god—the Quinotaur
or Quino-Tau-r) were supposedly born with a red cross between
their shoulder blades. The Tau cross is also strangely used by those

practicing sacred geometry as a "marker" for buried treasure, whether physical or spiritual.

Sacred geometry at play upon this Masonic tomb in St. Peter's, Rome

This buried treasure is truly the center, the point in our minds and hearts where we find the original self. This original center (heart means center) was seen to be connected to the Universal Mind, and only by accessing this center of ourselves could we access the Universal Mind or God. This in turn stops time, we become one with all, and we believe we are immortal. The Tau marks this place, either on the forehead or in the chest (between the shoulders), revealing to others those who can access the point in time where God resides. The word *temple* from whence Templar derives has another meaning: *tempos* simply means "time." The true temple is that place that has power over the cycling energy of the serpent. The true temple, like the one on our brow, is within us.

13

The *Da Vinci Code* Fiasco

We have spoken much of the Grail in this book because it is the goal or quest of the individual. For this reason it is seen as central to the symbols of the secret societies. There has recently been a lot of excitement about the Grail—a cyclical phenomena in humanity for the past 2,000 years. There are huge implications today with the Grail being a secret of various secret societies and I want to investigate this before we move on.

One question regarding the Holy Grail that the early medieval writers asked was "whom does it serve?" Well, let's have a look at the current Grail world and see if it is serving us—or are we serving it? We shall also discover just who it is behind this fiasco that has been manipulating the story from the very earliest of times.

Very briefly and for those among us who have been on the planet Sanity for the last few years, the *Da Vinci Code* is a *fiction* based around a man who discovers a code that reveals the true identity of the Holy Grail to be nothing more than the very bloodline of Jesus Christ and Mary Magdalene.

Unfortunately the author of this work, Dan Brown, claimed his now infamous book to be based upon real factual organizations and events. This could not be farther from the truth.

Let's take it apart.

Priory of Sion

This supposedly ancient and enigmatic group allegedly once had Leonardo da Vinci himself as a Grand Master, not to mention several other notables such as Nicolas Flamel and Isaac Newton. However, there is no truth in it at all. Sion was the name of a hill nearby the residences of Pierre Plantard and Gerade de Sede—the two original creators of the Priory of Sion hoax.

The documents of the Priory secreted in the Biblioteque Nationale in Paris have been proven to be forgeries. In fact, the only truthful copies of anything for Mr. Plantard in the Paris Library are newsletters from the 1950s for a rather boring housing association, complaining about the state of the streets—and even this is in extremely poor French.

All the instigators of this surrealist hoax have admitted their creation on record. On the one hand they said it was a surrealist joke; on the other, a kind of egotistical ploy to be accepted by society. Yet the world still goes mad with every new bloodline myth.

Sang Real

One of the main pieces of evidence for the books about the bloodline of Christ, from *Holy Blood, Holy Grail* to the *Templar Revelation*, has been the interpretation of the original term used for the Holy Grail—San Graal. In the 1980s book *Holy Blood, Holy Grail*, by Michael Baigent et al, we find that it is interpreted differently, placing the *g* from *graal* onto the end of *san*, making *sang real*. This then translates as royal or holy blood. Mistaking a simple error by a 15th century writer—the only time the error was ever made until the 1980s—an entire theory is based upon something that was simply not true. Sir Walter Skeat, one of the greatest etymologists in England, said, 100 years ago, that this error was "very early falsified," and for what ends he did not know. He pointed out that the original concept meant "mixing bowl," which relates entirely with the theory I put forward in *The Serpent Grail*.

Leonardo da Vinci

So, now that we know the true etymology of San Graal and that the Priory of Sion never existed, we should also know that da Vinci could not have been a grand master of a nonexistent order that protected a secret that also didn't exist.

The Holy Chalice in St.Peter's Rome

In fact, all the historical background and information on da Vinci reveals that he was a skilled and wonderful artist—no great revelation there.

However, there are those strange elements of his paintings, which the *Da Vinci Code* and other works of fiction pick up on. Take the female-looking character in the *Last Supper*, for instance: Many have pointed to the fact that this individual looks remarkably feminine. Well, he does. Others have pointed to the *Mona Lisa* as being not quite feminine enough, and that surely the sitter must have been a boy. Using these assumptions many have claimed that da Vinci was, therefore, homosexual. It is more and more amusing by the day just how far this rubber band can be stretched, before it comes hurtling back and hits somebody in the face.

So what is the truth? Is that a lady in the *Last Supper*? No.

There was a tradition of painting the disciple whom Christ loved, John the Evangelist, as a slightly boyish individual, thereby bringing questions to the mind of many as to whether Jesus was gay.

I discovered this to be part of an ancient Gnostic tradition whereby the two Johns (John the Baptist and John the Evangelist) were two sides to the duality—male and female, positive and negative—which needed to be rejoined in order to be complete. Therefore, John the Evangelist was perceived as the feminine principle in this relation, and John the Baptist was the manly, bearded, wild figure.

It was also part of the hidden tradition of the painter's guild of the time to include androgynous elements within their paintings—hence Mona Lisa seeming a little boyish. This androgynous element is there a symbol of the third force, the union of opposites mentioned before, of man and woman, of male and female, of the two sides of our mind that need to be brought into union once again to form the perfect human. There is no evidence whatsoever pointing to da Vinci being involved in any secret society, but the theories of the union of opposites was a rising current in the renaissance world in which he lived, and so that influence would have been absorbed by this perfectionist of a painter.

Did Jesus and Mary Marry and Have Children?

Who would have thought that such a simple question would raise such a controversy and even be taken seriously? To answer this one we need to break it down.

Firstly, if Jesus married Mary Magdalene then we have to admit that Jesus and Mary existed in the first place. Although we have a substantial amount of textual evidence for these biblical characters, this is due to the sheer amount of copying being carried out hundreds of years after the supposed event. We have no actual texts naming either character from the period; most of the texts date to hundreds of years after.

Even if we do admit that these people were real, then we would have to admit that Jesus did walk on water, cast out demons into pigs, and die and resurrect. That, or we would have another option: That the character of Jesus, just like that of Robin Hood and King Arthur, was based upon a real man somewhere, and all the extra mythical and mystical elements were added into the story. Just as Robin married Marion (Mary), and Arthur married Guinevere, so too in this mythical way, Jesus may have married Mary—even though there is no textual evidence for this.

Marion and Mary are the same and imply water and wisdom. Guinevere comes from similar roots, especially as the queen of heaven, which was a title for Mary the mother of Jesus and Isis the mother of Horus. And, as many scholars have pointed out, the two Marys may be amalgamations of a much older myth.

Guinevere is also the queen of serpents and, therefore, knowledge and wisdom, and her name is related in etymology to Eve, which means female serpent and is an indication of wisdom.

Just as the early Christian Church was forming groups such as the Gnostic Ophites or serpent worshippers, raising their communion cup to the good serpent, they were also splitting the three-fold mother goddess—Mary—into distinct parts. First the Mother Mary, then the Sister Mary, and then Mary Magdalene, a mysterious element, and we shall see why.

Mary the mother is Isis the mother of Horus. As Horus is the son and in fact reincarnation of Osiris, so Isis or Mary is also his sister and lover. She is all three, the feminine trinity. Mary Magdalene therefore is the hidden lover of Jesus who is both God and the son of God, just like Horus. And all of this mystery tradition relates back to the ancient serpent cult, as Isis, Osiris, and Horus had strong associations with the creative, wise, and immortal serpent.

Jesus was eventually likened to the Mosaic "brazen serpent in the wilderness" and imaged hundreds of times as a serpent upon the cross. Here we have that parallel with Arthur, whose name, Pendragon, means "head serpent" or "head of the serpent."

Now we can see with just these few examples that there is a real code afoot—an ancient code going right back into ancient Egypt and beyond, through Osiris and Isis and to Enki and Ninkhursag in Sumeria and Mesopotamia, who were known themselves as serpent priests or doctors.

But what is this code telling us?

Simply that in order to give birth to our own messiah or anointing, or in order to save ourselves, we need to be in union with wisdom, which is symbolized as both water and the serpent—hence Arthur Pendragon and his wife the queen of serpents, or the early Enki and Ninkhursag, who were serpent deities or Shining Ones and were therefore symbols of enlightenment.

As God was upon the face of the waters of the deep in Genesis, so too must we submerge ourselves in wisdom to bring about the divine creation within us.

So, now we understand that Jesus and Mary, in union, could be a metaphor or a copy of this ancient system. But what are we left with?

There are characters such as Yeshua who, it seems, may have been a real character of the 1st century or thereabouts, and who did preach a new Gnosis. But, there was also Apollonius of Tyana.

Apollonius of Tyana

He was born in the 3rd or 4th year B.C. in Tyana in Cappadocia. At age 16, he apparently became a disciple of Pythagoras, renouncing flesh, wine, and women (so he obviously could not have been that clever). He wore no shoes and let his hair and beard grow long—the first hippy.

He soon became a reformer and fixed his abode in the Temple of Aesculapius, who was a serpent healing deity and is still seen in the sky as Ophiucus, the serpent handler. Here it was said that many sick people came to be cured by him, and so we can only conclude that he learned the methods of healing from this serpent-worshipping cult.

Apollonius was claimed to have been a wise man, which is probably due to the fact that the Nagas of Kashmir in India taught him. These Nagas were the followers of the serpent cult found across the globe and often known in the West as Ophites—the very early Christian Gnostics who perpetuated the hidden wisdom of unification of the opposites. These Ophites were also connected to the Essene community, otherwise known as followers of Isis and who worshipped the serpent, *and* who are picked out by scholars to be the very people who created the Christ myth.

The biographer of Apollonius, Philostratos, tells us of his journey to Kashmir and the "emerald valley set in a rim of pearls" and of the tales that Apollonius told to his trusted friend, Damus, of dragons that lived in the hills, meaning the Naga serpent sages.

The hill where these wise men lived was defended on all sides by immense piles of rocks. As soon as the travelers had dismounted, a messenger from one of the Masters appeared, wearing, of all things, a serpentine Caduceus on his brow indicating the 6th chakra of the kundalini or coiled serpent enlightenment process. Platitudes were given, and in conversation, Apollonius learned that these Nagas had delivered their wisdom to the Egyptians and that Cush "was inhabited by the Ethiopians, an Indian nation." We can only take this to mean that the idea of serpent-worship found a brotherhood in Ethiopia, and it only became named after the serpent following influence from the Naga sages of India.

Apollonius more than passed on wisdom wherever he went, and according to many he lived to be well over 100 years old. Others say that he never died at all, but simply disappeared from view, much like Nagajurna (who gained his wisdom from the same sources and is a possible original of John). This idea of never dying often tends to imply that the "secret Gnostic wisdom" of the sage continued in a sect of some kind—in this case, most likely the Gnostic Ophites.

According to theosophist H.P. Blavatsky, a wise prince of India, a Naga, skilled in magic, made seven rings for the seven planets, which he gave to Apollonius. The great sage wore one for every day, and it was via these, it is said, that he maintained good health and long life. Of course, it may be that he was very small, lived in a mound, and was called Bilbo.

In the Valley of Kashmir, where Apollonius went, there is a place called SriNagar, meaning serpent king. Founded by the Buddhist King Asoka in 300 B.C. there is a local tradition that a great sage or adept came from Europe in the 1st century and eventually died there. Some have said that this was Apollonius, others that it was Jesus himself. There may be some truth in this, as Philostratos does mention a "Temple of the Sun," which matches very closely with one just a few miles away from SriNagar called the Temple of Martland.

Aurelian vowed to erect temples and statues to his honor, "for was there ever any thing among men more holy, venerable, noble, and divine than Apollonius? He restored life to the dead; he did and spoke many things beyond human reach" (*The Magus* by Francis Barrett).

Truly, temples and statues were erected to Apollonius in many places, including his own town of Tyana, even though later

Christians destroyed many of them. Unlike Jesus, there is evidence to prove that Apollonius actually existed. As Moncure Conway said in his book *Modern Thought*, "The world has been for a long time engaged in writing lives of Jesus." Even though they were writing about a man with no provenance.

In the fourth gospel it is said: "There are also many other things that Jesus did, the which, if they should be written every one, I suppose that even the world itself could not contain the books that should be written. Amen."

The library of such books has grown since then. But when we come to examine them, one startling fact confronts us: All these books relate to a person concerning whom there does not exist a single scrap of contemporary information—not one! Nobody can say with any conviction in truth, and not faith, that Jesus was a real person.

Rostau Modern Mound

On the other hand and by accepted tradition, Apollonius was born in the reign of Augustus, the great literary age of the nation of which he was a subject. In the Augustan age, historians flourished; poets, orators, critics, and travelers abounded. Yet not one of them mentions the name of Jesus Christ, much less any incident of his life. Jesus left us nothing in writing, although there is a growing speculation that the Gospel of Thomas was written by his hand. This is growing due to modern Christian propaganda. If, indeed, he existed, then he traveled only in Judea and Egypt. Apollonius traveled extensively and wrote extensively. The Emperor Marcus Aurelius admitted that it was to Apollonius that he owed his own philosophy, and erected temples and statues in his honor. No statues or temples were erected to Jesus.

Faust said, "Everyone knows that the Gospels were written neither by Jesus nor by his apostles, but long after their time by some unknown persons, who, judging well that they would hardly be believed when telling of things they had not seen themselves, headed their narratives with the names of the apostles or disciples contemporaneous with the latter."

Conversely, the written record of the life of Apollonius is very sound, and Philostratos, who wrote the *Life of Apollonius*, was the close friend of Damus, who had related the whole thing in person.

Philostratos said:

> Some consider him as one of the Magi, because he conversed with the Magi of Babylon and the Brahmans of India and the Gymnosophists of Egypt. But even his wisdom is reviled, as being acquired by the magic art, so erroneous are the opinions formed of him. Whereas Empedocles and Pythagoras and Democritus, though they conversed with the same Magi, and advanced many paradoxical sentiments, have not fallen under the like imputation. Even Plato, who traveled in Egypt, and blended with his doctrines many opinions collected there from the priests and prophets, incurred not such a suspicion, though above all men on account of his superior wisdom.

But the end was near. The very fact that Apollonius was in danger of usurping the "idea" of Christ with his own "factual" life caused much consternation among the early Christians. Justin Martyr, one of the Church Fathers of the 2nd century, said, "How is it that the talismans by Apollonius have power over certain members of creation, for they prevent, as we have seen, the fury of the waves, the violence of the winds, and the attacks of wild beasts. And whilst Our Lord's miracles are preserved by tradition alone, those of Apollonius are most numerous, and actually manifested in present facts, so as to lead astray all beholders?"

The book by Philostratos was therefore, and not surprisingly, kept back from translation and distribution. In fact, the books of the New Testament did not appear until at the very least 100 years after the *Life of Apollonius*. Even the birth of Apollonius bears some remarkable similarities to the fictional life of Christ. While his mother was pregnant with Apollonius, Proteus, the Egyptian god appeared to her and said, "Thou shalt bring forth me!" The mother of Apollonius was to bring forth a god.

Incidentally, Proteus was known to take the form of a snake, and so wisdom gave birth to the real Christ.

Perhaps the fact that so much was written about Apollonius made it impossible to "use" him as the new religious icon. The new creation of the Christian Church needed a fresh start, which would include as many elements of other Pagan beliefs as possible in order to maximize its effectiveness. According to Phillimore, Apollonius actually founded a church and a community, made up of his disciples. It is highly likely that these were connected to a branch of the Essene, known as the Therapeuts and Nazarenes.

Indeed there was a group known as the Apolloniei, the adherents of Apollonius, who actually survived some centuries after his death. These constituted what became the Christian Church, after the Council of Nicaea—so Apollonius did indeed begin Christianity, based upon serpentine myths and traditions of the oldest order.

Eunapius stated that Philostratos should have called his book "The Sojourning of a God Among Men." Instead Philostratos' book was titled the *Life of Apollonius*—and once the decision had been made to plump for the newly created Christ, the name Apollonius was repressed. It is basically because of books such as the one of Philostratos that the ancient libraries at places such as Alexandria were torched. Destroy the evidence of the opposition and there appears to be no opposition. As Dr. Lardner pointed out in his book, *Credibility of the Gospels*:

> It is manifest, therefore, that Philostratos compared Apollonius and Pythagoras; but I do not see that he endeavored to make him a rival of Jesus Christ. Philostratos had never once mentioned our Savior, or the Christians, his followers; neither in this long work, nor in the Lives of the Sophists... There is not so much as an obscure or general description of any men met with by him, whom any can suspect to be Christians of any denomination, either Catholics or heretics.

However, the same is true of Apollonius, who is not mentioned in the New Testament. Or is he? In 1st Corinthians 3:3–6 it says, "for while one saith, I am of Apollos, are ye not carnal? Who, then, is Paul, and whom Apollos, but ministers, by whom ye believed, even as the Lord gave to every man? I have planted, Apollos watered; but God gave the increase."

I could so easily have overlooked this had it not been for a chance discovery of an ancient version of 1st Corinthians found in a French monastery by a Huguenot soldier entitled the *Codex Bezae*. The name Apollos is spelled Apollonius! In the *Encyclopaedia Britannica,* the name Apollo in this context can also mean Apollonius. Indeed this Apollos was said to have even visited Paul (the apostle who did not suffer from snakebites) and he was called an Alexandrian Jew. Now we can understand how Paul managed to "see" the Lord on the road to Damascus. It is possible that Apollonius brought back a new gospel of Chrishna or Christna from the Kashmir interlude, and it was this that gave birth to the Christ of Chrishna and the idea of Christ being the serpent god.

In many respects this answers the issue of Jesus marrying Mary, as this tradition of the uniting of opposites is most profound in the Indian kundalini expressed through the rising serpents upon the rod, which is the third force. This rod became the tree or cross in Christianity with the male Jesus and the female Mary both in association.

The truth of the *Da Vinci Code* is more real than people know. Jesus and Mary did marry, in the Gnostic sense and not the literal sense. They did spawn a child and he was known simply as Gnosis. However, the evil twin brother known as Catholicism tried to wipe him out, as Seth tried to destroy Osiris, or Mordred killed Arthur, or the sheriff of Nottingham killed Robin. In the end, Seth, Mordred, and the sheriff were themselves brought down, so what will be the verdict on the Catholic Church? It is possible that a Gnostic revival could occur now that the *Da Vinci Code* has done us the service of raising the questions of the doubtful validity of the literal Jesus myth. It is possible, but, with greed, lust, and hatred being powerful tools in the mind of men, I doubt it. Maybe, by understanding that religion should be more than the rules written by man, we will question our existence again—looking for an answer we thought we already had.

At the center of each one of us, at the very core, there is a place where we become conscious of our unconscious state. Where we wake up to a whole new world that resides within us. This inner world is at peace and is in perfect balance. It is interconnected through the world of the subatomic particle to the very universe. Just as our eyes see the sun, our unconscious senses feel the warmth and absorb the goodness, without our conscious mind giving it a second thought. There is a whole world within us untapped and unknown to modern science, but one that was perfectly understood by the ancients, and they left clues for us to decipher. They understood how to remain conscious and to perceive the unconscious world of senses, and they gave voice and imagery to their experiences, and these became spirits, demons, and gods. We have a lot yet to learn, that has already been forgotten. There is a world full of Gnosis awaiting us.

The question now is, whom does it serve?

14

The Illuminati

Many people will have heard of the infamous Illuminati. Others will be wondering what on Earth they could be. Ever since their inception, this 18th century secret society has garnered the imaginations of millions. However, to understand the Illuminati, we must understand two specific institutions—the Freemasons and the Catholic authorities.

Freemasons

The history and origin of the Freemasons is not a simple subject. In fact, it is virtually impossible to decipher the truth from the myriad histories fed into thousands of books on the subject. The reason for this is simply that it is a large organization, but it is split into many facets, each one holding virtual autonomy. Through time, differences of opinion and ritual have arisen. Although we have already taken a look at the serpent origins of Freemasonry, there are elements we need to address in order to better understand their link with the Catholic Church and the Illuminati.

Many Masonic historians try desperately to claim that their lineage stretches right back to the Temple of Solomon and the builder Hiram Abiff—they are even told it as fact in their ceremonies. Others claim descent from Roman and Greek stone masons and the Roman Augurs whom we know had "special knowledge" of the lay of the land and energies related to our modern-day perception of ley-lines and Feng Shui. There can be no strict proof for any of this, although the "secret knowledge" has been passed down the centuries from one adept and initiate to another.

The general consensus has the Freemasons emerging from medieval stonecutters who are known as operative masons. These are the skilled craftsmen who built the great cathedrals and churches of Europe *for the Catholic Church*, and who included many mysterious images and secrets within their amazing carvings (soft masons or Freemasons, as the carving was free work or soft stone). This version of the history of the Masons claims that the Lodge evolved from the huts erected on site by those medieval masons. As time progressed, the Masons grew in power due to demand for their services, and formed groups or unions, which became known as Lodges.

By the 1600s the Lodges began admitting men who were not operative Masons and were termed gentlemen Masons. The terms developed through time, within the operative Masonic Lodges, and were taken on by these gentlemen Masons—becoming part and parcel of their ritual nature.

However, there are problems with this version of history. The facts state something quite different, although there is no reason to deny that gentlemen did begin to grow in number within the ranks of the Masons. There is indeed plenty of evidence to show that in the 14th century the Masons were already a well-established group, and accepted, or were evolved by, the inclusion of the Knights Templar that had escaped Catholic suppression to Scotland.

The first official documentation is from 1356 from England. It describes the formation of the London Masons Company and the ordinances governing the Lodge that was already established at York Minster. However, these are only the papers that have survived and speak of groups that were forming—it does not deny the fact that there must have been preexisting groups that do not have "paperwork to prove their preexistence." The only hard evidence we do have is the symbolism being employed within the great building works of Europe from the 11th century.

Understanding that this great building exercise erupted with such a vengeance following the first crusade and the setting up of such organizations as the Knights Templar and Cistercians (who were instrumental in bringing back building skills to Europe), is the first part of the puzzle. The Templars and their non-warrior cousins, the Cistercians, were more than incidental in both bringing back the seed of alchemical enlightenment from the crusades and the building skills of the Islamic Middle Eastern world. This is seen in the arch and the octagonal designs incorporated into most Templar and Cistercian buildings, as well as other building works carried out under their tutelage.

Also built into these structures are huge amounts of numerological symbols and "mystical" metaphors. These methods were understood and carried on by the Freemasons who today ritualize these ancient ways, and many probably do not even understand their correct purpose. These mystical building metaphors are as ancient as Stonehenge or the Great Pyramids—even if the term Freemason is not.

By the mid 17th century, there is definite evidence of large scale Masonic Lodges, as Elias Ashmole, the creator of the Ashmolean Museum in Oxford, records in his diary. He was made a Mason in the Lodge at his father-in-law's house. Many today split up the Masonic Lodges into Operative, Accepted, and Freemasonry; however, they are much like the Catholic Church's sub groups and monasteries, such as Cistercians, Franciscans, and even Jesuits—they are all from the same original source.

The Bible and specifically the Temple of Solomon gave the Freemasons a religious and acceptable framework to work on, and the symbolism employed with the operative mason's tools was worked to match the ancient mysteries such as the "as above, so below" Hermetic principle.

A Timeline of Known Dates:

A.D. 1250 Matthew Paris drawing shows Henry II in conference with operative Masons.

A.D. 1356 The formation of the London Masons Company and ordinances governing the Lodge at York.

A.D. 1376 The first use of the word Freemason.

A.D. 1390 The Regius Poem from Salisbury Cathedral is Masonic.

A.D. 1410 The Cooke Manuscript written for the Masonic school at Salisbury.

A.D. 1425 Henry VI forbids the yearly congregation of Masons.

A.D. 1599 Minutes taken at Aichisons Haven Lodge and St. Mary's Lodge in Edinburgh.

A.D. 1646 Elias Ashmole is initiated into the Masons.

A.D. 1717 The formation of the first Grand Lodge of London.

A.D. 1733 The first American Lodge is opened.

Today the Freemasons are a global phenomenon, with members from across the business community, religious establishment, and politics. The influence they have is obviously huge and universal. They have links with many other "orders," such as the Sovereign Order of the Knights of Malta, and have had over the years a lot of bad press for the influence they have brought to bear. They eventually swallowed up other institutions such as the Weishaupt Illuminati (which we will discuss shortly). Part of this influence has been shown by hundreds of authors to have had effect all over the world and to have been more than incidental in the instigating in full or part the revolutions in France, Russia, and even the American Revolutionary War.

Some quotes from these sources:

> Conventional wisdom says the Philippine Insurrection of 1896 was ignited because of native opposition to the power of the Catholic Church in the Islands. The revolutionary fire was fuelled by the writings of Jose Rizal, augmented by the political leadership of Emilio Aguinaldo.
>
> In reality the Philippine Insurrection was orchestrated by Freemasonry, and while Emilio Aguinaldo indeed led that revolution, he did so as a dedicated member and tool of the Craft.
>
> That insight into Philippine history was suppressed by the United States Government for 45 years, until it finally was revealed by historian John T. Farrell in 1954.
>
> The Scottish Rite monthly [New Age] added: "The first Revolution in March 1917 is said to have been inspired and operated from these lodges and all the

members of Kerenski's government belonged to them." (*Behind the Lodge Door*, Paul A. Fisher)

Freemasonry has worked in a hidden but constant manner to prepare the revolution [French]. We are then in complete agreement on the point that freemasonry was the only author of the revolution, and the applause which I receive from the Left, and to which I am little accustomed, proves, gentlemen, that you acknowledge with me that it was masonry which made the French revolution. (Taken from the chamber of Deputies during the session on July 1, 1904 and stated by the Marquis de Rosanbo)

According to Fisher, again, the rebellion in Italy against Papal governments during the 1830s "was known as the Risorgimento, which, in reality, was a classic Masonic revolutionary movement. Its leaders were Giuseppe Mazzini, Giuseppe Garibaldi, Camillo Cavour and King Victor Emmanuel II—all ardent Freemasons." (King Victor Emmanuel II was later poisoned by his son, Prince Umberto, who it is then claimed was assassinated by the order of Masonic Lodges.)

Mazzini, according to the Grand Commander of Scottish Rite Freemasonry in America, was the first head of modern Freemasonry in Italy.

One historian, Charles Heckethorn, in his book, Secret Societies, says the chilling word "Mafia" is an acronym meaning "Mazzini Autoriza Furti, Incendi, Avelenameti:" that is: "Mazzini authorizes thefts, arson and poisoning." (*Behind the Lodge Door*, Paul A. Fisher)

Practically all the heroes of Italian liberty were Masons. (*New England Craftsman* 1920)

A great part of Europe—the whole of Italy and France, and a great portion of Germany, to say nothing of other countries—are covered with a network of these secret societies, just as the superficies of the Earth is now being covered with railroads. And what are their objects? They do not attempt to conceal

themselves. They do not want constitutional government. They do not want ameliorated institutions;
they do not want provincial councils nor the recording of votes. (Benjamin Disraeli, future Chancellor of
the Exchequer of Great Britain and Prime Minister—
Hansard's Parliamentary Debates, 1876)

A lot of these quotes seem to point at a war between the Catholic Church and the Freemasons. This is an interesting point and one that confuses many people when they see that the Masons are actually linked and were created by the Catholic Church (or the other way around). This is a standard ploy used by secret society people across the world, and even to be found within the Statutes of many secret societies and even religious orders. It was the "done thing" to appear on the outside to be against the powers of authority, while all the time working for them.

The Freemasons can clearly be shown to have evolved from esoteric sects emanating from within and even before the Catholic Church and as a direct result of Templar influence in Scotland. So the Masons could be traced back to the Catholic Church.

This goes back to the Templars, a Catholic order. It also goes back to the Knights of St. John or Knights of Malta. Both the Templars and the Knights of Malta have reemerged from within the Masons and are now orders themselves—in various forms. Most still owe allegiance to the Masons, but are distinct. The Knights of Malta can directly be traced back to their origin and are now located in the Vatican.

Now the Jesuits are spoken of elsewhere in this book, but they certainly are part of the Catholic Church and, in my opinion, originally influenced the Illuminati. This created a secular and separate society that later formed back into the Masons—who were created by the Catholics anyway—do we see a picture emerging here?

There is a glimmer of that central part of the wheel to which all the spokes seem to be attached. Before the Illuminati merged into the Masons, they had been implicated in the creation of several other groups such as the Rosicrucians, Golden Dawn, and even the Lutherans and Protestants!

Even South America was regained via the Spanish under guidance of Jesuit and other Monastic Orders—all Catholics.

Rosicrucians

The earliest real documentation for the Rosicrucian ideals is from 1597. It is said that a certain alchemist traveled across Europe seeking to begin a society to carry out his newly discovered alchemical ideals. The Fama Fraternitas and the General Reformation of the World appeared in 1614 as fully fledged documents, so he must have succeeded. The founder is claimed to be a Christian Rosenkreuz, which is obviously a false name and means the rosy cross of the Christians.

It is claimed that this character traveled across Arabia, studied at Fez in Egypt and returned to Europe with his message—a message that is decidedly ancient. The origin of this enigmatic group is false and was, therefore, created by whoever did begin the order. What clues do we have?

The rosy cross, the Rosicrucian symbol clearly on display at Rosslyn Chapel, Edinburgh

The coat of arms of Martin Luther, that staunch anti-Catholic, included the rose and the cross. There are also parallels with Arabic Illuminati schools such as those of Abdelkadir Gilani, who was known as the shining rose. However, when we look at the origins of Masonry and the rituals and beliefs held within, we find they are not dissimilar. It appears that Rosicrucianism is yet another form of that Catholic-bred Diaspora—just like the Jesuit creation of the Illuminati, drawing on the undercurrents of mysticism to create a seemingly anti-self organization. The easiest way of winning a football game is to own both sides.

Just like the Freemasons, the Alumbrados (Illuminated Ones), the Illuminati, and dozens of other groups around at the time, the Rosicrucian ways were linked to the influential Sufi mystics, who had influenced the world for such a long time. The methods required the deepest of concentration upon "the master," so that absolute adherence to the "way" was normal. It was another method of control. The void left behind by the strictness and rigidity of Catholicism was easily filled by hundreds of such groups—including the emerging Protestants.

Today the Rosicrucians are a worldwide order with thousands of members—but their influence on the world now is minimal. Although there is a hint in one of their books, which tells us that the influence of the person or soul they call the Ego will keep returning to constantly make alterations to the way forward for mankind.

In this small piece we are told that it is the same source (Ego) from where all "spiritual illumination" has derived—and I would agree.

> Many centuries have rolled by since the birth, as Christian Rosenkreux, of the individual who we know and honor by the name—the Founder of the Most Holy Order of The Rosicrucians.
>
> Though by many outsiders his existence is regarded as a myth, it is nevertheless true that his birth marked the beginning of a new epoch in the spiritual life of the western World. That particular Ego has also been in continuous incarnation ever

since, in one or another of the European countries, taking a new body as his successive vehicles outlived their usefulness, or circumstances rendered it expedient that he change the scene of his activities. Moreover, he is incarnate today—an initiate of high degree; an active and potent factor in all affairs of the West—although unknown to the world.

As are all such individuals, he is a representative of the Central Conclave of the Elder Brothers of humanity. His mission was and is to show the spiritual significance of all scientific discoveries, thus counteracting as far as possible the deadening influence of materialistic science, which, for reasons previously given, the Elder Brothers dread more than any other manifestation of human activity.

To this end he labored with the Alchemists centuries before the advent of modern science. He, through an intermediary, inspired the now-mutilated works of Bacon. Jacob Boehme and others received through him the inspiration which makes their work so spiritually illuminating. In the works of the immortal Goethe and the masterpieces of Wagner the same influence meets us. (*The Rosicrucian Cosmo-Conception* by Max Heindel, 1910)

This particular Ego has been manifesting itself throughout time—and I would agree. However, I also say that it is the same Shining influence throughout man's history that has been making these moves, stepping in and out of the scene as cerebral evolution has moved mankind forward. These Rosicrucians call this influence the Central Conclave of the Elder Brothers. The text continues and tells us who can "see" these secrets:

It hides from the profane, but reveals to the Initiate the more clearly how he is to labor day by day to make for himself that choicest of all gems, the Philosopher's Stone—more precious than the Kohinoor; nay, than the sum of all earthly wealth!

Apparently Christ himself wrought this marvelous Stone while incarnate in the body of

Jesus....The Reichs-Anzeiger said, in one article: "Yes, there is a Philosopher's Stone. It is an Elixir of Life. It is all, and much more than has ever been claimed for it. Moreover, most people have had it in their hands often, but know it not!"

How absolutely and unqualifiedly true that is, yet at the same time how thoroughly misleading, none can guess save those who know the secret, but even the eavesdropping traitor who had listened and overheard the words spoken among the brethren, could have profited thereby."

The writer then points out that:

To those who are entitled to the knowledge, many a mystery will reveal itself "between the lines" in this work, suggested but not spoken, for to reveal them, save from the lip to ear to worthy persons and under proper circumstances, would be a grievous breach of faith, not to be contemplated.

The secrets held within the pages of that 1910 book are simple to behold and, upon reading the text, reveals nothing more than the enlightenment experience.

We are even told that in order to become an initiate we cannot simply apply. We will be watched from the sidelines and our merits in this life counted towards being offered the "golden key to the temple." Of course, in 1910, there was no World Wide Web, and today we find this once-influential secret society now offering courses with credit card payments. Although they still claim to be teachers of the Mysteries and custodians of the Sacred Teachings of a spiritual power more "potent in the life of the Western World than any of the visible Governments; they may not interfere with humanity so as to deprive them of their free will." Reading "between the lines," this implies that they are an invisible government.

This secret government takes the form of seven Brothers who, Heindel continues, "go out into the World whenever occasion requires; appearing as men among other men or working in their invisible vehicles with or upon others as needed; yet it must be strictly kept in mind that they never influence anyone against their will or contrary to their desires; but only strengthen good wherever found."

Of course a person's "will" is dependent upon what has already influenced him or her, and "good" is relative. Is it really our "will" to run up huge debt while trying to obtain the elusive happiness we are fed by the mass media?

The Illuminati

In *Essai sur la secte des Illumines*, 1789, Mason de Luchet wrote:

> There are a certain number of people who have arrived at the highest degree of imposture. They have conceived the project of reigning over opinions, and of conquering, not kingdoms, nor provinces, but the human mind. This project is gigantic, and has something of madness in it, which causes neither alarm nor uneasiness; but when we descend to details, when we regard what passes before our eyes of the hidden principles, when we perceive a sudden revolution in favour of ignorance and incapacity, we must look for the cause of it; and if we find that a revealed and known system explains all the phenomena which succeed each other with terrifying rapidity, how can we not believe it?

The Illuminati are, for many, the "Men in Black," the silent masters in the background who plot our futures. To others they are a fable, a boys club, created by frustrated Freemasons in the 18th century. There is, as ever, truth in all, but we must understand that most of the time we end up believing exactly what the marketing and propaganda wants us to believe.

Sweeping aside the Christian Bible Belt influence of anticonspiracy theorists, and those crazy ideas of the conspiracy theorists such as "they came from outer space," we have to get back to the basic facts as we know them.

Standard history tells us that the Illuminati was started by Jean Adam Weishaupt, the founder of the Order of the Illuminati. Weishaupt was born in Bavaria on February 6, 1748. His father, Baron Ickstatt, was a professor at the University of

Ingolstadt, having married the niece of the curator. The baron secured a scholarship at the Jesuit College for Adam, who then went on to become a law student at the age of 15. Ingolstadt was a steadfastly Jesuit area and had been for more than 200 years. Dissent was not permitted, even though they had been partially suppressed in 1773 by Clement XIV. It has been said of the Jesuits that they were the world's largest and most powerful secret service—due mainly to the fact that they were feared by many in the Catholic Church, and that a universal "confession" could be well utilized for blackmail.

The Jesuits were founded by St. Ignatius of Loyola and *nine* companions, just like the Knights Templar.

Interestingly, Nicholas Poussin, the infamous painter of the *Shepherds in Arcadia,* was also a Jesuit, and it seems, from the pages of history, that the Jesuit Order has been at the center of many outrages. They are intimate with the Vatican, and history has shown that there is little in the politics of the world that the Vatican has not had a hand in. According to a converted nun, M.F. Cusack:

> The Jesuits offer the world at large a system of theology by which every law, Divine or human, may be broken with impunity, and by which the very Bulls of Popes may be defied. It is a ghastly religion; it is a religion to be abhorred by all honest and honerable men. (*The Trail of the Serpent*, Inquire Within)

So according to this 19th century writer, they were even above the Bulls of the Pope. Edwin A. Sherman, an American Freemason, also wrote, in the 19th century:

> The Jesuits laugh at us; and during their hilarity, the rattlesnake is coiled at our feet, climbing to strike us in the heart.

And even President Lincoln, who was finally assassinated after numerous attempts, said:

> The Jesuits are so expert in those deeds of blood that Henry IV said that it was impossible to escape them, and he became their victim, though he did all he could to protect himself....I know that the Jesuits never forget nor forsake.

Amazingly, in the conspiracy theorists' world, the Jesuits have also been implicated in the creation of the anti-Semitic *Protocols of the Elders of Zion*, as they had already been shown to have been implicated in *The Secrets of the Elders of Bourg-Fontaine*, another "stirring" work.

We must also note that the Jesuits have hundreds of links with the Masonic Order and Templar symbols. In the Jesuit Extreme Oath of Induction, as recorded in the Journals of the 62nd Congress, 3rd Session of the U.S.A. (from which it was removed at a later date and quoted here from the book *Subterranean Rome* by Charles Didier, 1843), we find that:

> On either side stands a monk, one of whom holds a banner of yellow and white, which are Papal colors, and the other a black banner with a dagger and a red cross above a skull and crossbones [a Templar symbol].

According to this same text, the letters I-N-R-I are established, and mean Iustum Necar Reges Impius (Exterminate impious kings). The superior then states:

> ...among Roman Catholics to be a Roman Catholic, and to be a spy even among your own brethren; to believe no man, to trust no man...and obtaining their confidence, to seek even to preach from their pulpits and to denounce with all vehemence in your nature our Holy Religion and the Pope; and even to descend so low as to become a Jew among Jews, that you might be enabled to gather together all information for the benefit of your Order....You have been taught to plant insidiously the seeds of jealousy and hatred between communities, provinces, states that were at peace, and to incite them to deeds of blood, involving them in war with each other, and to create revolutions and civil wars in countries that were independent and prosperous...to take sides with the combatants and to act secretly with your brother Jesuit, who might be engaged on the other side. You have been taught your duty as a spy, to gather all statistics, facts and information in your power from

every source; to integrate yourself into the confidence of the family circle of protestants and heretics of every class and character, as well as that of the merchant, the banker, the lawyer, among the schools and universities, in parliaments and legislatures, and the judiciaries and councils of state, and to be all things to all men.

It seems to be a peculiar world that the Jesuits inhabit. On the one hand they fraternise with Freemasons, royalty, and presidents, and on the other, they take an oath that puts them at odds with just about everybody who is not Catholic.

It is into this world that Weishaupt was brought up.

By 1775, Weishaupt was professor of canon law at Ingolstadt, and it was this year he or somebody else chose for Weishaupt to form a plan of an association of which he would head. This association would "oppose the forces of superstition and lies"—which implies religion. The thoughts of many commentators are that Weishaupt so hated the Jesuits that he thoroughly intended to do away with them once and for all. Others believe that Weishaupt was in fact trained by the Jesuits for the purpose of raising a worldwide army of spies who would constantly be feeding back information—information that the Jesuits could not get anymore through their confessions. In fact, the Illuminati even set up their own confessions in line with those of the Jesuits: "this means consisted mainly in the introduction of an obligation of unconditional obedience, reminiscent of Loyola's Constitutions; of a far-reaching mutual surveillance among the membership of the order; and a kind of auricular confession, which every inferior had to make to his superior."

All of this surveillance and confession were fed back to the Jesuits from the very people who were supposed to be against them. How better to find out what was in the mind of the opposition than to *be* the opposition? This is a standard double ploy utilised for centuries by the secret services of all religions and states. After all, it is the very reason for the double 0's on James Bond's code name.

They even fed the anti-Semitic rhetoric, which suited the Catholic Church down to the ground.

Through associations with the Freemasons, the Jesuits managed to get information from and influence to the Freemasons of the globe. Just how much influence the Illuminati finally had (or have) is unknown—that is the idea of secrecy. But what can be seen is that following Weishaupt's amazing creation, out of the order of a much older institution, we suddenly have several worldwide revolutions and the balance of powers shifting like never before. However, even though Weishaupt and his close friend Zwack were banished and never seen again, there can be nothing read into this. It could be that they were simply rewarded with a long holiday out of the way, or were, as some believe, sent to Saxe-Coburg and the Netherlands to start the whole thing again.

There are older links for the Illuminati though that stretch right back into the realm of Afghanistan. This link is with the Roshaniya or Illuminated/Enlightened Ones, and reference to them comes from the House of Wisdom in Cairo—a veritable fount of esoteric knowledge predating the Roshaniya by hundreds of years.

Again, initiation and ritual match up between the Roshaniya and others such as the Muslim Assassins, who influenced the Templars and hence Christianity, Freemasonry, and so on.

The earliest leader we know of is Bayezid Ansari, who claimed descent from the "helpers" of Mohammed. Who exactly these "helpers" were nobody knows; suffice to say their existence in helping Mohammed escape Mecca pinpoints them in space and time, if nothing else.

It is claimed that Bayezid was indoctrinated by the Ismailis—themselves close to the Assassins and having "hidden lodges" around the world. These Ismailis came about to protect a great secret of Islam after the Crusades, in much the same manner as the heretical Cathars protected some strange secret knowledge.

It seems that the Ismailis recruited well, as the Illuminated Ones grew fast. Bayezid taught a series of supernatural exercises that were believed to lead to enlightenment and the great secret—an obvious allusion to the fact that the great secret is enlightenment. To obtain this illuminative aspect of the secret, they had to undergo the usual meditation and fasting called the khilwat—silence. Using merchants and soldiers, Bayezid eventually spread his message across the world by word of mouth, and those

Gnostics and Mystics who heard the message already understood the secret of illumination. Eventually Bayezid, who was now known as Pir-I-Roshan (sage of illumination) founded a great city at Hashtnagar with the message of human fulfillment emanating from its center. It was understood that utilization of the human mind, in the enlightened aspect, could bring about wonders.

Eventually Bayezid died and his sons as successors were not really up to the job. However, only 40 years after the last leader of the illuminate ones died, Weishaupt started his Illuminati. As Arkon Daraul says in *Secret Societies*:

> Coincidences of date and beliefs connect these Bavarian Illuminati with the Afghan ones, and also with the other cults which called themselves "illuminated." The beginning of the seventeenth century saw the foundation of the Illuminated Ones of Spain—the Alumbrados, condemned in an edict of the Grand Inquisition in 1623. In 1654 the "Illuminated" Guerinets came into public notice in France.
>
> Documents still extant show several points of resemblance between the German and Central Asian Illuminists: points, which are hard to account for on the grounds of pure coincidence.

Which social order do I sign up for? Author at military museum, Malta

The Roshaniya have some telling symbols and rituals. The priests were identified with a secret sign in which they crossed over both hands flat on the forehead—the place of the third eye and illumination. The colors of the Roshaniya and the Ismailis were red and white—a color utilized by hundreds of those linked with the ancient enlightenment—especially the Knights Templar, who also had a red cross on their white clothes. The red and white are symbolically important for the enlightenment process, the movement of the sun and moon, and many other elements.

Red and white were also incredibly important in the Far East where we find more Illuminated Ones known popularly as the Triad.

So the Illuminati seem to have emerged from the Catholic Church as a cover name of a secret society supposedly set up to circumnavigate the Church's authorities. There could be claims that due to the name Illuminati simply meaning "enlightened ones," it could be that their origin then lies in a great many places. One of these is the Brethren of the Free Spirit in 14th century Europe, but this group can easily be traced back to a pantheistic heretical movement that was quickly suppressed by the Church. And in fact this is the same in all cases. Where alternatives to Weishaupt's Illuminati are found, they are soon quickly explained away. During its supposedly short life, it gained the membership of many well-known and influential people across Europe, and this is the exact point of the process. It was a method used for centuries, and still used to this day, to find out those who oppose you under the guise of real enlightenment or illumination.

The true history of the Bavarian Illuminati, like that of the Freemasons who erected the Church's buildings, is now so clouded in mystery that it is almost impossible to decipher. In the past few decades so much madness has been written and subtle links glorified that the popular perception has the Illuminati still in existence today, ruling the world like some sci-fi elite. The fact remains though that the links we do have reveal that the Illuminati were a group created subtly by the Catholic Church to stave off dissent within Europe's privileged and influential. Regardless of the evidence, however, the Church and even its opponents still maintain that the Illuminati were and even are opponents of the

Church and even state, even though there is precious little evidence for this. In those places that the Illuminati have been powerful, the Church is to this day still a big force, and yet in those countries, such as England, that no longer have a powerful Catholic contingency, the Illuminati were not. This is evidence in opposition to the normal belief.

15

The Nazi Code

In the late 19th and early 20th century, Germany was in a peculiar political position. It needed to rediscover its own identity following the loss of its Holy Roman imperial power. To this end various secret societies sprang up under the guise of esoteric and philosophical schools. From this base emerged what was to become one of the world's most dangerous secret societies—the German Order.

One man, more than any other, can be identified as the driving force behind this new wave—Baron Rudolf Freiherr von Serbottendorff. It was von Serbottendorff who was more than incidental in growing the Thule Gesechafft, which came out of the German Order. This Thule Society was a new secret group based supposedly upon ancient Nordic mythology, but in reality was more Eastern than most writers realize.

In 1918, von Serbottendorff purchased the *Munchener Beobachter*, a weekly Munich newspaper, which he transformed into an anti-Semitic scandal sheet and the Thule Society's official publication.

The Thule society, as we will discover, went on to give birth to the Nazi Party and the rest is history.

However, I wondered just who was this von Serbottendorff and why is it that he would be so implicated in the proposed takeover of the world?

It amazingly transpires that von Serbottendorff was an adopted Turkish citizen with links in the now infamous Sufi tradition and an adept of the mysteries. No wonder then that the later Thule Society and the Nazi Party should have mystical leanings. It has also been claimed that his real European name was Adam Alfred Rudolf Blauer and that he was involved in Bavarian anti-communist struggles. Amazingly, he was also a Freemason, and just prior to World War I he had made several trips to the Near East, where he became involved in the mystery tradition.

In the Balkan War of 1912–1913, he was implicated in directing the Turkish Red Crescent and was made Master of the Order of the Rose Garland (Rosenkranz). All of this is at the height of Rosicrucian fame in Europe, and as some would have it, the Rosicrucians were more "potent in the life of the Western World than any of the visible Governments."

In 1910, while living in Istanbul, Serbottendorff controlled his own secret society based on a combination of Islamic Sufi mysticism, masonry, alchemy, and anti-Bolshevik ideology—the perfect occult base for the Nazi party.

It transpires that he eventually established a sect of devotees along the lines of the "fedayeen" or Assassins, who were guided by their spiritual leader, the Old Man of the Mountain. He had basically set up a semi-religious and militant secret society whose purpose was to change the world.

According to Dr. Walter Johannes Stein, the Thule Society was a "Society of Assassins" holding secret meetings and issuing death orders. This murderous method of political change had been brought to the German Thule Society by von Serbottendorff, who spread the word though his newspaper interests. Franz Gurtner, the president of police in Munich, was a member of the inner circle and later became minister of justice under the Third Reich.

The Thule Society served as the recruiting and political platform front of the German Order. In 1918, the Worker's Political Circle, with the Thule Society representative Karl Harrer as chairman, was set up, and in 1919 this became the German Worker's Party. Only one year later this became the NSDAP (Nationalsozialistische Deutsche Arbeiterpartei) or Nazi Party under the later leadership of Adolf Hitler.

We know that there were links between these organizations as Serbottendorff himself stated: "Thule members were the people to whom Hitler first turned and who first allied themselves with Hitler."

I found that the ancient Sufi tradition had influenced the West to a greater degree than I had previously believed. But, here with the Thule Society, I had Serbottendorff bringing Sufi and Islamic mysticism directly into the German political state.

Serbottendorff is even on record as having stated that Muslim Masters had entrusted him with "Illuminating Germany," and he did so by allying Sufism to ancient Aryan mythology.

Following the rise of Adolf Hitler, who discovered the Society after he had been ordered to spy on them, Serbottendorff's newspaper was bought out by Dietrich Eckart, a Bavarian Catholic who had helped form the German Worker's Party—and thus the newspaper was now under German rule, for obvious reasons.

It was Eckart who introduced Hitler to the more esoteric ways of the world, and it was Eckart who transcribed *Mein Kampf*. When they came to power, Hitler set up the SS, a secret Order of the Silver Star who went out initiating people into the mysteries. Close ties to Turkey were still in place, as the mass exterminations of both countries show. Eckart himself was highly influenced by the Eastern mysticism and was a follower of Aleister Crowley's movement. In fact, some researchers have even claimed that Crowley influenced the Nazi occult movement to such a degree that it may have been through him that the "secret brotherhood" were working and thereby influencing Hitler and his motley crew. The occult was rife within the Nazi Party as Himmler's Death Head Units were to show with their ritualized murders, harking back to Celtic head cults. Not to mention Himmler's occult-inspired SS, who were headquartered at the castle of Wewelsburg in Westphalia, where there was a round table with 13 seats.

In 1935, Himmler's SS established the Ahnernerbe (Ancestral Heritage) to seek out occult secrets that would aid the Nazi Party to victory. They traveled across the world to Tibet, South America, Rennes le Chateau and other special places of occult interest.

Without doubt the whole remit of the Nazi Party was to establish an occult-based theology in a political forum. It was their attempt to reestablish something that they perceived had already been lost. It was nothing new. The same thing had already been done in America, where the Masonic influence had established a Masonic constitution, and the political family of the United States was and, would be forever, based around arcane Masonic and occult secrets.

So what was this Thule, and does it give us any clues as to the secrets of this occult takeover bid?

Thule was named after a fabled island much like Atlantis or Lemuria. It was believed to have been situated somewhere in the north and was lost a long time ago, along with its highly developed and intelligent civilization. But the secrets of this ancient race were not lost; they were, instead, to be found within the myths and mysteries of the ancient world. Amazingly, followers of the Thule Society believed that there were masters hiding in the background who occasionally influenced the human race, just as the theosophists and Rosicrucians believed. These were called the Great White Brotherhood—or Shining Ones.

It was believed that only the true initiate could establish contact with these masters, through magic and ritual, and once contacted the initiate would be empowered with great skills and superhuman strength. These extra skills were given to enable the initiate to create the conditions for the master's race—the Aryans—to populate the Earth and, thus, exterminate the inferior races.

This element of extermination was more obvious before and during the war, with the Holocaust. But it was also used to undermine the strengths of other countries. In Bavaria, left-wing socialists proclaimed the Bavarian Soviet Republic. However, this communist movement was not to be tolerated, and so a counter movement was set up, not surprisingly called the "whites." They were called the Frei Corps and were financed by the Thule Society, bringing swift defeat to the newly formed Soviet Republic, and yet another example of how a secret society, grounded on the ancient mysteries, could influence the world.

Hitler had been on the ground in 1919, as a soldier who went in after the revolution had been put down. His purpose was to select new recruits and to investigate those who had opposed the revolution, which he did ruthlessly. This in turn led to Hitler being given a role in the intelligence division of the German Army—he was now both inside the official army, and on the outside, a member of a secret society with intentions of taking power. Through the rantings of Gottfried Feder of the Thule Society and others like him, Hitler was secured as a recruit and was more and more intrigued by the anti-Semitic rhetoric of the group. Soon, Hitler was in charge of propaganda in the Thule Society.

There are literally hundreds of instances I could cite to show that the Thule Society and other secret societies were inciting all kinds of changes within Europe, but just these few collated facts, I believe, sufficiently show that the politics of the day was not all that I had previously believed it to be. In fact, there were influences at play, which even I was surprised about—namely the Sufi influence.

This is also shown in yet another Germanic society called the Order of Teutons, a magic Lodge set up in 1912 before the Thule Society by Theodor Fritsch, Philipp Stauff, and Hermann Pohl. All three have been implicated as anti-Semitic and racist in general. The Order was set up along the same lines as the Rosicrucians and the Freemasons, with slightly different degrees of initiation. Only those of Aryan descent were permitted to join. Again, like the Thule Society, this group was linked with Rudolf Blauer (aka von Serbottendorff), who brought with him Sufi ideals and mystic leanings.

The Nazi Party outlawed the Freemasons, and, yet, allowed the Bavarian Order to continue. It was believed that the Masons had been infiltrated by the Jews and it was time to purge them from the most holy Orders. One Order changed its title to The Frederick the Great Association, as Frederick had been the founder of Masonry in the Germanic states. They also removed any obvious Jewish liturgy from their rituals.

The Catholic Part

According to the official statements, the Catholic Church simply kept quiet during the Hitler reforms. They even claim that many Catholic priests were victimized by the Nazis for their part in freeing Jews and other undesirables. This is true: The Catholic Church did remain quiet, and there were individuals within the

Church that stood up for the rights of man. However, there is a darker side to the Catholic role in the running of the Nazi war and Holocaust machines.

As a child, Adolf Hitler attended classes at a Benedictine monastery, which is where he first saw the now infamous swastika. Here he sang in the choir and claimed that he dreamt of one day taking holy orders. (*The Rise and Fall of the Third Reich* by William Shirer, Simon & Schuster)

"I am now as before a Catholic and will always remain so," he is reported to have said to one of his generals (*Adolf Hitler* by J. Toland). The Catholic Church never excommunicated him and, when we consider that a person could be excommunicated for minor misdemeanours such as giving water to an infidel, then this is quite a turn-up.

The stark fact remains, that the Catholic Church turned a blind eye to the Nazi oppression, especially as it had just spent the last few centuries trying to rid the world of Jewry itself. In fact, taken to this end, and the hidden links between Freemasonry and the Catholic Church, we can start to see a picture of a Christian purging of the Jews in process—a process that appears to have been going on for an awfully long time. Some have claimed, however, that this was a balancing act in that the Jews were getting too powerful in Europe at the time and needed "trimming."

Author in Rome. Mighty St. Peter's HQ of the Catholic Church

The Catholic deal with the Nazis involved having further privileges for its priests and even permission to get involved in the public school system, with a massive $400 million in state aid. It also lead to a clearing of anti-Catholic lawsuits, as by 1940 Hitler had erased or quashed over 7,000 legal cases against Catholic priests. All in all, the Catholic Church was doing quite well out of the process.

A Concordat with the Catholic Church in 1933 stated:

> The German Reich guarantees the freedom of the profession and the public exercise of the Catholic Religion.

Catholics "shall enjoy the protection of the State in the same manner as the employees of the State."

> The teaching of the Catholic religion in the elementary, vocational, secondary and superior schools shall be a regular subject and shall be given in conformity with the principles of the Catholic Church. (*Hitler's Third Reich: A Documentary History* edited by L. Snyder, Nelson-Hall)

To the Catholics, this was all perfect, so why should they make life hard for the Nazis? The Nazis gained prestige and, seemingly, backing from the Roman Catholics. They also needed to ensure that their allies of the future, Italy, would not be upset.

Many authors have shown that even following the end of the war, the Nazis were aided in their escapes by their brothers in the Catholic Church—escaping via monasteries and nunneries and into deeply Catholic countries in South America—especially with the aid of certain Jesuits. It would not do to call people into a secret society and then leave them high and dry when the whole thing collapses. In fact, I was to wonder whether the plan had collapsed at all—I was now wondering whether the plan was carried out perfectly well.

Frans von Papen was the chancellor of Germany between June 1932 and 1933, and first vice chancellor of the Third Reich under Adolf Hitler. Papen has been called Hitler's mentor, and to this end he should have theoretically known what Hitler was thinking. Papen gives us an insight into these thoughts in his book *My Conversations with Hitler*:

"Hitler has put into practice the high ideals of the papacy." What exactly Papen means by this I really cannot say, but it implies the obvious—that Adolf Hitler was working directly for the pope.

So, I thought, who is this von Papen?

It turns out that without Papen, Hitler would have struggled to gain power. Papen made the way smooth for Hitler's rise to power as is shown by him receiving the vice chancellery following Hitler gaining the chancellery.

Papen was born to a very wealthy Catholic family in Westphalia and served in World War I in Turkey, of all places, where he was to serve again during World War II as ambassador. On his return from World War I, he joined politics on the far right and, in 1932, was plucked from obscurity by President Hindenburg to be chancellor. It was this friendship that allowed Hitler's rise to power—as previously Hindenburg had said that he would never allow Hitler to become chancellor.

Franz von Papen, it seems, was a highly influential individual in the politics of Nazi Germany, and he was also a Jesuit! High ideals of the Catholic Church, indeed!

Papen saw through several elements, which helped the integration of the Catholic "ideals," including mixing the Catholic youth with the Hitler youth and signing the Concordat between the Vatican and Munich. Incidentally, the cardinal secretary of state, who signed the document on the Vatican's behalf was Archbishop Eugenio Pacelli who was later to become Pope Pius XII. Upon taking his position of pope in 1939, just as Hitler's troops were marching into Poland, Pope Pius wrote to Hitler:

> To the illustrious Herr Adolf Hitler, Fuhrer, and chancellor of the German Reich! Here at the beginning of our pontificate we wish to assure you that we remain devoted to the spiritual welfare of the German people entrusted to your leadership. During the many years we spent in Germany, we did all in our power to establish harmonious relations between church and state. Now that the responsibilities of our pastoral function have increased our

opportunities, how much more ardently do we pray to reach that goal? May the prosperity of the German people and their progress in every domain come, with God's help, to fruition.

Pope Pius began a tradition of holding a birthday party for Hitler sending "warmest congratulations to the Fuhrer in the name of the Bishops and diocese of Germany."

Here is what Hitler himself thought of the Jesuit Order:

I learned much from the Order of the Jesuits. Until now, there has never been anything more grandiose on the earth, than the hierarchical *organization* of the Catholic Church. I transferred much of this organization into my own party.
(*www.missiontocatholics.com / Library / Books / Smokescreen / index.htm*)

The S.S. organization had been constituted by Himmler *according to the principles of the Jesuit Order*. Their regulations and the Spiritual Exercises prescribed by Ignatius of Loyola were the model Himmler tried to copy exactly. Himmler's title as supreme chief of the S.S. was to be the equivalent of the Jesuits' 'General' and the whole structure was a close imitation of the Catholic Church's hierarchical order. (Walter Schellenberg, former chief of Nazi counter-espionage quoted from *Homeland Security: The Jesuit Gestapo* by Michael Bunker)

Indeed, we even find that a lot, if not all, of *Mein Kampf* was believed to have been written by Bernard Staempfle, a Jesuit priest (*Secret History of the Jesuits*, Edmond Paris).

It would not be the first time that the Catholic Church has been implicated in the running of a state, and it would not be the last.

During the research of this subject, I have contacted many people;one of them was Dianne DiNicola of the pressure group ODAN or Opus Dei Awareness Network. Dianne, after having checked me out, allowed me to use some of their material. The following extract is from their Website *www.odan.org* and implicates the Opus Dei in the Franco regime in Spain:

Letter From Escriva to Franco

In the following letter, Opus Dei founder, Escriva, congratulates Spanish dictator Francisco Franco on the union of church and state in Spain. According to Giles Tremlett, "Opus Dei's 84,000 members around the world deny [Escriva] actively supported Franco;" however, this document shows that at the very least Escriva admired Franco.

Opus Dei also denies that the organization has a political agenda, and claims that its members have complete freedom as well as personal responsibility for their actions. However, the following quote from Escriva's book *The Way,* which Alberto Moncada describes as a summary of Escriva's "national catholicism," illustrates how difficult it would be for a member of Opus Dei to reconcile this personal freedom with his counsel:

> Nonsectarianism. Neutrality. Those old myths that always try to seem new. Have you ever bothered to think how absurd it is to leave one's catholicism aside on entering a university, or a professional association, or a scholarly meeting, or Congress, as if you were checking your hat at the door?

Letter From Josemaría Escrivá de Balaguer to Francisco Franco, May 23, 1958

The following letter, translated from Spanish (original Spanish text found here) was published in the January-February, 2001 issue of *Razón Española* (magazine title means *Spanish Reason*). Copies of this and other letters from Msgr. Escrivá de Balaguer to Franco are kept in the Fundación Nacional Francisco Franco (National Foundation of Francisco Franco) (Marqués de Urquijo, 28, 28008 Madrid, Spain). The originals belong to Generalísimo Franco's only daughter, Carmen.

To his Excellency Franciso Franco Bahamonde, Head of State of Spain

Your Excellency:

I wish to add my sincerest personal congratulation to the many you have received on the occasion of the promulgation of the Fundamental Principles.

My forced absence from our homeland in service of God and souls, far from weakening my love for Spain, has, if it were possible, increased it. From the perspective of the eternal city of Rome, I have been able to see better than ever the beauty of that especially beloved daughter of the church which is my homeland, which the Lord has so often used as an instrument for the defense and propagation of the holy, Catholic faith in the world.

Although alien to any political activity, I cannot help but rejoice as a priest and Spaniard that the Chief of State's authoritative voice should proclaim that, "The Spanish nation considers it a badge of honor to accept the law of God according to the one and true doctrine of the Holy Catholic Church, inseparable faith of the national conscience which will inspire its legislation." It is in fidelity to our people's Catholic tradition that the best guarantee of success in acts of government, the certainty of a just and lasting peace within the national community, as well as the divine blessing for those holding positions of authority, will always be found.

I ask God our Lord to bestow upon your Excellency with every sort felicity and impart abundant grace to carry out the grave mission entrusted to you.

Please accept, Excellency, the expression of my deepest personal esteem and be assured of my prayers for all your family.

Most devotedly yours in the Lord,
Josemaría Escrivá de Balaguer
Rome, May 23, 1958

I did find in my own research that Opus Dei were more than incidental in the Franco regime and helped with the financial organizing of the regime's political desires. It was Opus Dei members who were in charge of the Ministries of Finance to such an extent that some Spanish writers called them the Spanish Mafia.

The one question I still have though, is why does it appear on the surface that secret societies such as the Freemasons seem to be against the Catholic Church, and vice versa, when all along they are connected?

The answer can only be, that to win a football game, you need to back both sides. By appearing to be against the Masons, you ensure that your side remains loyal. But by owning the other team, in this case the Masons, you get to hear and control all of those who are truly against you!

A trip down the Internet boulevard will give you a whole host of weird and wonderful theories from "the Masons infiltrate the Catholic Church" to "the Pope is a reptile." Whichever you end up believing, ask the following questions:

- What possible gain is there?
- Who controls the most?
- How long has this been going on?
- Have the proven methods of manipulation and control used in the past been only used once?

History is more than just the words on the page. It is more than some documentary on TV. History is the stark reality of mankind's cyclical nature. What we did before, we shall do again. All I can say is, watch this space, for man shall inevitably repeat his mistakes....

16

Secret Societies Today

We have seen much of the symbolism and historical background of the various secret societies. We have seen where their enlightenment concepts originated and what they mean. We have seen what their symbols refer to and we have reinterpreted much that is known.

There are many modern-day conspiracy theories about aliens, the Kennedy family, Princess Diana, and even Elvis. There is even a growing madness that many of the world's leaders are shapeshifting reptiles as espoused by the author David Icke. However, as you may have gathered, much of the so-called proof for this is the mythology and history of the serpent-worshipping cults of the globe, and now that we know the real reason for this, we have a more down-to-earth approach.

I do not intend, however, to look at these, preferring instead to concentrate on the "why" and "when" of real secret societies. I have not yet touched upon the Far East and China.

Unfortunately, finding the origins of most Chinese secret societies is nearly impossible, as they are so couched in myth and mystery. One thing is sure: Secret societies have changed the course of China—the Boxer Rebellion of 1900 was led by a secret society. These Boxers, or Fist for Protection Society, were initiated in much the same way as any protection society across the world. Placed in darkness, they were made to fast and meditate, opening up their minds to cleansing. This Boxer Society came from an older group known as the Big Swords, and this was another name used by the Triads.

In the 12th century at the time of the Crusades there were gatherings of men who took oaths to "regard the stars as our brothers and Heaven and Earth as our father and mother." These same men then drank each others' blood mixed with wine.

By the 14th century, the White Lotus Society was formed, and eventually China was scattered with secret societies. However, most of these organizations can be linked together and form the Triad we know of today. This group of societies was believed to have been formed for a popularized royalist myth—to bring back the Ming dynasty.

However, hundreds of years and even the attainment of power have not resolved this supposed goal. But, the reason for this non-attainment is simple—Ming actually means "Light" and is the real element these secret societies wish to see restored. It is the light of the Shining Ones, spreading back hundreds if not thousands of years, even in the heart of red China, that the secret societies still strive for. We know that this is the case, because once the Lotus Society had installed the Ming dynasty to the throne in the 14th century, it was only by the 17th century that they were deposed again, by the same society.

One thing is clear: whether East or West, the center rule of the secret society is "light" or "illumination."

Bildebergers

The Bilderberg Group is an informal secretive trans-atlantic council of key decision makers, developed between 1952 and 1954....It brought leading European and American personalities together once a year for informal discussions of their differences....The formation of the American wing of Bilderberg was entrusted to (Gen.) Eisenhower's psychological warfare co-ordinator, C.D. Jackson, and the funding for the first meeting, held at the Hotel de Bilderberg in Holland in 1954, was provided by the Central Intelligence Agency. Thereafter much of its funding came from the Ford Foundation....The subjects over which the annual meetings ranged were wide...but it is clear

that the [1957] Treaty of Rome was nurtured by discussions at Bilderberg the previous year. (Reproduced
from an article by Richard J. Aldrich, lecturer in
politics at Nottingham University, in *Diplomacy and
Statecraft* for March 1997. Dr. Aldrich is the author
of *The Hidden Hand: Britain, America and Cold War
Secret Intelligence*)

This modern-day group of the powerful elite has been accused,
on an international basis, of forming the brains behind a new world
order. On the other hand, they claim that the Bilderberg Group is
simply a meeting of those in power in order to discuss, in a free
and easy way, the concerns of the world leaders.

What does appear to have come out of the meetings are two
other groups also called to account by the conspiracy theorists—
namely the Trilateral Commission and the Council on Foreign
Relations.

One of the key institutions that has fostered unity
and cooperation with the Atlantic Community beyond
the old concepts has been the Bilderberg Group.
(*Bilderberg: The Cold War Internationale*, 1971,
Eugene Pasymowski and Carl Gilbert)

The origins of this group rest with one man, Joseph Retinger,
a Catholic who had links to the Jesuit Order. He even recommended
the turning of Hungary, Austria, and Poland into a tripartite state
under the guidance of the Jesuit Order. The plan was dropped.

I remember Retinger in the United States picking
up the telephone and immediately making an
appointment with the President, and in Europe he
had complete entrée in every political circle as a kind
of right acquired through trust, devotion, and loyalty
he inspired. (Sir Edward Bedington-Behrens. "The
Bildeberg Group," *Nexus Magazine*, Volume 3 [1])

With a good war record, Retinger was certainly involved in
secret and underground works, even parachuting into occupied
Germany at the age of 58.

He founded the European Movement, which gave rise to the Council of Europe in 1949, which then set up in Strasbourg where Retinger worked.

Retinger believed in unity, and to that end it did not really matter how the unity was brought about. He certainly liked to involve big business and the influence that they created within the general public. We are, after all, tied to our television screens and led by marketing men. The political and religious differences in the world, which created the disunity between certain states, he believed, could be brought together through a corporate ideal— if everybody wanted the same thing they would all be the same. A market-led revolution was and strangely still is taking place. Russia (as the USSR) collapsed and now is in the process of commercialization; the same will be and is true of China. This commercialization is creeping across the world like an invading force. In many respects this could be seen as a kind of communism by the back-door, which has been claimed was instigated by the Masons on the orders of the Catholic Church or Illuminati. Retinger did have left-wing policies, and with his connection to the Jesuits there are obvious links to take into consideration— not least of which with the Catholic Church.

Involving Prince Bernhard of the Netherlands, who was implicated in the Lockheed bribery scandal in 1976, Retinger began his crusade by starting on America, which he believed to be essential to world "peace." The prince held an important position in Royal Dutch Petroleum, or Shell, and was involved in several international corporations, and so had influence that the Americans and others would respect.

In 1952, Retinger proposed that there should be an open and frank discussion between the disparate organizations and individuals that controlled the world. This should be in secret to allow those taking part to air their views without the worry of it appearing in the newspapers the next day.

This was the birth of the Bilderberg Group, which was named after the hotel in Oosterbeek where the meetings were originally held in May 1954.

> In short, Bilderberg is a recognized, flexible, and
> informal international leadership forum in which

different viewpoints can be expressed and mutual understanding enhanced. (Bilderberg Meetings, 1989)

The Trilateral Commission

The Trilateral Commission was formed in 1973 by private citizens of Japan, Europe (European Union countries), and North America (United States and Canada) to foster closer cooperation among these core democratic industrialized areas of the world with shared leadership responsibilities in the wider international system. Originally established for three years, our work has been renewed for successive triennia (three-year periods), most recently for a triennium to be completed in 2006. (From the Trilateral Commission Website)

The Trilateral Commission is a private organization, at the initiative of David Rockefeller. It consists of over 300 private citizens from the three areas of Europe, Japan, and North America, and is there "to promote closer cooperation between these three areas."

There has been a lot of scrutiny of the Trilateral Commission, and it has been implicated strongly in many conspiracy theories—however, with as many members as it has, there is no surprise that some of them will be connected to other organizations, such as the Knights of Malta (Catholic), Jesuits (Catholic), and Freemasons. Not least of these is Mr. Rockerfeller, former president of the Chase Manhattan Bank and corporate king.

The Rockerfellers actually have their origins in a traveling salesman John D. Rockefeller, who sold what was to become Nujol, a petroleum-based laxative. John, evading accusations of horse stealing, reemerged as William Rockefeller, only to disappear again and come back as Dr. William Levingston. Eventually he became director of the United States Steel Corporation and the Rockefeller legacy began. By starting the Rockefeller Foundation, the family later had a firm basis in helping the people of America—and later still the world—with charitable contributions.

The Rockerfellers are often linked with the Rothschild's in the conspiracy world. I will leave it up to the readers to do their own research on these two families.

Rosicrucians

There are many Rosicrucian movements in Britain, Europe, and the United States, and around the world, with a great many teachings. Some are extremely open, and others are more secretive. The secretive Rosicrucians tend to save their hidden teachings for the higher degrees of Freemasonry. Probably the most famous organization is AMORC (the Ancient and Mystical Order of the Rosy Cross), who advertise widely, and to date have more than 300,000 members. They offer correspondence courses and hold meetings around the world.

The earliest real documentation for the Rosicrucian ideal is from 1597, and most of these early documents can now be traced to a Lutheran priest, Johann Valentin Andreae (1586–1654), who actually created the symbolic myth of Christan Rosenkreuz in an attempt to stimulate interest in the concepts, which, therefore, must have been already in existence. During the late Middle Ages, a wide network of operative guilds, companies, and orders operated and spread their beliefs far and wide. These were the Masons, and the Rosicrucian movement is implicitly linked with them due to this early spread. These early Rosicrucians were said to be bound by strict oaths of secrecy and worked toward knowledge and enlightenment. It could be that the dispersal of the Knights Templar and their Gnostic secrets found its way across Europe. The rose was often used as a symbol of hidden or secret knowledge.

Much like other groups of the time, the Rosicrucians were linked to the Sufi mystics, whose influence was prolific throughout the world. The Sufi methods required the deepest concentration on "the master" and absolute compliance with the "way"—a method of control that easily filled the void left by the strict and rigid ways of Catholicism.

Contemporary Rosicrucians are still a worldwide order, but their influence in today's society is minimal. However, Rosicrucians have a book that details the influence of the person or soul they call the Ego, who will keep returning to make alternations to mankind's path forward. The Rosicrucians call the influence of this Ego the Central Conclave of the Elder Brothers, but I call it the Shining Ones. The same process of illumination is held within the secrets of Rosicrucianism as that of the ancient Shining Ones, and each group's beliefs in the secrets of the rose and the cross signify this connection.

The Order of the Golden Dawn

Although the Hermetic Order of the Golden Dawn (OGD) is no longer properly in existence, its influence was and is felt in other Orders. The amazing element here is that the whole basis of the OGD was false. The Order collected thoughts and teachings from many other organizations, collated them together, and presented them as their own.

In the late 19th century Dr. William Wynn Westcott, Samuel Liddell "Macgregor" Mathers, and Dr. William Robert Woodman got together, and using Westcott's original concept, created the OGD. Anybody who has any understandings of the OGD and the Freemasons will spot almost instantly that the OGD was itself mostly based around the core doctrines of the Freemasons. There are also many elements of the Kabballah, astronomy, alchemy, and astrology. Westcott and the others actually invented the Order from scratch, and even created a fictional character in the same fashion as the Rosicrucians. This fictional character was Fraulein Sprengel, the chief adept who granted the charter for the OGD, thus creating a provenance that was simply false.

Within a year the OGD was up and running with degrees and an emphasis on magical theory and ritual—taking it a little beyond the Rosicrucians and Freemasons in that respect.

The OGD became incredibly influential and included, within its ranks, the poet W.B. Yeats, the esoteric and magical writer and historian A.E. Waite, and the anti-Christ character himself Aleister Crowley, who would later on take the OGD in Britain and turn it into the OTO (Ordo Templi Orientis). The links that Crowley would develop were phenomenal, and included the spy writer Ian Fleming. Interesting then, the links between Crowley, the German OGD, Rosicrucians, and that Fleming should, later on, use the occult services of Crowley in the Second World War. These same links between Crowley, the Germans, and even the Irish Nationalists, brought him the attention of the United States secret services.

We can even see that Crowley was inspired by the ancient worship of the serpent as he speaks of rising the kundalini and:

> Take a substance symbolic of the whole course of nature, make it God, and consume it. The magician becomes filled with God, fed upon God, intoxicated with God. Little by little his body will become purified by the internal lustration of God; day by day his mortal frame, shedding its earthly elements [like the snake], will become in very truth the Temple of the Holy Ghost. (*Magick*, Aleister Crowley, 1929)

Of course this language is Gnostic and derived from the earliest Ophite Gnostics and their belief in the self as the temple of God and the rising of the serpent energy within—the kundalini. We can see this in the following:

> The blood is the life. This simple statement is explained by the Hindus by saying that the blood is the principle vehicle of the vital Prana. It was the theory of the ancient Magicians, that any living being is a storehouse of energy varying in quantity according to the size and health of the animal, and in quality according to its mental and moral character.

Gnostic concepts of balance in relation to the Grail are also related, in exactly the same way that I revealed in the *Serpent Grail:*

> The priestess enters with a positive child on the right and a negative child on the left and having placed the paten before the Graal on the altar—that is the material basis for the operation and the astral light or vital force with which it is to be united—she, followed by the children moves in a serpentine manner involving three and a half circles of the Temple....It represents the rousing of the kundalini serpent with its three and a half coils at the base of the spinal column. (*The Trail of the Serpent*)

Opus Dei

Although not necessarily a secret society, the Opus Dei certainly act as if they are, so I decided I ought to include them.

In the last chapter we saw how the Opus Dei were implicated in the Franco regime in Spain and how the Opus Dei Awareness Network were working tirelessly to uncover the truth. I did find in my own researchers that Opus Dei were in fact more than incidental in the Franco regime and in fact helped with the financial organizing of the regime's political desires. It was Opus Dei members who were in charge of the ministries of finance to such an extent that some Spanish writers called them the Spanish Mafia.

The question I have that I brought up earlier in the book, is why does it appear that secret societies, such as the Freemasons, seem to be against the Catholic Church, and vice versa, when they are so closely connected?

In my mind, the answer is that by appearing to be against the Masons, the Catholic Church ensures that its adherents remain loyal. The truth to this conundrum can also be found in the fact that there are two distinct streams of Freemasonry—the rational and the illumination.

> One could easily conclude the existence in Freemasonry of two currents which appear contradictory, and which are merely complimentary—the rationalists and the Illumines. What unites and binds them together is the ritual. The rationalist politicians have inspirers: these are the occultists of the lodges. Freemasonry is the place from whence the diverse sects draw their elements; it is for them a preparatory school, a filter, a discipline. (*La Trahison Spirituelle de la Freemason*, J. Marques-Rivere)

What better society is there to hold influence? A society with links directly backwards into Ophite worship and forwards into a great many secret societies—all emerging from ancient serpent worship.

So, I thought, what about the Opus Dei? What further evidence could I find on my own?

I had already found that the Opus Dei were a relatively new Catholic Order with close links directly to the pope. They are not huge, but have a lot of influence. They have centers strategically positioned in or outside colleges and universities across America, where they gather information, money, and recruits— for their "good works." They have built themselves multi-million-dollar buildings, and do not deny accusations that they target the rich. The Opus Dei lost more than $50 million when the bank of Roberto Calvi collapsed, even though the money seemed to have been siphoned back into the Catholic Church. Calvi turned out to have been a member of P2 (Freemasons), and was banker for many Catholic orders. The Opus Dei are incredibly secretive—even admitting the fact. In their own magazine, entitled *Cronica*, they tell their members to keep their slates clean:

> Dirty clothes are washed at home. The first manifestation of your dedication is not being so cowardly as to go outside the Work to wash dirty clothes. That is if you want to be saints. If not, you are not needed here.

A Jesuit priest told ABC News:

> I think they really fly under everybody's radar screen and that they're a lot more powerful than a lot of people think. (Rev. James Martin speaking to ABC News 2001)

During the late 1950s and the 1960s, Opus Dei members came to control the economic ministries of Spain as well as other important cabinet posts. This was in keeping with the organization's aim of influencing the development of society indirectly. Opus Dei recruited its members from among the brightest students, which encouraged a sense of elitism and belonging. Because of this tightness of community and the secrecy that surrounded the organization, some critics have termed it the "Holy Mafia."

> But Father Gonzalo Munoz, a Melbourne Catholic priest, believes Melbournians should be wary of the group. 'The more we expose them the better....My concern is really that they are trying to influence

the church with values that are contrary to the Gospels. It's about elitism, it's about wealth and prestige," Father Munoz said. "My concern is that they are going to infiltrate universities." (Church Storm, Sunday, April 2001)

Ok, I thought, all is not completely well in the Catholic world. What about that other Order, the Knights of Malta?

There's nothing secret about the order, but a lot of people think there is." The fact that five of the six US ambassadors to the Vatican have been members of the Knights of Malta is "sheer coincidence," he said. ("Knights of Malta Fight New War," John Travis, Catholic News Service, in an interview with Fra. Andrew W.N. Bertie)

This Order can truly be traced right back to the Crusades in one long and perfect historical line, without wondering whether it reformed or not. There are some modern Orders that have similar names, but they are mimicking the true Order, which is now in Rome, after having been kicked out of Rhodes and Malta by several invading armies. As the Knights of St. John they were highly influential, much like the Templars, and were linked as the Hospitallers on Malta. When the Templars were disbanded, a lot of them simply merged with the Knights of St. John, and took with them their mystical ways and knowledge. Now, they have connections across the world and are a sovereign order, which means they have ambassadors and hold political sway as well as the all-important diplomatic immunity. It maintains diplomatic relations with Europe, North America, South America, and Asia with the authority of the Holy See. The Knights of St. John has specialized agencies in the United Nations and other international organizations. In the United Kingdom the Order of St. John of Jerusalem is the branch of the Knights of Malta, and out of it came the Order of the Garter—to which the main players in old politics in the United Kingdom must be affiliated.

They are directly responsible to the pope and have been linked by hundreds of conspiracy theorists to many scandals.

For instance, in the 1980s, Colonel Oliver North authorized an exchange of guns for drugs to finance the Contras in Nicaragua. In order to sort this out, Colonel North needed connections in the underworld and got involved with the Mafia, the CIA, and many other shady organizations and characters. One of these was Al Carone, who was a colonel in the United States Army—he was also a member of the Sovereign Military Order of the Knights of Malta.

So far I had found nothing new about the world. All of this information was widely available at the click of a mouse. But what is new is that all of these are branches of just one tree. They have all been spawned from the same mother and father, and they can all be traced down the evolutionary timeline and back to ancient Sumeria and the "Shining Ones."

Take the Freemasons, for example. They are supposedly a God-fearing Protestant organization doing good for the community. They can be proven to have come from the Catholic Templars. The Templars showed allegiance to the Catholic Church and the pope. The Catholic Church sprang from a Roman Imperialistic intrusion into the world of religion. These religions (we shall give them all a cover title of Christianity even if it is not strictly correct), were all basically following the same beliefs (as I have set out in this book), and all emerged from the creation of the Sons of Light—the Essene. The Christian play, that of Jesus, was a set-up by the Essene, the Shining Ones, who stretch back into Egypt, and from Egypt the ideas were mixed from Sumeria.

I know this is a vast over-simplification of the whole thing, but I wanted to keep this chapter small in answer to some of my critics, who have said that I should reveal the Shining Ones today.

There can be no revealing of them today, as their beliefs have dissipated into the mother Church of Catholicism. If any organization on the globe is still the Shining Ones, then I do not need to look at secret societies, bankers, or business men; I do not need to turn to Illuminati and Men in Black; I do not need to have a go at a few innocent Freemasons who have no idea what it is they are really worshipping. The true Shining Ones are out in the open and are still proselytizing like never before; they are still forming new branches; still grafting onto the vine. They paradoxically hide behind others and yet fear no man. They are the most powerful nongovernmental organization on the globe and have been for centuries. They have wealth that even the United States would envy and, yet, declare poverty. They

17th century pharmacy sign Paris, the real grail

have a presence in every single country in the world, like no other. They have their hands in just about every cloak-and-dagger society we could mention and instigated most of them. They feverishly cling to secrecy and declare openness. They control the minds of billions of people and influence the rest. They make policy that governments have to adhere to. They are the Catholic Church.

> Pope John Paul II rang in the New Year on Thursday with a renewed call for peace in the Middle East and Africa and the creation of a New World Order based on respect for the dignity of man and equality among nations. (CCN News, January 2004)

17

The Holy Vehm

The only nation in the world that knows right from wrong is the German nation, and Germany must fulfil her mission, otherwise European civilization will be ruined.

—Dr. Rudolf Steiner, Stuttgart, 1918

Germany has seen the rise and fall of many secret societies and has harbored or fostered the growth of more than most European countries. From the Rosicrucians to the Order to the Golden Dawn, from the Freemasons to the early days of the Nazi Party, Germany has had its fair share of intrigue. The Catholic Church and even the *established* Nazi Party had tried, in vain, to stamp them out, but the fire created by the methods of secret societies is difficult to quench. No sooner has it been stamped out in one place than it starts up again in another, like a forest fire that refuses to die. One secret society with such a voracious fire was the Holy Vehm. This unique society had, for centuries, brought fear to the German people, both powerful and weak. It was open in its goal—revolution—and its vigilance was such that the name of the Holy Vehm was known across the world. Although they were believed to have disappeared at the end of the 16th century, their symbol of a red cross on a white background survives to this day in the International Committee of the Red Cross, and their disappearance seems to have occurred at the same time as the appearance of the Rosicrucians (rosy or red cross). Members even saw themselves as "seers" and "illumines" (Wissend or Wise Ones) and outsiders were known as those "who had not seen the light."

In the old acts, still retained at Dortmund, the members of these tribunals were often designated under the name of Rose-Croix; there were three degrees of initiation: the Francs-juges, the real Francs-juges who executed the sentences of the first, and the Saints-juges of the secret Tribunal, whose duty it was to observe, to scour the country, and report on what went on. They had signs and words for recognition. In 1371, after the Peace of Westphalia, they reinforced by the wandering and proscribed Templars, according to Clavel [Clavel wrote Histoire Pittoresque de la Franc-maconnerie et des Societes Secretes in 1843], established themselves throughout the whole of eastern Germany, the Red Country....[1]

But what was their origin and how did they become so feared?

The standard orthodox history claims that by the middle of the 13th century and at the height of Templar power, Westphalia in Germany was suffering from a state of lawlessness and oppression from loosened warriors, mercenaries, and bands of outlaws. It seemed no innocent man could travel between the rivers Rhine and Weser, and so the Chivalrous Order of the Holy Vehm or Fehm was secretly created to counter this state of affairs. It was created by ex-outlaws and freemen who now had families and business concerns of their own to worry about and so, with the initial backing and aid of the Holy Church, they took up arms and horse and chased down the tyrants. Eventually the Holy Vehm began to take the law into their own hands and held secret sessions wherein they judged those they had caught and sentenced them often to death. The term *fehm* or *vehm* is derived from the Latin *fama*, a law of common or agreed form. It can also mean to be "set apart," just as they saw themselves. *Fehm* can also mean "black" or "wisdom."

During this time, secrecy was paramount because of reprisals from the outlaws and soon oaths and rituals were part of the bargain. For instance, during the initiation the candidate would swear on oath to kill himself and his family should he reveal himself to be a member of the Holy Vehm. The judge or Stuhlherren would then place his sword across the candidate's throat and draw a few drops of blood to seal the oath and serve as a reminder of the judgment he would receive. The initiate would then kiss the cross on the hilt. These oaths were taken at receptions, which were often held in caves or the depths of the forest, and went something like this:

> I swear to be faithful to the secret Tribunal, to defend it against myself, against water, sun, moon, stars, foliage of trees, all living beings, all that God has created between heaven and earth; against father, mother, brothers, sisters, wife, children, finally all men, the head of the Empire alone excepted; to uphold the judgement of the secret tribunal, to aid in its executions and denounce to the present or any other secret Tribunal all misdemeanors against its jurisdiction, which may come to my knowledge....[2]

Although the "receptions" were held at night and sometimes in caves, the actual judgments were in open, public places, and often in the morning, as dawn broke.

Within the space of a few short years, the Holy Vehm had initiated nearly a quarter of a million freemen and commoners, each one sworn to eradicate heresy, traitors, and lawbreakers, and to uphold the Ten Commandments, going well beyond their initial reason for forming. Because of this amazing rise to power, secrecy became less and less a problem, and soon judgments were made openly in public places such as town halls and market squares. That said, these judgments, or Heimliches Gericht, were always held at midnight. Because these judgments almost always resulted in execution, those charged, more often than not, tried to escape and fled the country. That was not the end of the matter, and soon the mighty arm of the Holy Vehm reached far and wide, and special executioners were sent to hunt the outlaws down and kill them without trial.

Eventually such lawlessness itself became too much for the Church and state to ignore and the Holy Vehm, once again, went underground as they were closed off by officialdom by the end of the 16th century. Indeed it seems the rot may have set in from before the end of the 15th century, as no less than three court sessions summoned the emperor himself, who of course refused to turn up. On the surface, though, by 1568, they had ceased to exist and little more was heard from them. They remained, hidden and secret, being heard of in the early 19th century when the French under Jerome Bonaparte legislated against them at Munster. But they reemerged again with true vengeance in the 1930s during the Nazi period of Germany, this time focusing on the Jewish "heresy" and doing much of Hitler's dirty work. By almost all accounts the Vehm disappeared at the same time as the Nazis, but there is more....

Through my own contacts in various secret societies, I decided it was time to try and track them down, to see if indeed they still existed. I first called on a friend I had in the Ordo Templi Orientis, a secret society partially recreated by that anti-Christ himself, Aleister Crowley. It was late in the evening when I finally arrived in a little village in Surrey, and I was hungry and thirsty. The rain was beating down hard like it always does in the British summertime, and I ran from the car, across the gravel forecourt, and banged on the white Edwardian front door. I could see the lights inside flickering through the rain that almost blinded me, and I was overjoyed as the door swung wide and my old friend ushered me in. Within minutes, I was sat before a log fire with a large glass of wine, listening to all the latest "insider" gossip. I was surprised to find that most recent intrigue was about the then new Pope Benedict and how the Spanish and French had been arguing over who should follow him.

Eventually, though, we got around to my mission, and my friend immediately knew who to contact—in fact he was positively excited by the prospect of finding out himself. Going through a Golden Dawn contact in Berlin he was able to find out that the Vehm—or at least a modern recreation of them—were alive and well in Germany to this day. I wanted more and so I pushed him to check that these weren't just pseudo-Nazis. He checked, and word came back that these guys were in fact not modern day versions of the Chivalrous Order of the Holy Vehm, but were in fact a continuance of the very same medieval order that supposedly disappeared finally in the late 1940s. I was invited over to Berlin to speak with them. so I accepted.

Within days, I was on a plane to Berlin, a city I had never visited before. I flew alone and with only hand luggage, a camera, recording equipment, and a map.

Berlin is the capital of Germany and is a vibrant and very cosmopolitan place. There are still back streets that evoke a sense of the cold war, especially closer to the old border, but, as a whole, it appears fresh and newly built. My very first impressions were simply that it was ordered and clean.

I landed late in the afternoon and made my way to the hotel. I was set to meet three English-speaking Germans the following day at the Altes Museum, the Berlin Dome at Lustgarten. I slept, woke, had breakfast (which wasn't so pleasant), and then had the concierge order me a cab. By 11 a.m. I was outside the beautiful Berlin Dome building awaiting the three gentlemen. I had no idea what they looked like, but I was assured they would know me, so I stood taking pictures of the building and enjoying the German sun. I did not wait long before I was tapped on the shoulder by an elegant-looking older gentleman with short gray hair and a dark suit. Behind him were two others, similarly gray with one in a tweed-style jacket and the other in short sleeves. They all smiled at me and I was quickly put at ease.

"Come, let us drink." Said the man who had tapped me on the shoulder, and with a large grin on his face he led me away a short distance to a waiting car—a large black Mercedes.

We drove for a while through the bustling streets and out of Berlin's center. I was asked not to take pictures and to swear on oath that I would not reveal their true identities. I had little choice but to promise, or otherwise I would surely have been back to England on the next flight. Eventually, we arrived at a small café where it seemed the three elderly gentlemen were well-known and they were welcomed with what looked like to me almost Masonic handshakes. We sat, ordered coffee, and I noted how each of the three men sat almost solemnly and turned their knives, forks, and spoons towards the center of the table in an almost ritual fashion. I was only later to discover that this indeed had been an ancient secret sign of the Holy Vehm to others in the room.

All three men spoke perfectly good English, so I had no problem communicating with them. I probed them for their backgrounds. They had all fought during sWorld War II as young men and somehow survived. All three had been officers and had come together during the war as they were asked to join the Vehm.

They were unashamed of their past and told me with total confidence, and almost contempt, that they would fight again to restore power to the Fatherland and rid Europe of the "scourge" as they called the Jewish race. I was shocked to find such anti-Semitism still alive, although I probably should not have been. It turned out that they had become members of the Vehm during the war and had even held secret judgments against the "oppressors" of the German people in the woods of Germany and France. After the war they and others maintained the membership of the Vehm, and they claimed that it was still very much alive and well today in Germany and Austria and was in fact growing within the anti-European contingents. They had initiated many hundreds of younger Germans in the last few years and each of them were Freigraf, or court presidents, although judgments were few and far between these days.

I asked why they had allowed me to meet with them, as surely they must have known that I would wish to report on the meeting. They replied that their oaths were pure as they had not revealed their true identities and were revealing no new secrets, other than the contemporary existence of the Holy Vehm.

My time with these gentlemen was one of mixed emotions. On the one hand, I was almost afraid that they may take me off into some dark wood and exercise their judgment against me; on the other hand, I was excited by the whole intrigue. It felt a little like a James Bond movie—meeting outside a museum, being driven off in a black Mercedes, and talking about wartime exploits behind enemy lines. At the end of our meeting we said goodbye and I was driven back to my hotel, where I simply couldn't rest through excitement. The next day I was back in the UK and life returned to normal, but I couldn't help but wonder about those words of Rudolf Steiner from the early 20th century:

> *The only nation in the world that knows right from wrong is the German nation, and Germany must fulfil her mission, otherwise European civilization will be ruined.*

18

White Powdered Gold

My final word will be on a modern-day deception—white powdered gold. Whether wittingly or unwittingly, this substance is being prostrated before the world as if it were some kind of wonderful new snake oil. What's it all about and why is it so popular?

A book by Laurence Gardner, titled *Lost Secrets of the Sacred Ark*, attempts to prove that the ancients transformed gold into a white powder, which they used to help items levitate and to transport themselves through interdimensional portals. It is also proposed that the substance was taken orally as a kind of Elixir. The book has sold hundreds of thousands of copies and *claims* backing from certain scientists. Because of the release of my books *The Serpent Grail* and *Gnosis: The Secret of Solomon's Temple Revealed*, I have been getting hundreds of e-mails from people asking my opinion on these discoveries by Gardner et al, and so I decided to investigate a little further.

I have read most of Gardner's books and always found them very entertaining. Laurence is a nice man and I have absolutely no issues with him personally. However, my aim in all things is to get to the truth, and I am constantly pressed by e-mails, letters, and calls to get to the bottom of this white powdered gold issue, and so I simply had to push my questions out there. The fact remains that Gardner and others now claim that white powdered gold was secretly used by the Freemasons and other secret societies, so it comes under the remit of a book about secret societies. Just what is the truth?

ORMUS

The word ORMUS is today used extensively by the exponents of this substance and is derived from Orbitally Rearranged Monatomic Elements or ORMEs. It was supposedly discovered in the late 1970s by David Hudson, a farmer from Arizona, who noticed some strange materials on his land while he was mining for gold. Apparently Hudson then spent millions trying to understand the substance and has since created ORMUS from gold, water, and even "manna." The claim is that ORMUS is a new form of matter that "appears to have the properties of Spirit." They claim that the substance transits between the material plain and the spiritual plain and can thereby be used as a communication device to the Otherworld. There is, however no science at all to back these claims—just thousands upon thousands of assumptions.

The word *Ormus* in fact was originally another name for the Zoroastrian deity Ahura Mazda (Ormazd), and seeped into the Christian world in the 4th century via the Armenians, who converted to Christianity and who previously worshipped Armazd (Ormus). Ormus also became the name of one of the most important ports in the Middle East in the 16th and 17th centuries in the Persian Gulf at the Straits of Hormuz (Ormus). From here huge quantities of certain products were shipped across the entire area, as we shall see, and which reveal the truth of the original white gold! The city-state of Ormus can in fact be dated back to at least the 13th century and was extensively used for the slave trade in later years. Due to the strategically important location of the Straits of Hormuz, it has been fought over for centuries.

The strict etymology of the word is divided. Most scholars claim that Ormus/Ormuz is derived from the Persian word *Hur-mogh*, meaning simply "date-palm." Others claim that *orme* is the ancient word for worm or serpent (which I found in my other work to be no different to the fire of thought—illumination). In fact, the date-palm and the serpent share symbolic similarities. The palm itself is symbolic of several important myths. Firstly, it was the sign of the "Flaming Column" found on the coinage of Carthage. The palm also stood for fire and the Tree of Life. The leaves were never changing, and in this they signified the unchangeable Lord. The Phoenicians also held the palm in high esteem, and their coinage displayed the serpent coiled around its trunk—the fire of the tree (spine—see entries on the kundalini earlier in the book). The name of the deity "Baal Tamar" meant "Lord of the Palm," and "Tamar" means "resplendent Sun Fire." So we simply have a circular argument here. Let me explain. Ahura Mazda was a fire god or shining illumination of the Persian Zoroastrians that have been implicated by many Gnostic scholars as progenitors of much Gnostic thought, and were extreme mystics in outlook. Ahura Mazda is therefore the same as the palm and is indeed imaged by the palm. The name itself means simply "Lord of Wisdom," and mazda is in fact a feminine noun, which reveals a hidden Gnosis behind the name.

> Wise One, I realise you to be powerful and progressive because You help with Your own hand. You give rewards to both the wrongful and the righteous, by means of the warmth of your Fire, which is mighty through Righteousness and through which the strength of Good Mind comes to me. (*Gathas*: Song 8:4)

You see, true Gnosis or knowledge or indeed wisdom (the "good mind" above) can only be gained through balance, and this was often imaged in ancient times as balance between the sexes. The world saw this feminine principle in the myths of Sophia, the female element of wisdom and from where we derive "philo*sophy*." In fact, what Zoroaster was saying here was that true wisdom lies in the balanced state, and this balance was imaged by the world axis or tree—perfectly upright and running between the opposites ("wrongful and the righteous"). The palm as a symbol of fire and Ormus (Ahura Mazda) as the deity of wisdom and fire was simply "illuminated" or "enlightened." It was the image of perfection. And so, what we end up with is the etymology and the actual hidden Gnosis in the name, giving us the real truth behind the name our modern pseudo-scientists have given to a particular substance. Nowhere in this wonderful ancient philosophy do we find a peculiar substance that enables other-dimensional travel.

Science

The scientist often used by Laurence Gardner and others in their work is Dr. Hal Puthoff, director for advanced studies in Austin, who was quoted by Gardner as backing his theories.

Here's what is supposedly said by Puthoff: "Since gravity determines space-time, Puthoff concluded that the powder was 'exotic matter' and was capable of bending space-time." As Puthoff is so often used as backing the substance, I decided to ask!

I actually discovered to my surprise that Dr. Puthoff was not at all happy, and is a little perturbed at having to keep answering questions regarding the matter, especially as he never backed the theory in the first place. However, I convinced Hal to give me a quote:

> Hi Philip.
>
> The Story is this. Early on (several years ago) someone brought Dave Hudson [who helped Gardner write his book] by and he told me about anomalous effects concerning his white powder. One of his claims was that under certain conditions the mass decreased, i.e., an antigravity effect showed up. In response, I said that, from a physicist's viewpoint, **IF** that were true, then there would have been a spacetime effect. (This is probably the source of the oft-stated quote attributed to me "The powder bends the spacetime metric.") Of course, I said no such thing about the powder because I do not know whether the statement about the powder is true. I offered that if he provided me a sample of the powder, I would check it out. He said he would. He never did. I never heard anything from him after that visit. But I hear a lot about the attributed quote from my colleagues, which I keep correcting!
>
> Best regards,
> Hal Puthoff, Ph.D.
> Director,
> Institute for Advanced Studies at Austin

As can be seen by this quote, Dr. Puthoff never backed the theory, and even wanted to help to see if there were any truth behind the claims by testing the substance claimed by Gardner to be derived from gold. I was told by Edmund Marriage of the Patrick

Institute, who helped Gardner on the book, that it was tested by Oxford University and no gold was found. So what is the truth?

Dr. Sarfatti of the Global Advanced Intelligence Agency (a mock and comical title) also said that, "I think this is a false allegation....I know Hal very well and this is an obvious distortion, if not a bald lie."

Puthoff also said, "I have absolutely no idea what David Hudson's white powder does. Don't know where this quote comes from, which keeps showing up in the Internet, presumably from David Hudson. I am totally skeptical."

I have had all manner of claims given to me via e-mail, and none of them have any scientific basis. Some have claimed that ingesting the substance took them on journeys to other dimensions or even made them float. I have always asked if the individual knew what was in the substance and from where it was bought. In each case, nobody has a clue what was actually in the powder.

Question: Has anybody seen any credible objective scientific evidence for the claims made by Gardner et al? Has anybody actually levitated anything with this substance? Or even passed an article into another dimension? I ran these questions on my Website and on various other forums. Not once did I get back any scientific answers. I did have hundreds of e-mails arguing the matter from an historical point of view, that shewbread or showbread of the ancient Israelites was white powdered gold or monatomic substance, but no science. In fact when I proposed the question to my good friend and author, Crichton Miller, he answered simply: "it's salt." You see, let's just try and understand our ancestors from a position that most modern alternative historians seem to forget—survival.

Survival

Ancient man, just as we are today, was interested in his own survival. There is little difference between us and our ancestors. We too follow the same evolutionary drive to survive. Look at it this way: We hoard goods because in our subconscious we need to ensure that we have sufficient reserves to see us through the winter or a poor harvest. This is something we have learned over the millennia, which could be said to be at the root of greed. However, one of the things our ancestors needed as an addition to their diet was salt, and so in essence salt became one of the most valued things. It was hoarded and it was sanctified.

Most people think of salt as simply the white granules they shake over their dinners, but it is much more. It is an essential element of the diet, not just for humans but for animals too, and even many plants. Our ancient hunter-gatherer ancestors simply had to take in salt daily to stay alive in order to balance his water intake, and incredibly to him, it was from the sea that salt would seem to come, so the very etymology implies "from the sea." With the coming of agricultural times, man took on roughly 150 grams per day of salt, and also used it extensively for tanning hides and preserving foodstuffs.

In fact, it was even used to preserve bodies after death and was used by the ancient Egyptians and others in mummification. This preservation quality has come down to us today in symbolic form as an Elixir—extending life in the Otherworld.

Because of the incredible need and desire for salt, it became one of the most valuable substances in the world, and was sought far and wide. Great trading routes erupted, transporting it across land and sea, and even battles were fought over the control of these trade routes. One place that rose to a meteoric position of power was the port of Ormus that I have already mentioned, and we even find that salt was traded for slaves. The worth of salt has even crept into our language: "Salt of the earth" is used to describe somebody of great value with down-to-earth attitudes; "Taken with a grain of salt" to describe something of no worth (only one grain!). In fact, salt actually became money in a great many places, and even gave us our word "salary." The art of high etiquette in places such as Serbia was to offer visitors a piece of bread and some salt—a very valuable gift indeed. And this isn't something new—it is as old as mankind, and animals were seeking out salt long before homo erectus stood up. About 4,700 years ago the *Peng Tzao Kan Mu* was written in China, and copies of it are still in existence. This book deals with pharmacology and explains the worth of salt, with more than 40 kinds being used in all manner of ways. In Egypt, there is evidence of salt-making and mining from 1450 B.C., and similar evidence can be found the world over, including the Bible, where there are over 30 references to it.

> Let your speech be always with grace, seasoned with
> salt.... (Colossians 4:6)

This alone reveals that salt was here being used as a reference to a work upon the "self," to purify our thoughts and words.

Salt became a symbol for purity and was *used on altars*—becoming "holy salt." In this way, the "showbread" of Laurence Gardner is really just partly salt! This makes much more sense as manna bread and as a survival tool in the wilderness.

So just what is this showbread? Well, in Exodus 25:23–30 we are told to make a specific table or altar whereupon can be laid the bread made from fine flour. The exponents of white powdered gold claim that this fine flour was in fact fine powder—hence white powdered gold. The bread was called shew or show bread simply because it was on show. The method of making the bread is, in fact, not a chemical activity as we are lead to believe; it is instead a way of self-improvement—an esoteric psychology. We are to take fine flour, bake it, and it is to be unleavened. We are to make 12 cakes and place them in two rows of six on the pure table. This could be seen as one of the very original alchemical treatises, for the fine flour was "from the earth," the base substance or anima mundi—our base self. Then we are to bake or put in the furnace—this is simply to rigorously check ourselves and burn off all impurities, which is demanded with the "unleavened" element, which means nothing artificial must be placed in the bread. The 12 cakes or pieces of bread are the whole extent of the sky—the Zodiac—through which the opposites work, the sun and moon, and is representative of our whole life, always in balance. Placing them in two rows of six indicates the six-month growing cycle for grain to turn into bread. The loaves themselves also indicate the tribes of Israel because "grain" was equated with mankind and the tribes were made up of many grains like a loaf.

The fire or illumination can only come through understanding this balance within ourselves and gaining knowledge and wisdom. For sure there are many biochemical reactions within the mind, such as the Indian kundalini and the Hebrew spirit of God, often brought on by drugs or meditation, but there is often a merging of this symbolism. This fire or internal energy was known the world over by the name of the serpent. The reality we see here before us is also that of ordinary psychology and self-improvement.

Previously, we saw that orme (the root of Ormus) meant worm (little serpent) or serpent, and the serpent has been associated with salt for thousands of years. Bacchic ceremonies in Greece were consecrated with the serpent, and in the procession, a troop of virgins from noble stock would carry the reptile in golden baskets with *salt and bread*. This is seen in many of the rituals of the early Ophite Gnostic Christians, where *ophite* means serpent worshipper. These Ophites would actually consecrate their bread and wine with the kiss of the serpent and a sprinkle of salt. Even in Jewish tradition we are told "The bread of the serpent is dust" (*Yeshayahu* 65:25), and it was in the "dust" that the serpent was made to creep. In Babylon, the goddess of the specific salt water was Tiamat, the dragon or serpent mother, and in alchemy salt is represented by the image of a serpent. Of course we must also remember that on the very real practical level, salt was a major ingredient in bread, and as is true in much of the world, salt was often given as a gift with bread.

Conclusion

If there is truth to the claims made for this white powdered gold, then surely more research should be done by top scientists, as the claims made for it are scientifically outstanding if not outlandish. When I uncovered the ancient practice of ingesting snake venom and blood (not to be tried at home **please**) I went to several scientific establishments and sought the advice of medical institutions. I do not propose anybody takes venom and blood, as the mixtures are quite unique and hidden in secretive ways, but people are taking this white powdered gold (if that is truly what it is) and are claiming to have either hallucination experiences or actually entering altered states of consciousness as a result. And so, to this end, I ordered a bottle of fluid said to contain the monatomic substance. After a week the bottle arrived, and, keeping it in its container, I quickly took it down to a friend I have at a local university. Running the substance through his various pieces of machinery, he found no gold and no salt. In fact, all he found was water and some trace elements of iron. This small plastic bottle of water cost more than $30. Makes Perrier look cheap.

If we are to propose our theories in public and to claim scientific support for them, then we have to be able to back up those claims. At present, apart from some experiential and convoluted history-making, we have no hard verifiable evidence that monatomic substance or white powdered gold exists, nor especially that ancient man developed it or used it.

What the evidence does reveal is that salt was the real money or white gold of its day, and that this mineral found its way into our food (bread) and religion as a gift of God or the gods. The symbolism of this and the internal psychological tools of theology and philosophy merged together via the image of the serpent, and the resultant etymology serves as a testament to this.

The fire of the serpent and the need for salt are holistic symbols.

But one final enlightening thought was brought to me by my practically minded father-in-law—Alan Dickson. The proponents of "white powdered gold" claim that it made things levitate and go to great lengths to show how this can be found in ancient symbolism. Now that we know what true white gold is, we would do well to remember that salt water makes solid objects float, and that the Ark, which Laurence Gardner claims was levitated by this white powder, was in fact a copy of an Egyptian b'arque—a boat. Regardless of how arrogant we are about our ancestors we have to give them credit for such beautifully intricate mysteries.

So we know that white powdered gold is salt. We know that the whole thing is a farce of the highest order. Why then is it being presented before us as if it were the best thing since sliced bread? I would at this point also draw in the concept that the proponents of this "substance" are also the same people who feed us the concepts of the Royal Bloodline from Jesus and Mary— another myth. I do not intend to answer this conundrum because there is a depth here that is ultimately dangerous, so I will leave the reader this final code to break.

Conclusion

For centuries there have existed certain esoteric schools of mystical philosophy originating apparently in several Oriental currents of thought meeting in the Levant, Egypt, and the near East. We find in these schools elements of Buddhism, Zoroastrianism and Egyptian occultism mingled with Grecian mysteries, Jewish Kabalism, and fragments of ancient Syrian cults. Out of the hotch-potch of Oriental philsophy, magic, and mythology arose in the earlier centuries of the Christian era numerous Gnostic sects, and after the rise of Mohammedanism, several heretical sects among the followers of Islam— such as the Ismaelites, Druses, and Assassins—which found their inspiration in the House of Wisdom in Cairo. To the same sources may be traced the ideas that inspired such political-religious movements of the Middle Ages as those of the Illuminati, Albigenses, Cathari, Waldenses, Troubadours, Anabaptists, and Lollards. To the same inspirations must be assigned the rise of early secret societies. The Templars are said to have been initiated by the Assassins into anti-Christian and subversive mysteries, and we find similar traces of an old and occult origin in the Alchemists, the Rosicrucians, and the later mystical cults of which Swedenborgian is a familiar example. (From an article publish in the *Patriot* by G.G. or "Dargon" titled "The Anatomy of Revolution," 1922)

In this short extract, "Dargon" gives us a summary of what will be found by any serious investigator of the secret societies of the world—that they are all connected and all derive from a similar if not the same source. This same source may also be traced through the infamous Essene—the Jewish brotherhood who took themselves off to Damascus, Qumran, and there set about reinvigorating their strict methods of control based upon their very ancient religious belief systems, which themselves may indeed be traced into Egypt. From these white-robed "Shining" brothers can be found a connection that speaks volumes, and I recommend any serious reader to look their way for answers on origin. One thing is sure, as Le Couteulx de Canteleu said in his *Les Sectes et Societes Secretes* published in 1863:

> All secret societies have almost analogous initiations, from the Egyptian to the Illuminati, and most of them form a chain and give rise to others.

This "analogous" form running through all secret societies, apart from the strict method of control, is the underlying belief in and worship of the stars—the sky. It is this element that named them the Shining Ones, and it is this element that is still at the root of so much misinterpreted symbolism. Even the Holy Vehm were "wissends" who had the sun and the stars as symbols of power. This worship of the stars was known as Sabeism and the high Mason Albert Pike in *Secret Societies and Subversive Movements* by Nesta H. Webster pointed out:

> The seven great primitive nations, from whom all others are descended, the Persians, Chaldeans, Greeks, Egyptians, Turks, Indians, and Chinese, were all originally Sabeists and worshipped the stars.

The very power of understanding the stars was jealously guarded by all priesthoods around the world—from Aztec to Egyptian. In each case, the role of the priest was to interpret the movements of the stars, sun, and moon, in order to better predict the future, and for navigation. This jealousy forged ciphers, codes, and symbols. It forced the hiding and destruction of implements and tools of the trade. Many of the Freemasonic symbols we see today were never meant for building—they were meant for astronomy. The Holy Vehm also had a secret that reveals this—the stick, stone, string, and grass were implements used to measure. The stone tied to the string, attached to the stick, and placed in the ground were used for "ruling" the ground, a mystical and also very real device.

These secrets of the stars were deemed mystical—for the populace could not understand how such magic was done and these secrets were passed from one generation to the next by initiates and adepts. This is how the long thread has been woven—generation following generation, passing on knowledge and keeping it hidden. Eventually and often, the secret brotherhoods no longer know why they keep their odd symbols secret and why they say the strange invocations. But, through their traditions and by their dedication to their brothers, they keep alive a rich tapestry that can be broken down and reinterpreted. The truth is almost never to be found in the picture we see before us, and so we must pull hard on the thread and begin to unravel the tapestry one generation at a time. My good friend and author Crichton Miller summed this up in the very title of his book the *Golden Thread of Time*, which itself reveals the true astronomy (naming of stars) and indeed astrology (logic of the stars) of our ancient friends. According to Le Couteulx de Canteleu, the priests or leading men of the organizations followed the Egyptian hierarchy. In the first instance there was the priest, who alone could do magic and contact the gods. In the second we shall find the greater initiates, those chosen from amongst the people and who must maintain secrecy at all costs and protect the priesthood. Thirdly, the lesser initiates who were only told things that were deemed proper.

In this hierarchical trinity we see an exact plan of most if not all of the world's secret societies. The majority of Freemasons today would fall into the category of the lesser initiates—they are only aware of what they are told, and being kept at this distance and level of knowledge they seek no more, because they know of no more. Only at the highest degrees in Freemasonry are the real secrets maintained, and yet there have been some who claim to have been higher level initiates or indeed "priests" and who have since "spilled the beans." Anybody who has seen these supposed secrets of white powdered gold and even Jewish conspiracy plots will know that this is misinformation at best and money-making at worst.

In this unique compendium of thoughts and research from across a spectrum of subjects relating to secret societies we have learned a great many things. One of those things is not to believe everything we are told. I should not have to state this so obviously in the 21st century, because ancient philosophers told us this a long time ago. The sad fact is that due to new generations emerging all the time we tend to learn very little and to leave the past behind. Each generation has to start from scratch and tends to look forward, forgetting that our past holds intelligent and thought provoking answers to questions that are and will always be relevant. Because we begin each generation fresh and new, we also do not "see" the thread running through each generation from the one before—the thread of the secret society.

In the last century we had the emergence of psychology and psychoanalysis and the clever new words that came with them. But are we so arrogant to think that we invented the discovery of human psychological problems? This is of course utter rubbish, Psyche herself was a Greek goddess. For thousands of years man has sought answers to his own inner reality, the only thing that has changed radically is the wording. Now we say somebody is psychotic, our ancestors would have said they were touched by the spirits. But are we any more advanced than our ancestors? 90 percent of the globe still believe in God; we still rage war in the name of religion; we still pollute the environment and destroy our own home. There is in fact anthropological evidence to prove that very ancient man was actually peaceful, living in harmony with his neighbour and even respected the earth and lived in balance with it. The evidence then shows that as society grew and more people occupied smaller spaces, minor wars erupted and even, violent sacrifices. The evidence also shows that small bands of men gathered together to control those who fought. These small bands emerged as our kings and queens, medicine men and priests and of course our secret societies.

There is a lesson here for us all. Just one hundred years ago there was one billion people on the planet. Now there is six billion and it is growing out of all proportion. Six billion people can do a lot of harm to themselves and the environment, thus destroying the whole for everybody. Without balance, without wisdom, without knowledge, then where are we heading? I never once mentioned greed, money, capitalism did I? They do not enter into the equation of such a simple debate, but they are dark sides of the anthropological argument.

We have seen in the various articles in this compendium that man also collects himself together into groups, like fish in a school or birds in a flock. These groups become religions, secret societies, governments, in fact just about any group. There is a simple reason for this grouping and it is exactly the same for the animals. We form together for protection against predators—there is strength in numbers. Whether you are a Freemason or a Boy Scout, the ultimate reason you join forces with others of like-race and like-mind is because you see strength and protection. Why is it then that some individuals take themselves away from these groups? I myself have been invited to join many secret societies and groups. I have even turned down offers of honorary degrees. Why? Because I am confident, self empowered and have my own mind. I fear no man, I fear no society or culture. I strive to learn more about them all and to thereby be yet more empowered, because knowledge builds strength and joined with my own will it creates a confidence that is true enlightenment.

We may think and believe that the kundalini or some other spark in the bio-chemical and electric brain is enlightenment, but it is not. Our masters feed us filth and keep us in the dark. We are told what to be like, what to buy, what to do and say. We no longer need to know ourselves, the television has all the answers. But the fact is, what we see on the television is a reflection of greed, money and capitalism and these can easily be the dark forces of human nature. Light and dark are opposite sides of the same coin. Balance is like a coin placed upon its edge and like a coin it can easily be knocked over.

I desire a good life for my family, but that does not have to include a range of cars, a yacht in every port or another million. I am not a communist, I am a realist and the reality is that while one man has, another does not. My evolutionary instinct is to gather goods, property and wealth for the bad times ahead, to see me through the winter or the coming storm. The down side of this is that we grow that divisive side of our nature, greed, and somebody somewhere suffers.

The ancient Chinese texts tell us that mankind has been in this situation before many times and that his greed and "noise" has brought his civilisation crashing down to the ground. How close are we to doing it yet again? How "noisy" are you?

Notes

Chapter 1

1. *In the Blood* by Steve Jones (Harper Collins) 1996.
2. *The Copper Scroll Decoded* by Robert Feather (Thorsons) 1999.

Chapter 2

1. *Woman's Mysteries*. Esther Harding (Rider) 1971.
2. *Human Antiquity*. Feder and Park (Mayfield Publishing) 1993.
3. Stars and Snakes and Shining

   The stars are relevant to the story we have portrayed here, and they will take on more importance the deeper we probe into the history of the Shining Serpents. The major players have of course been immortalized themselves in the stars, and we can see with Ophiucus and Serpens their position in the sky was very important. The very act of placing them in the sky as gods with celestial power shows their importance. In fact it is highly likely that often the human on the ground was simply a mirror image of the pattern and movement of the celestial objects in the sky.

   Ophiucus is positioned between Sagittarius and stretches just east of the head of Hercules to Scorpio. Partly in the Milky Way, it is divided equally by the celestial equator. The classical scholars united Opiuchus (serpent holder) with Serpens (the snake) and created a great image in the sky of Aesculapius—the ancient snake healer. "He who holds the serpent...they will struggle forever, since they wage war on equal terms with equal powers." One to poison and one to heal—the two opposites seen in the enlightenment experience and giving rise to the Shining.

Aesculapius was the ship's surgeon on the Argo—associated with Jason and the Argonauts who went in search of the Golden Fleece, guarded by serpents/dragons and said to bring people back to life and bestow immortality. The word *hygiene* comes from Hygeia, one of the daughters of Aesculapius, and *panacea*, the cure-all, comes from his other daughter, Panacea.

Serpens was seen by the ancients as the healing one in the sky, and with Ophiucus he is one of the Psylli of Libya, the snake healers.

Biblical writers said this constellation was Aaron with his serpent staff, or Moses.

The annual birth of the sun and therefore Christ/Dionysus/Krishna and many more solar deities, is accompanied by the bright star, which was Sirius or Sothis, or even the planet Venus. It is also joined by the 3 stars of Orion's belt, which are the three wise men or Magi.

The sun enters each zodiacal sign at 30 degrees and so the sun king or god enters his ministry at 30 years.

The sun is the carpenter that builds the mansions of the zodiac.

When it is said that Christ (or indeed the others) walked on water, this is a mirror of the sun, which appears to walk on water with its reflection.

The sun loses its strength at the end of the year, at the same time the Scorpio constellation is seen in the sky. Scorpio is Judas Iscariot—the backbiter, which is an analogy of the method that scorpions use to strike.

Chapter 3

1. Kashyapa warned Buddha that there was only one hut available, and that a malevolent Naga occupied it. Buddha was not phased by this and went to the hut regardless. However, a terrific struggle ensued culminating in the hut bursting into flames. The onlookers drenched the flames, but they had to wait until morning to find that Buddha had survived. The Buddha emerged with his begging bowl in his arms and inside was a peaceful, coiled snake. The Buddha had slain the dragon of its fiery notions and emerged with a beneficial result.

2. See *The Serpent Grail* by Philip Gardiner with Gary Osborn (Watkins), 2005.

3. *Baphe* means to submerge, *metis* means wisdom, and therefore Baphomet could simply mean "to be submerged in wisdom."

4. The blood of course is seen the world over as the life force, or life energy of the body. It was sacred to the Hebrews especially, but not in isolation.

Christ spilling his almost Tantric energy into the place of the skull is therefore invigorating the skull into which it falls—making Golgotha a very sacred place or relic.

5. The Nagas are serpent worshippers from India.

6. The seven days are of course an allusion to the seven levels of the coiled serpent, or kundalini awakening, whereby the serpent energies are visualized and raised in balance into the head, and one becomes a Buddha or enlightened one.

Chapter 5

1. Shining Serpent

   In Genesis 3:1 the fundamentalist Christians believe incorrectly that they have sighted the first mention of Satan. He is to them called "the serpent." One of the Hebrew words for serpent is nachash and means "to shine" or "shining, upright creature." This is a positive indication that the nachash were not really snakes at all, but instead Shining upright beings and that serpent and shining go hand in hand.

   In Chaldee it means brass or copper, because of its shining, just as the word *Nehushtan* means "a piece of brass," in 2 Kings 18.4. Note how it was the Lord who ordered Moses to lift up the Brass Serpent in the wilderness, so that people might be saved. Moses was indeed a Shining One. (Num. 21.8—"make thee a fiery serpent" or "make thee a shining serpent"). Nachash seems to be interchangeable with Saraph or Seraph, to shine. In 2 Corinthians 11.3 the Nachash that fooled Eve is spoken of as an angel of light or a shining one. Eve as the female serpent was responding to a Shining One.

   Adam too is implicated as a Shining One when we discover that in the Hebrew Genesis, "His skin was a bright garment, shining like his nails; when he sinned this brightness vanished, and he appeared naked" (Targ. Yer. Gen. iii. 7; Gen. R. xi.; Adam and Eve, xxxvii.).

   The Aztec Quetzalcoatl—the plumed serpent—is seen in many dialects of the area. In Itzan it was Cuculcan and in Quichuan it was Amaute. But what we find in all of these is the same etymology. In all instances he is the plumed serpent, but also wise teacher. He is also the "golden or shining serpent."

   In Norse myth, and more specifically the work of Ulf, we have the serpent that Odin battles referenced:

   "Vidgymnir of Vimur's ford [Thor] struck the ear-bed [head] from the shining snake by the waves."

The etymology of that other serpent creature the dragon also reveals some impressive insights. According to the Oxford English Dictionary (1966), *dragon* is derived from the Old French, which in turn was derived from the Latin dracon, which in turn was derived from the Greek *spakov*, which means "serpent" and is from the Greek verb *spakelv* or "to see clearly." It is thus always related to sight. In the Sanskrit *darc*, which means "to see"; Avestic *darstis* means "sight," Old Irish *derc* is "eye," Old English *torht*, Old Saxon *torht* and Old High German *zoraht*, all meaning "clear," "bright," or "shine."

The roots of the word can be traced back to early Indo-European tongues and right into the Indian continent—the home today of the serpent Kundalini enlightenment experience.

2. *Giant* comes from ge genis meaning "from the earth." *Giants* also comes from the word *Gigantes*, as in the Maltese giant stones Ggantija. So breaking the word down gives us *gi gant*. *Gant* is "stones" and *Gi* or *Ga* is "big"—*giant* is therefore "big stone." The Watchers who were also called giants are therefore also big stones and are now associated through etymology to the big stones of the world. These stones were seen as stars on Earth, fallen like the meteors and worshipped by the likes of the Calani.

Anak was the giant of the Bible who spawned the Anakim, living on both sides of the river Jordan like the Rephaim. The Nephilim were the offspring of the sons of God (Watchers, Angels and giants) and ordinary women.

Charlemagne was said to be a giant and was so strong he could squeeze together three horseshoes.

Goliath of Gath's height was said to be 6 cubits.

Og was the King of Bashan and the remnant of the Rephaim.

Uranus and Gaia were hurled to the earth by Hercules and buried under Mount Etna.

Scandinavian giants inhabited Jotunheim.

Jack and the Beanstalk is like the David and Goliath story of the Bible—a giant-slaying legend. Jack originated in Cornwall. According to tradition, he lived for 3,000 years and walked beside the ark (or even crept inside it).

Porus was an Indian Giant King who is said to have fought against Alexander the Great.

The Giant's Causeway in Ireland is a natural formation of 40,000 basaltic columns projecting into the sea, fabled to be the beginning of a Giant's road. Similar natural phenomena are claimed to be the doing of Giants such as:

Giant's Loom, Giant's Well, Giant's Organ, Giant's Peep-hole, Giant's Eye-glass, and Giant's Chair. The Giant's Ring in County Down is a stone circle similar to Stonehenge. St. Michael's Mount in Cornwall is said to have been built by the giants Cormoran and Cormelian.

War—the giants had a war with Zeus in Greek myth. This was a revolt by the giants against Zeus, which was put down with the aid of Hercules, who threw Uranus and Gaia to earth. It strangely matches the war in heaven between the Watchers and the Shining Ones—where Lucifer and other "angels" are cast down to earth.

3. Taautus (Taut) or Hermes

Said by Eusebius to be the originator of serpent worship in Phoenicia. Sanchoniathon called Thoth a god and says that he made the first image of Coelus and invented hieroglyphs. This links him with Hermes Trismegistus, also known as Thoth in Egypt. Taautus consecrated the species of dragons and serpents, and the Phoenicians and Egyptians followed him in this superstition. This Taautus could very well be a memory of the first group who began the worship of the serpent after the flood or end of th last ice age 12,000 years ago. The idea of Taautus links precisely with the stories of Thoth, who later became a great sage of Gnostic and alchemical beliefs. Thoth was deified after his death (a time that nobody knows) and given the title "the god of health" or "healing." He was the prototype for Aesculapius and identified with Hermes and Mercury. All healers, all wise, all teachers, all saviors, all associated with the serpent for their powers, and all central to the belief systems of secret societies. Indeed, it was as the healing god that Thoth was symbolized as the serpent—whereas he is normally represented with the head of an Ibis and Baboon.

The Letter or Symbol "Tau" is the first letter of Taautus, Tammuz and Thoth, and is thought to be the "Mark of Cain," a symbol of hidden treasure.

4. Cord

The cord is seen in many of the world's religions and all have similar meanings. It can mean to tie oneself to the divinity, thus linking it to the other aspect of freedom from the bonds. The Golden Cord of Zeus holds the universe, and to connect to this universe is the prime directive of the Shaman. In the Iranian myths the cord is passed around the waist three times for good action, thought, and word.

The Shaman uses a cord to symbolize his own umbilical cord, and with it he can access "other worlds"—or the enlightenment aspect. The cord was also symbolic of the serpent encircling the globe. In the form of a rope the Tibetans saw it as a connective device between heaven and earth—as did several other groups. It was also seen as a ladder, a tree, and a bridge to heaven. In Hinduism, Gnosis was termed the "hidden rope of ascension." In Babylonian and Sumerian myths, the rope was the bond or union between god and mankind, known as the mystical link.

The Knights Templar were accused of using a cord in their rituals: "Item, that they surrounded or touched each head of the aforesaid idol with small cords, which they wore around themselves next to the shirt or the flesh."

Chapter 8

1. See: *www.greatserpentmound.org*.

2. John Bathurst Dean in *Worship of the Serpent Traced Throughout the World and its Traditions Referred to the Events in Paradise* (1830). Deane also believed that the Kaaba or Caabir of the Muslims—which was a conical stone—resolved itself into Ca Ab Ir—the "Temple of the Serpent Sun."

   Avebury is a huge British temple and stone monument erected at least 2000–2600 B.C. in the shape of a serpent if seen from the sky. Today it is a world heritage site, and one of Europe's largest, encompassing a small hamlet and enclosed by a massive ditch, which required the movement of 200,000 tons of rock, chipped away by the crudest of tools. The circle itself was originally composed of 98 stones (but alas only 27 remain) and was erected around 2500 B.C. The two smaller inner circles were probably erected around 2600 B.C. Leading away from this is the avenue that snakes along, and it was Stukely, the antiquarian, who first noted that the ground plan of the Avebury complex was the representation of a serpent passing through a circle—forming what he believed to be a popular alchemical symbol.

   In essence, the serpent is the symbol of the power or energy and indeed wisdom that is derived from the sun—something our ancestors closely associated with life. Of course, the precession of the earth is also built into Avebury, so one could easily discover, as if by magic, where and when in the great cycle one was. This skill was past down from priest to priest as a sacred secret, for power was truly wielded by those who knew such things—in fact it was the ability to "measure" or "rule." It aided the growth of crops, the navigation of the seas and land, and matched the great cycles of the gods in heaven.

   The archaeology of the area shows that people used to walk outside of the pathway of the serpent, leaving the inner pathway for the priests.

This was the way of the living to new life. The dead had their own methods—via places such as Newgrange in Ireland, but here in Avebury, via the tombs such as those of West Kennet close by.

Tyrian cousins frequently depicted a serpent squeezing between two upright stones, which the Greeks called Petrae Ambrosiae; noting that Ambrosia is the nectar and Elixir of the gods. According to 19th century archaeologist, Bryant, Stonehenge was seen as these amber stones, as nearby is Amesbury—previously Ambrosbury.

On a recent trip to Avebury I was perplexed at the shape of a large number of the stones in the main circle. They appeared to be great arrows that had fallen down to earth, burying the tip in the ground. Then I recalled the three snakes found in the heart of Meich (Irish myth). Could these be precursors to the heart shape we know today? Could this be where the symbolic shape for the heart came from? It is a long stretch of the imagination to see this though, and taking into account the fact that every other stone is tall and straight, we have to assume that they were male and female shapes. Indeed I have just returned from Malta where I noted the walls of the great Mnadjra temple was made up in exactly the same way: tall upright, large oblong. Remembering that these structures were contemporary and that Malta was itself overrun with serpent and mother deity worship, there is little doubt that these ancient stone monuments are related in some way.

Of course, in other parts of the symbolical world the snake's head is seen as an arrowhead or spearhead and the body a straight line. We also cannot discount the fact that serpents were seen quite often as entwining the great phallus in the Caduceus form of fertility. In this respect we would have the various and most ancient images of the serpent, not just in layout but also in structure.

"On the ancient Norman font in Abury Church there is a mutilated figure, dressed apparently in the Druidical priestly garb, holding a crozier in one hand, and clasping an open book to his breast with the other, although when we visited the church the 'book' could easily also be a chalice. Two winged dragons or serpents are attacking and biting the feet of this figure on either side. May not this be designed to represent the triumph of Christianity over Druidism, in which there was MUCH VENERATION entertained for this serpent and serpent worship?"

These are remarks made by a past Vicar of Avebury. After spending many hours in the cool, fusty air of the little church at Avebury, staring at the image, it is my view that the serpents "biting" the druid's feet are actually subdued by the priest rather than attacking him. He is revealing his wisdom, controlling the serpents of opposition, order, and chaos, just as so many thousands of other depictions from around the world reveal.

Close to Avebury is West Kennet Long Barrow, situated on a high rise of land that overlooks Silbury Hill—Europe's largest man-made mound, built up with stepped chalk and covered in chalk to smooth it off. This hill was pure white in its heyday, shining across the landscape; much like the whitewashed Great Pyramid in Egypt, built at the same time.

West Kennet is a small but magical place, built similar to Newgrange in a cruciform shape from the air. Archaeologists also discovered that there was a semicircular ceremonial area at the top of the T cross, making an Ankh if viewed from above.

Another strange coincidence that struck me, and one I later confirmed against other sites, was the layout of the interior of the tomb. Imagine an upright with two parallel horizontals at equal distances apart and you have the Cross of Lorraine. This would not really have struck me had it not been for the blatant fact that the Cross of Lorraine was a symbol for poison, the trinity (the Celtic goddess trinity, Tricephalic Heads, and so on) and a symbol used by the Templars. These relationships should have nothing to do with each other but for the fact that the thread of the snake connects all these areas. But, add into this the fact that nobody is sure where the Lorraine symbol originated, and then we indeed have a mystery. Other burial mounds viewed from above look just like the cross, as if the bodies and ceremonies were being somehow played upon this "sacred shape." It is a shape that is hidden beneath the ground and not a shape seen openly—as if this were the three-dimensional aspect of the symbol, a stairway to the other realm. In fact, many of the actual stairways from the period that we know of were in this very shape, indicating a kind of copycat symbolism—from reality into mystery.

3. Hargrave Jennings, *Ophiolatreia*.

4. Deane, *The Worship of the Serpent Traced Throughout the World*.

5. *Chivim* is a Hebrew word, meaning "sons of the female serpent" (or Eve) and may imply a greater knowledge of this journey from a Judaic perspective.

Chapter 9

1. Borchant, *Mysticism*.

2. James Pritchard, *Solomon and Sheba* (1974), p.35.

3. Wilhelm Bacher and Ludwig Blau, *Shamir*.

Chapter 11

1. Brahma is the subtle life-force or the spirit itself and Saraisvati was the River of Life. See *The Wonder that was India* by A. L. Basham, Fontana Ancient History, 1967.

2. Mahadeva, one of Siva's names, is often represented with a snake entwined around his neck, arms, and hair. His consort, Parvati, is likewise represented. Bhairava, the Avatar of Siva, sits upon the coils of a serpent, whose "head rises above that of the gods." According to Hyde Clarke & C. Staniland Wake in *Serpent and Siva Worship,* Siva is the same as Rudra, the healer, and is called the King of Serpents. He is depicted with a garland of skulls, symbolizing time measured in years, the changing of ages. He is called sometimes Nagabhushana Vyalakalpa or "having serpents round his neck" and Nagaharadhrik or "wearing serpent-necklaces" and also Nagaendra, Nagesha, or "king of Nagas" is also known as Nakula, the "mongoose," which means one who is immune from the venom of the snake.

3. See *Gnosis: The Secret of Solomon's Temple Revealed* by Philip Gardiner.

4. The word *emerald* comes from the Greek *smaragdos*, which simply means "green stone"—although true emeralds have been popular for well over 4,000 years. Cleopatra, the famous Queen of Egypt who died from the bite of an Asp, was fond of them—and more than any other gem! She had the emerald mined near Aswan. The emerald is found on Jewish breastplates and is used as Indian Talismans. Spaniards stole it during the conquest of South America and the Incas held it in high veneration. It is said to cure fevers, epilepsy, leprosy, dysentery, opthalmia, bleeding, liver problems, and stings from venomous beasts. It was also strangely said to "blind" serpents.

    The Emerald Tablet is a summary of alchemical thought—existing in Arabic and Greek—and mainly having roots in Roman and Greek alchemy, especially that of Hermes—thus bringing to mind that it must originate from the same source as the Dionysiac Architects or the Roman Collegia.

    One of the earliest recordings of its existence is from an 8th century Arabic work. Some relate the Emerald to the Sacro Catino of Genoa, the supposed Holy Grail, said to have been in the possession of the Queen of Sheba, and was made from green or emerald glass.

    It was believed that a physician named Galienus, who called it the Table of Zaradi, recovered the Tablet from the Thrice Great Hermes. Many believe Galienus to be the surgeon Galen, but others believe it to be a mistranslation of Balinas (Apollonius of Tyana). If this is the case, then the Emerald Tablet of the great serpent deity, Hermes, would be coming directly from the sage who visited the Naga (serpent) kings of India and Kashmir and who is himself said to be long-lived.

The term *Zaradi* derives from the word for "underground cave" or "chamber" and alludes to an "otherworldly" domain—possibly the Shamanic Underworld.

Other people said to have discovered the Tablet are equally incorporated into the serpent worship story: Alexander the Great and Zara (Sarah)—the wife of Abraham—who is said to have taken it from the hands of Hermes just after the flood.

Chapter 12

1. Coelus was the Roman god of the heavens and is identified with Uranus of the Greeks.

2. Labyrinth means double-headed axe just like the Hammer of Thor, and Thor's name is linked with that of Thoth.

3. John Bathurst Dean, in *Worship of the Serpent Traced Throughout the World and its Traditions Referred to the Events in Paradise* (1830).

Chapter 17

1. *The Trail of the Serpent*, by Inquire Within, no publisher, 1940s.

2. Ibid.

Bibliography

Abdalqadir as-Sufi, Shaykh. *The Return of the Kalifate*. Cape Town: Madinah Press, 1996.

Ableson, J. *Jewish Mysticism*. London: G Bell and Sons Ltd., 1913.

Acharya, S. *The Christ Conspiracy: the greatest story ever sold*. Stelle, Ill.: AVP, 2003.

Andrews, R., and P. Schellenberger. *The Tomb of God*. London: Little, Brown and Co., 1996.

Anon. *The Trail of the Serpent*. publisher, date, and author not stated.

Appollodorus. *The Library-Greek Mythography*. NP, 2nd Century B.C.

Ashe, Geoffrey. *The Quest for Arthur's Britain*. London: Paladin, 1971.

Baigent. *Ancient Traces*. London: Viking Press, 1998.

Baigent, Leigh. *The Elixir and the Stone*. London: Viking Press, 1997.

Baigent, Michael, Richard Leigh, and Henry Lincoln. *The Holy Blood and the Holy Grail*. London: Jonathan Cape, 1982.

———. *The Messianic Legacy*. London: Arrow, 1996.

Baigent, Michael, and Richard Leigh. *The Dead Sea Scrolls Deception*. London: Arrow, 2001.

———. *The Temple and the Lodge*. London: Arrow, 1998.

Balfour, Mark. *The Sign of the Serpent*. London: Prism, 1990.

Balfour, Michael. *Megalithic Mysteries*. London: Parkgate Books, 1992.

Barber, Malcolm. *The Trial of the Templar*. Cambridge, Mass.: Cambridge University Press, 1978.

Barrett, David. *Sects, Cults and Alternative Religions*. London: Blandford, 1996.

Barrow, John. *Theories of Everything*. London: Virgin, 1990.

Basham, A.L. *The Wonder that was India*. London: Fontana Collins, 1954.

Bayley, H. *The Lost Language of Symbolism*. London: Bracken Books, 1996.

Bauval, R. *The Orion Mystery*. Oxford: Heinemann, 1996.

Beatty, Longfield. *The Garden of the Golden Flower*. London: Senate, 1996.

Begg, E. *The Cult of the Black Virgin*. London: Arkana, 1985.

Begg, E. and D. Begg. *In Search of the Holy Grail and the Precious Blood*. London: Thorsons, 1985.

Bildeberg Group. *Nexus Magazine* 3 (1) (Dec. 1995–Jan. 1996).

Blackfoot, Emery. *Chance Encounters*. Boston: Serendipity Press, 1987.

Blaire, Lawrence. *Rhythms of Vision*. New York: Warner Books, 1975.

Blavatsky, H.P. *Theosophical Glossary*. Whitefish, Mont.: R.A. Kessinger Publishing Ltd, 1918.

Borchant, Bruno. *Mysticism*. Maine: Weisner, 1994.

Bord, Colin, and Janet Bord. *Earth Rites: Fertility Practices in Pre-Industrial Britain*. London: Granada Publishing.

Bouquet A.C. *Comparative Religion*. London: Pelican, 1942.

Boyle, Veolita Parke. *The Fundamental Principles of Yi-King, Tao: The Cabbalas of Egypt and the Hebrews*. London: W & G Foyle, 1934.

Brine, Lindsey. *The Ancient Earthworks and Temples of the American Indians*. London: Oracle, 1996.

Broadhurst, Paul, and Hamish Miller. *The Dance of the Dragon*. Cornwall: Mythos, 2000.

Bryant, N. *The High Book of the Grail*. Cambridge: DS Brewer, 1985.

Bryden, R. *Rosslyn—A History of the Guilds, the Masons and the Rosy Cross*. Rosslyn: Rosslyn Chapel Trust, 1994.

Budge, E.A. Wallis. *An Egyptian Hieroglyphic Dictionary, Volume 1*. Dover: Dover Publications, 1978.

Butler, E.M. *The Myth of the Magus*. Cambridge: Cambridge University Press, 1911.

Callahan, Philip. *Paramagnetism: Rediscovering Nature's Secret Force of Growth*. Acres, USA, 1995.

———. *Ancient Mysteries Modern Visions: The Magnetic Life of Agriculture*, Acres, USA, 2001.

———. *Nature's Silent Music*. Acres, USA, 1992.

Campbell, Joseph. *Transformations of Myth Through Time*. London: Harper and Row, 1990.

Cantor, N.F. *The Sacred Chain*. London: Harper Collins, 1994.

Carr-Gomm, Sarah. *Dictionary of Symbols in Art*. London: Duncan Baird Publishers, 1995.

Cavendish, Richard. *Mythology*. London: Tiger, 1998.

Carpenter, Edward. *Pagan and Christian Creeds: Their Origin and Meaning*. London: Allen and Unwin Ltd., 1920.

Castaneda, Carlos. *The Teaching of Don Juan*. London: Arkana, 1982.

Ceram, C. W. *Gods Graves and Scholars: The Story of Archaeology*. London: Victor Gollancz & Sidgwick and Jackson, 1954.

Childress, David. *Anti-Gravity & The World Grid*. Stelle, Ill.: Adventures Unlimited Press, 1987.

Chadwick, N. *The Druids*. Cardiff: University of Wales Press, 1969.

Churchward, Albert. *The Origin and Evolution of Religion*. Whitefish, Mont.: R.A. Kessinger Publishing, 1997.

Churton, Tobias. *The Golden Builder*. Lichfield: Signal Publishing, 2002.

Cicero. *De Senectute*. Publisher unknown.

Clarke, Hyde, and C. Staniland Wake. *Serpent and Siva Worship*. Whitefiesh, Mont.: R.A. Kessinger Publishing Ltd., 1877.

Coles, John. *Field Archaeology in Britain*. London: Methuen, 1972.

Collins, Andrew. *Twenty-First Century Grail: The Quest for a Legend*. London: Virgin, 2004.

———. *From the Ashes of Angles, The Forbidden Legacy of a Fallen Race*. London: Signet Books, 2004.

———. *Gods of Eden*. London: Headline, 1998.

———. *Gateway to Atlantis*. London: Headline, 2000.

Cooper, J.C. *An Illustrated Encyclopaedia of Traditional Symbols*. London: Thames and Hudson, 1978.

Croker, Thomas Crofton. *Legend of the Lakes*. out of print and publisher unknown.

Crooke, W. *The Popular Religion and Folk-lore of Northern India*. Whitefish, Mont.: R.A. Kessinger Publishing Ltd., 1997.

Cumont, F. *The Mysteries of Mithra*. Dover: Dover Publications, 1956.

Currer-Briggs, N. *The Shroud and the Grail; a modern quest for the true grail*. New York: St. Martins Press, 1987.

David-Neel, Alexandria. *Magic and Mystery in Tibet*. Dover: Dover Publications, 1929.

Davidson, H.R. Ellis. *Myths and Symbols of Pagan Europe*. Syracuse: Syracuse University Press, 1988.

Davidson, John. *The Secret of the Creative Vacuum*. London: The C.W. Daniel Company Ltd., 1989.

Deane, John Bathurst. *The Worship of the Serpent Traced Throughout the World*.

De Martino, Ernesto. *Primitive Magic*. Dorset: Prism Unity, 1972.

Devereux, Paul. *Secrets of Ancient and Sacred Places: The World's Mysterious Heritage*. Beckhampton: Beckhampton Press, 1995.

———. *Shamanism and the Mystery Lines*. London: Quantum, 1992.

———. *Symbolic Landscapes*. Glastonbury: Gothic Image, 1992.

Dinwiddie, John. *Revelations—the Golden Elixir*. Writers Club Press, 2001.

Dodd, C.H. *Historical Tradition of the Fourth Gospel*. Cambridge: Cambridge University Press, 1963.

Doel, Fran, and Geoff Doel. *Robin Hood: Outlaw of Greenwood Myth*. Nottingham: Temous, 2000.

Duckett-Shipley, Eleanor. *The Gateway to the Middle Ages, Monasticism*. Michigan: Ann Arbor Paperbacks—the University of Michigan Press, 1961.

Dunstan, V. *Did the Virgin Mary Live and Die in England?* Rochester, N.Y.: Megiddo Press, 1985.

Davies, Rev. Edward. *The Mythology and Rites of the British Druids*. London: J. Booth, 1806.

Devereux, Paul. *Places of Power: measuring the secret energy of ancient sites*. London: Blandford, 1999.

Devereux, Paul, and Ian Thompson. *Ley Guide: The Mystery of Aligned Ancient Sites*. London: Empress. 1988.

Dunford, Barry. *The Holy Land of Scotland: Jesus in Scotland and the Gospel of the Grail*. Perthshire, Scotland: Sacred Connections, 2001. *www.sacredconnections.co.uk*.

Eliade, Mircea. *Shamanism: Archaic Techniques of Ecstasy*. Princeton, N.J.: Princeton University Press, 1964.

Ellis, Ralph. *Jesus, Last of the Pharaohs*. Cheshire: Edfu Books, 2001.

Epstein, Perle. *Kabbalah: The Way of the Jewish Mystic*. Boston: Shambhala Classics, 2001.

Ernst, Carl. *Venomous Reptiles of North America*. Washington: Smithsonian Books, 1992.

Evans, Lorraine. *Kingdom of the Ark*. London: Simon and Schuster, 2000.

Feather, Robert. *The Copper Scroll Decoded*. London: Thorsons, 1999.

Fedder, Kenneth, and Michael Alan Park. *Human Antiquity: An Introduction to Physical Anthropology and Archaeology*. Mountain View, Calif.: Mayfield Publishing Company, 1993.

Ferguson, Diana. *Tales of the Plumed Serpent*. London: Collins and Brown, 2000.

Fergusson, Malcolm. *Rambles in Breadalbane*. London: 1891.

Fontana, David. *The Secret Language of Symbols*. London: Piatkus, 1997.

Ford, Patrick. *The Mabinogi and other Medieval Welsh Tales*. Berkeley, Calif.: University of California Press, 1977.

Fortune, Dion. *The Mystical Qabalah*. Maine: Weiser Books, 2000.

Foss, Michael. *People of the First Crusade*. London: Michael O'Mara Books, 1997.

Frazer, Sir James. *The Golden Bough*. London: Wordsworth, 1993.

Freke, Timothy, and Peter Gandy. *Jesus and the Goddess*. London: Thorsons, 2001.

Gardner, Laurence. *Bloodline of the Holy Grail*. London: Element, 1996.

———. *The Shining Ones*. Nottingham, UK 2002 *ww.radikalbooks.com*.

———. *Proof—Does God Exist?* Calif.: Reality Entertainment, 2006.

Gardiner, Samuel. *History of England*. London: Longmans, Green and Co., 1904.

Gascoigne, Bamber. *The Christians*. London: Jonathan Cape, 1977.

Gerber, Richard. *Vibrational Medicine*. Santa Fe: Bear & Company, 2001.

Gilbert, Adrian. *Magi*. London: Bloomsbury, 1996.

Goldberg, Carl. *Speaking With The Devil*. London: Viking, 1996.

Gould, Charles. *Mythical Monsters*. London: State, 1995.

Graves, Robert. *The Greek Myths: 2*. London: Pelican, 1964.

Gray Hulse, Tristan. *The Holy Shroud*. London, Weidenfeld and Nicolson, 1997.

Guenther, Johannes Von. *Cagliostro*. London: William Heinemann, 1928.

Hagger, Nicholas. *The Fire and the Stones*. London: Element, 1991.

Hanauer, J.E. *The Holy Land*. London: Senate, 1996.

Hancock, Graham. *The Sign and the Sea*. London: Arrow, 2001.

Halifax, Joan. *Shaman: the Wounded Healer*. London: Crossroad, Thames and Hudson, 1982.

Harbison, Peter. *Pre-Christian Ireland*. London: Thames and Hudson, 1988.

Harrington, E. *The Meaning of English Place Names*. Belfast: The Black Staff Press, 1995.

Hartmann, Franz. *The Life of Jehoshua The Prophet of Nazareth: an occult study and a key to the Bible*. London: Kegan, Trench, Trubner & Co, 1909.

Harvey, Clesson. *The Great Pyramid Texts. www.pyramidtexts.com.*

Heathcote-James, Emma. *They Walk Among Us*. New York: Metro, 2004.

Hedsel, Mark. *The Zelator*. London: Century, 1998.

Howard, M. *The Occult Conspiracy*. Rochester: Destiny Books, 1989.

Howard, Michael. a paper entitled *The Womb of Ceridwen*.

James, E.O. *The Ancient Gods*. London: Weidenfeld and Nicolson, 1962.

Jennings, Hargrave. *Ophiolatreia*. Whitefish, Mont.: R.A. Kessinger Publishing, Year unknown.

Johnson, Buffie. *Lady of the Beast: the Goddess and Her Sacred Animals*. San Fransisco: Harper and Row, 1988.

Jones, Alison. *Dictionary of World Folklore*. New York: Larousse, 1995.

Josephus. *Antiquities*. Indypublish.com

Kauffeld, Carl. *Snakes: The Keeper and the Kept*. London: Doubleday and Co., 1969.

Kendrick, T. D. *The Druids*. London: Methuen and Co., 1927.

King, Serge Kahili. *Instant Healing: Mastering the Way of the Hawaiian Shaman Using Words, Images, Touch, and Energy*. Los Angeles: Renaissance Books, 2000.

Knight, Christopher, and Robert Lomas. *Uriel's Machine: Reconstructing the Disaster Behind Human History*. London: Arrow, 2004.

Knight, Christopher, and Robert Lomas. *The Second Messiah*, London, Arrow, 1997.

Laidler, Keith. *The Head of God*. London: Orion, 1999.

———. *The Divine Deception*. London: Headline, 2000.

Lapatin, Kenneth. *Mysteries of the Snake Goddess*. Boston: Houghton Mifflin Company, 2002.

Layton, Robert. *Australian Rock Art: a new synthesis*. Cambridge: Cambridge University Press, 1986.

Larson, Martin A. *The Story of Christian Origins*. Village, 1977.

Leakey, Richard, and Roger Lewin. *Origins Reconsidere*. London: Doubleday, 1992.

Le Goff, Jacques. *The Medieval Word*. London: Parkgate Books, 1997.

Lemesurier, Peter. *The Great Pyramid Decoded*. London: Element, 1977.

Leone, Al. *The Totality of God and the Izunome Cross—Unlocking the Secret Riddle of the Ages*. unpublished at time of writing this but can be read in full at *www.gizapyramid.com/Leone1.htm*.

Levi, Eliphas. *Transcendental Magic*. London: Tiger Books, 1995.

Lincoln, Henry. *Key to the Sacred Pattern*. Gloucestershire: The Windrush Press, 1997.

Loye, David. *An Arrow Through Chaos: how we see into the future*. Rochester, Vt.: Part Street Press, 1983.

Lyall, Neil, and Robert Chapman. *The Secret of Staying Young*. London: Pan, 1976.

MacCana, Proinsias. *Celtic Mythology*. New York: Hamlyn, 1992.

Mack, B.L. *The Lost Gospel*. London: Element, 1993.

Maclellan, Alec. *The Lost World of Agharti*. London: Souvenir Press, 1982.

Magin, U. *The Christianisation of Pagan Landscapes*. In *The Ley Hunter* 116: 1992.

Mann, A.T. *Sacred Architecture*. London: Element, 1993.

Maraini, Fosco. *Secret Tibet*. London: Hutchinson, 1954.

Matthews, John. *Sources of the Grail*. London: Floris Books, 1996.

———. *The Quest for the Green Man*. Newton Abbott: Godsfield Press, 2001.

Maby, J.C., and T. Bedford Franklin. *The Physics of the Divining Rod*. London: Bell, 1977.

McDermott, Bridget. *Decoding Egyptian Hieroglyphs*. London: Duncan Baird Publishers, 2001.

Meij, Harold. *The Tau and the Triple Tau*. Tokyo: H.P , 2000.

Michell, John, and Christine Rhone. *Twelve-Tribes and the Science of Enchanting the Landscape*. Grand Rapids: Phanes PR, 1991.

Milgrom, Jacob. *The JPS Torah Commentary: Numbers*. New York: Jewish Publication Society, 1990.

Moncrieff, A.R. *Hope, Romance & Legend of Chivalry*. London: Senate, 1994.

Morgan, Gerald. *Nanteos: A Welsh House and its Families*. Llandysul: Gomer, 2001.

Morton, Chris, and Ceri Louise Thomas. *The Mystery of the Crystal Skull*. London: Element, 2003.

Muggeridge, Malcolm. *Jesus*. London: Collins, 1975.

Nilsson, M.P. *The Minoan-Mycenaean Religion and Its Survival in Greek Religion*, Oxford, Lund, 1950.

Oliver, George. *Signs and Symbols*. New York: Macoy Publishing, 1906.

O'Brien, Christian, and Barbara Joy. *The Shining Ones*. London: Dianthus Publishing Ltd., 1988.

Oliver, Rev. George. *The History of Initiation*. Whitefish, Mont.: R.A. Kessinger Publishing Co, 1841.

O'Neill, John. *Nights of the Gods*. publisher unknown.

Opponheimer, Stephen. *Eden in the East*. London: Orion, 1988.

Orofino, Giacomella. *Sacred Tibetan Teachings on Death and Liberation*. London: Prism-Unity, 1990.

Pagels, E. *The Gnostic Gospels*. London: Weidenfeld and Nicolson, 1979.

Paterson Smyth, J. *How We Got our Bible*. London: Sampson Low, 1998.

Pennick, N. *Sacred Geometry*. Chievely: Capall Bann, 1994.

Picknett, Lynn, and Clive Prince. *The Templar Revelation*. London: Corgi, 1998.

Piggot, Stuart. *The Druids*. London: Thames and Hudson, 1927.

Pike, Albert. *The Morals and Dogma of Scottish Rite Freemasonry*. Richmond: L.H. Jenkins, 1928.

Plichta, Peter. *God's Secret Formula*. London: Element, 1997.

Plunket, Emmeline. *Calendars and Constellations of the Ancient World*. London: John Murray, 1903.

Powell, T.G.E. *The Celts*. London: Thames and Hudson, 1968.

Rabten, Geshe. *Echoes of Voidness*. London: Wisdom Publications, 1983.

Radin, Dean. *The Conscious Universe*. London: Harper Collins, 1997.

Randles, Jenny, and Peter Hough. *Encyclopedia of the Unexplained*. London: Brockhampton Press, 1995.

Read, Piers Paul. *The Templars*. London: Phoenix, 1999.

Rees, Alwyn, and Brynley. *Celtic Heritag*. London: Thames and Hudson, 1961.

Reid, Howard. *Arthur—The Dragon King*. London: Headline, 2001.

————. *In Search of the Immortals: Mummies, Death and the Afterlife.* London: Headline, 1999.

Richet, C. *Thirty Years of Psychic Research.* n.p.: 1923.

Rinbochay, Lati, Locho Rinbochay, Leah Zahler, and Jeffrey Hopkins. *Meditative States in Tibetan Buddhism.* London: Wisdom Publications, 1983.

Rohl, David. *A Test of Time: The Bible—from Myth to History.* London: Arrow, 1995.

Roberts, Alison. *Hathor Rising: The Serpent Power of Ancient Egypt.* Rottingdean: East Sussex, Northgate, 1995.

Roberts, J.M. *The Mythology of the Secret Societies.* London: Granada, 1972.

————. *Antiquity Unveiled.* Health Research, 1970.

Robertson, J.M. *Pagan Christs.* London: Watts, 1903.

Rolleston, T.W. *Myths and Legends of the Celtic Race.* London: Mystic P, 1986.

Russell, Peter. *The Brain Book.* London: Routledge, 1980.

Schaya, Leo. *The Universal Meaning of the Kabbalah.* New Jersey: University Books, 1987.

Schele, Linda, and Mary Ellen Miller. *The Blood of Kings: Dynasty and Ritual in Maya Art.* George, New York: Braziller, 1992.

Scholem, Gershom G. *On the Kabbalah and It's Symbolism.* London: Routledge & Kegan, 1965.

Schonfield, Hugh. *Essene Odyssey.* London: Element, 1984.

————. *The Passover Plot.* London: Hutchinson, 1965.

Schwartz, Gary, and Linda Russek. *The Living Energy Universe.* Charlottesville, Va., Hampton Roads Publishing, 1999.

Scott, Ernest. *The People of the Secret.* London: The Octagon Press, 1983.

Seife, Charles. *Zero: The Biography of a Dangerous Idea.* London: Souvenir Press, 2000.

Seligmann, Kurt. *The History of Magic.* New York: Quality Paperback Book Club, 1997.

Signs, Symbols and Cipher. London: New Horizons, 1992.

Simpson, Jacqueline. *British Dragons.* London: B.T. Batsford and Co, 1980.

Sinclair, Andrew. *The Secret Scroll.* London: Birlinn, 2001.

Sharper Knowlson, T. *The Origins of Popular Superstitions and Customs*. London: Senate, 1994.

Smith, M. *The Secret Gospe*. London: Victor Gollancz, 1973.

Snyder, Louis L. *Encyclopaedia of the Third Reich*. London: Wordsworth, 1998.

Spence, Lewis. *Introduction to Mythology*. London: Senate,1994.

————. *Myths and Legends of Egyp*. London: George Harrap and Sons, 1915.

Stephen, Alexander M. *The Journal of American Folklore*. January/March, 1929.

Stone, Nathan. *Names of God*. Chicago: Moody, 1944.

Sullivan, Danny. *Ley Lines*. London: Piaktus, 1999.

Talbot, Michael. *The Holographic Universe*. London: Harper Collins, 1991/1996.

Taylor, Richard. *How to Read a Church*. London: Random House, 2003.

Temple, Robert. *The Crystal Sun*. London: Arrow, 1976.

————. *Netherworld: Discovering the Oracle of the Dead and Ancient Techniques of Foretelling the Future*. London: Century, 2002.

Thiering, Barbara, *Jesus The Ma*, London: Doubleday, 1992.

————. *Jesus of the Apocalypse*. London: Doubleday, 1996.

Thomson, Ahmad. *Dajjal the Anti-Christ*. London: Ta-Ha Publishers Ltd., 1993.

Thomson, Oliver. *Easily Led: A history of Propaganda*. Gloucestershire: Sutton Publishing, 1999.

Toland, John. *Hitler*. London: Wordsworth, 1997.

Tolstoy, Nikolai. *The Quest for Merlin*. London: Little, Brown and Co., 1985

Tull, George F. *Traces of the Templars*. London: The Kings England Press, 2000.

Vadillo, Umar Ibrahim. *The Return of the Gold Dinar*. Cape Town: Madinah Press, 1996.

Villars, de, Abbe N. de Montfaucon. *Comte de Gabalis: discourses on the Secret Sciences and Mysteries in accordnace with the principles of the Ancient Magi and the Wisdom of the Kabalistic Philosophers,* 17th century. Whitefiesh, Mont.: R.A. Kessinger Publishing, 1996.

Villanueva, J.L. *Phoenician Ireland*. n.p.: Dublin, 1833.

Vulliamy, C.E. *Immortality: Funerary Rites & Customs*. London, Senate, 1997. Previously *Immortal Man* published by Methuen 1926.

Waite, Arthur Edward. *The Hidden Church of the Holy Grail*. Amsterdam:Fredonia Books, 2002.

Wake, C. Staniland. *The Origin of Serpent Worship,* Whitefish, Mont.: R.A. Kessinger Publishing Ltd, 1877.

Walker, B. *Gnosticism*. Wellingborough: Aquarian Press. 1983.

Wallace-Murphy, Hopkins. *Rosslyn*. London: Element, 2000.

Waters, Frank. *The Book of the Hopi*. New York: Ballantine, 1963.

Watson, Lyall. *Dark Nature*. London: Harper Collins, 1995.

Weber, Renee. *Dialogues with Scientists and Sages: Search for Unity in Science and Mysticism*. London: Arkana, 1990.

Webster, Nesta H. *Secret Societies and Subversive Movements*, New Ed edition. A & B Distributors, 1994.

Weisse, John. *The Obelisk and Freemasonry*.Whitefish, Mont.: R.A. Kessinger Publishing Ltd. 1996.

Wheless, Joseph. *Forgery in Christianity*. Health Research, 1990.

Williamson, A. *Living in the Sky*. Norman, Okla.: University of Oklahoma Press, 1984.

Wilson, Colin. *The Atlas of Holy Places and Sacred Sites*. London: Doring Kindersley, 1996.

———. *Beyond the Occult*, London, Caxton Editions, 2002.

———. *Frankenstein's Castle: The Double Brain—Door to Wisdom*. London: Ashgrove Press, 1980.

Wilson, Hilary. *Understanding Hieroglyphs*. London: Brockhampton Press, 1993.

Wise, Michael, Martin Abegg, and Edward Cook. *The Dead Sea Scrolls*. London: Harper Collins, 1999.

Within, Inquire. *Trail of the Serpent*, Publisher and author (supposedly Inquire Within) kept a secret, circa 1940s.

Wood, David. *Genisis*. Baton Wicks Publications, no year.

Woods, George Henry. *Herodotus Book II*. London: Rivingtons, 1897.

Woolley, Benjamin. *The Queens's Conjuror*. London: Harper Collins, 2001.

Wylie, Rev. J. A. *History of the Scottish Nation 1*. n.p., 1886.

Zollschan, G.K., J.F Schumaker, and Dr G.F. Walsh. *Exploring the Paranormal*. London: Prism Unity, 1989.

Other Sources

Dictionary of Beliefs and Religions, Wordsworth. 1995.

Dictionary of Phrase and Fable, Wordsworth. 1995.

Dictionary of Science and Technology, Wordsworth Edition. 1995.

Dictionary of the Bible, Collins. 1974.

Dictionary of the Occult, Geddes and Grosset. 1997.

Dictionary of World Folklore, Larousse. 1995

The Apocrypha, Talmud, Koran, Bible, Dead Sea Scrolls—Damascus Document, The Community Rule, War of the Sons of Light with the Sons of Darkness, Messianic Rule of the Congregation, Temple Scroll; writings of Pliny the Younger, Flavius Josephus, Pythagoras, Plato, Hippolytus of Rome, Ephraim the Syrian, Carl Jung, Jeremiah Creedon (Guardian), Foundation for the Study of Cycles, The I Ching (Richard Wilhelm Translation), New Scientist, Nag Hammadi Gospel of Truth, Gospel of Mary, Gospel of the Egyptians, On Baptism; documents received from the following and used by their permission; Scientologists, Jehova's Witnesses, Mormons, Jewish Pentecostal Mission, Rosicrucians, Freemasons, Inner Light; *Websters Encyclopaedia, Encarta Encyclopaedia, The Unexplained* (Focus), *Encyclopaedia of History* (Dorling Kindersley), Staff at Lichfield Cathedral, *New Scientist* (21 March 1998 and 11 July 1998), Bible Explorer (Expert Software), Faith in Every Footstep (The Church of Jesus Christ of Latter-Day Saints press Information CD-Rom); Corroborations of Occult Archaeology, The Theosophical Society Publishing House 1935. A Guide to the Antiquities of the Bronze Age in the Department of British and Medieval Antiquities, printed by order of the board of Trustees, 1904, Oxford University Press.

Mythology

www.gardinersworld.com

www.elfhill.com

Index

About the Author

Philip Gardiner is the best-selling author of numerous books, including *Gnosis: The Secret of Solomon's Temple Revealed*; *The Ark, the Shroud and Mary*; *Secrets of the Serpent*; and *The Serpent Grail*. He has written and directed several DVDs, lectured extensively around the world, and appeared on more than 400 radio and television shows. His Website is *www.gardinersworld.com*.